TOWPATH TOURS

A GUIDE TO CYCLING IRELAND'S WATERWAYS

JOHN DUNNE

The Collins Pres

Published in 2005 by
The Collins Press,
West Link Park,
Doughcloyne,
Wilton,
Cork

British Library Cataloguing in Publication Data
Dunne, John
        Towpath Tours : a guide to cycling Ireland's waterways
        1. Towpaths - Ireland - Guidebooks 2. Walking - Ireland-
        Guidebooks 3. Cycling - Ireland - Guidebooks 4. Ireland -
        Guidebooks
        I. Title
        796.5'1'09415

ISBN 1903464757

Typesetting: The Collins Press

Font: Calisto, 11 point

Cover design: Jean McCord

Printed in Malta

For my father

CONTENTS

ACKNOWLEDGEMENTS

In writing this guide I owe a debt to Ruth Heard (Ruth Delany). When I was conducting my research on the inland waterways I quickly learned she is the expert on the subject, particularly the Grand Canal and the Royal Canal. Her books provided me with a quantity of information from which to draw and a huge inspiration to complete my work.

I am also indebted to the many people I have encountered on my travels who provided me with snippets from their own association with the waterways and their local knowledge. Thanks are also due to the maintenance crews of Waterways Ireland whom I meet frequently and who have always treated me with great courtesy and without whom my journeys would have been far more difficult.

A special thanks is also due to the Northern Ireland Tourist Board whose staff were at all times helpful, interested and encouraging and who showed a great interest in the waterways in their region and in providing facilities for cyclists.

AUTHOR'S NOTE

While every effort has been made to ensure accuracy in the information supplied, no responsibility can be accepted for any damage or loss suffered as a result of error, omission or misinterpretation of this information. The author and publisher shall have no liability in respect of any loss or damage caused arising from the use of this guide. This includes – but is not limited to – loss or damage resulting from missing signs, future changes in routes, accidents and lost or injured persons.

INTRODUCTION

Oh I would die beside a lonely river
Whose waves should pour a flood of eloquence upon my ear.
John Keegan Casey, 'Leo' (1846-1870)

For cyclists and walkers the towpaths and trackways of Ireland's inland waterways are the perfect amenity. They offer a hidden treasure trove of tranquil settings, constantly changing scenery and glimpses of our past, while affording the cyclist a safe and fume-free environment. This book aims to bring cyclists to areas of hidden Ireland that have hitherto been the preserve of boatowners and a limited number of intrepid hikers.

I was inspired to write this book by a desire to share the enjoyment I have been fortunate to experience over many years cycling along Ireland's waterways. Initially my desire was to escape the dangers of Dublin's traffic and to bring variety to my cycling. However, the more I visited the inland waterways the more I was intrigued by their origins and history, and the more I wondered why I encountered few people along my routes. I contrasted this with experiences I had cycling along waterways in

England and Europe. where I encountered dedicated cycling paths and information panels on both the canals themselves and local history.

The Irish canals and canalised sections of our rivers are marvellous feats of engineering that by and large are taken for granted, except for a small community of boatowners, anglers, walkers and, to a lesser extent, cyclists. In past years they have suffered neglect but fortunately, owing to the enlightened interest of local communities, voluntary groups, some public officials and, latterly, the cross-border state agency, Waterways Ireland, they are now receiving the attention and resources they deserve. They may no longer occupy an important place in our transport network but they offer a superb amenity to be enjoyed by those pursuing a variety of leisure interests.

In this book I have set out a total of 29 tours to be enjoyed along the banks of seven of Ireland's inland waterways. To be included, all the waterways had to have had towpaths along their banks that are still passable by bicycle. It will surprise many to learn that almost 650km of towpaths and trackways qualify under these criteria. The tours are recommendations and do not need to be religiously followed. There are many points along the routes where cyclists can begin and end their journey. There are also many opportunities for off-route excursions and there are a number of tours where such excursions are suggested so that local highlights are experienced. The book is intended to provide the reader with information to plan a route, as well as signalling items of interest along the way. It should be remembered that, with the exception of the Shannon-Erne Waterway, the distances quoted at the start of each tour are for the outward journey only and need to be doubled for a round trip journey distance. Some cyclists may prefer to make their return journey by road, to sample some of the nearby towns.

Several people have asked me how long each tour takes. I declined to include a time estimate for any of the tours as it would depend on too many variables, not the least of which is the cyclist's fitness. The canal towpaths and river trackways are relatively level but the surfaces vary and progress can sometimes be affected by the weather. Apart from the special circumstances of the Shannon-Erne Waterway and the filled-in section of the Lagan Navigation, they are all fully capable of passage even in the depths of winter when the paths provide a different challenge and the environment presents a different vista.

While this book was originally intended for cyclists it will be of keen interest also to walkers. Some of the tours embrace routes which are part of waymarked trails but the majority offer fresh excursions through unspoiled countryside and regions which few people are aware exist as potential walking routes. In addition, walkers will not encounter the access difficulties that have become all too familiar in our hills and mountains. Boatowners and those with an interest in Ireland's heritage will also find much to interest them within these pages.

WATERWAYS MISCELLANY

This chapter is a compendium of fascinating facts and snippets that reveal the character of the formidable engineering achievements that live on along Ireland's man-made inland waterways.

EARLY ORIGINS

Canals have been a feature of the world's landscape for a very long time. The word canal is taken from the Latin word *canalis* which is translated as 'artificial waterway'. There is evidence of their use by early Egyptian and Chinese civilisations and also by the Romans.

The first canal is credited to King Menes who built a canal in Upper Egypt around 4000 BC. The first Chinese canal dates back to 600 BC when the 419km (260-mile) Wild Goose Canal linked the Yellow River to the Huai River. The Romans were the first to build a canal in Europe linking Arles in southern France to the Mediterranean Sea in 103 BC. The first canal in the British Isles dates back to 120 AD when the Romans built the

Foss Dyke connecting Lincoln with the Trent River at Torksey. The earliest canal in Ireland is thought to be the Friar Island Cut which is said to have been built prior to 1150 to link Galway to Lough Corrib. These early canals were built for irrigation, to link adjacent lakes, to deliver drinking water and, to a limited extent, to transport goods more easily than on dry land.

It was the latter purpose that provided the impetus for the modern canal which quickly became the transport system facilitating the Industrial Revolution in the eighteenth century. Recognising that heavy loads could be transported more efficiently on water than on roads, the first commercial canal to be built in the British Isles was constructed in Northern Ireland at Newry between 1731 and 1741 to carry coal from Tyrone coalfields. This was quickly followed by the commencement of canal construction in England to service new factories sprouting up in locations such as Manchester. The Grand Canal in Ireland got underway in 1756 to be followed by the Royal Canal in the 1790s.

FAMOUS CANALS
Canals have played a huge role in changing the course of world commerce. Two canals in particular have had the most impact: the Suez Canal and the Panama Canal. Others, such as the Bridgewater Canal in England, have a special place in waterways history, having been built at the instigation of the 3rd Duke of Bridgewater, Francis Egerton, the man who is credited with introducing canals to England but, more importantly, the canal was the work of James Brindley, one of the greatest canal engineers in history.

SUEZ CANAL
The Suez Canal ranks as one of the great engineering

achievements in world history. Until the canal was opened through the narrow neck of land that separates Western Asia from Egypt it was necessary for ships sailing from Europe to Asia to circumnavigate Africa, adding thousands of miles to their journeys. Although it had occupied the minds of many engineers over the years it was the Frenchman, Ferdinand de Lesseps, who got the opportunity in 1859 to put his plans into practice.

There is an Irish connection, however. In designing his canal de Lesseps used a survey which had been made by an Irish military surveyor from Annalong, County Down, called Francis Rawdon Chesney (1789-1872). In 1829, acting on an army commission, Chesney carried out a survey that showed that a canal cut across Egypt's Suez peninsula was feasible. De Lesseps described the Irishman as the 'father of the Suez Canal'. The canal took over ten years to build and is 160km long with no locks and passes through several lakes on its way to the sea. It is cut to sea level so locks were not necessary. In order to facilitate ocean-going vessels it is cut to 10.4m (34 feet). The top of the canal is 91.4m (300 feet) wide while the bottom stretches to 60m (197 feet). It cost £20 million to complete but has since cost a multiple of that figure on ongoing maintenance. Dredging operations are constantly necessary to keep the channel open.

The Suez Canal had an immediate impact on European trade, especially to British trade with the Far East, Australia and New Zealand. Britain was at the time the greatest trading and exporting nation and it benefited enormously from the canal's opening. In more recent years the canal's benefits have been extended to many other countries, not least being the neighbouring oil rich nations of the Gulf area.

PANAMA CANAL

Spurred on by his great success in the Middle East, Ferdinand de Lesseps turned his attentions to cutting through the Isthmus of Panama, the long, thin neck of land that joins North and South America. The absence of a link between the world's two great oceans, the Atlantic and the Pacific, meant that ships wishing to pass from one side of America to the other were required to round Cape Horn and its treacherous seas at the foot of South America. As far back as 1601 Samuel de Champlain proposed a canal across Panama in his *Brief Narrative* which describes his voyage to the West Indies. It was not until 1882 that de Lesseps commenced construction of the canal.

De Lesseps was, however, thwarted in his plans. Two things stopped him. Firstly, his company ran out of money and, secondly, and of greater significance, he discovered that nature had its own way of stifling his ambitions. The land through which the canal had to be cut was infested with millions of malaria and yellow fever bearing mosquitoes. Thousands of de Lesseps' workers died in their efforts to build the canal before he was finally forced to give up.

Fortunately for world commerce and, in particular, for American trade, the United States Government came to the rescue. After a revolution in Panama, during which the only person to die was, curiously, a Chinese national, they purchased the strip of territory across the isthmus and set about completing the canal. In order to save work it was decided to temper the French ambition to cut a sea level canal and instead to construct a lock canal with an upper level over 24.4m (80 feet) above the sea. US engineer, John Stevens, was hired to supervise construction. Also appointed was a

Baltimore doctor called Gorgas whose contribution was telling. His first battle was with the Stegomyia and Anopheles mosquitoes. It may appear that he took things to the extreme but he was hugely successful in this battle. The following is an account of his actions:

> He screened up all the houses and ordered every household to cover up all vessels that held water. He drained lakes, swamps, ditches and ponds. Those that could not be drained he oiled so that the mosquitoes in them could not breathe. He cut grass jungles to the ground, destroyed all vermin and burned all rubbish. He raised all buildings up above the ground and covered them with wire screens. He screened every train and on every train he put a hospital car. He banned alcohol.

As one observer remarked at the time; 'Fifty thousand strong tee-totallers have done the greatest piece of work the modern world has ever seen.'

From an engineering perspective the greatest feat involved the cutting of a channel through the Culebra Mountain. Over 100 million tonnes of rock and earth had to be blown away to make a 11.3km (seven-mile) passage for ships through this mountain. Another 360 million tonnes of material were dug out to make the canal, which is 91.4m (300 feet) wide at the bottom.

The Panama Canal was formally opened for traffic on 15 August 1914 and is remarkable for the size of its lock gates. Each has two leaves and each leaf is 19.8m (65 feet) wide and 2.1m (7 feet) thick. They vary in height from 14.3 to 25m (47 to 82 feet). It takes a ship about two hours to pass through all the canal's locks.

THE BRIDGEWATER CANAL

The Bridgewater Canal was named after the 3rd Duke of Bridgewater, Francis Egerton, who is known as the father of inland navigation. He hailed from Berkhamstead in the heart of England, where he lived in a fine residence called Ashridge Hall about 6.4km (four miles) from the town. He was an owner of coalmines and the speedy transport of coal from his mines was something that regularly occupied his mind. In 1759, with the sanction of Parliament, he began work on a waterway that would carry coal from his mine at Worsley to Manchester.

While the canal was the Duke's brainchild it owes its success in engineering terms to James Brindley who at first worked under the direction of another engineer, John Gilbert. Born in 1716 at Thornsett, Derbyshire in humble circumstances, Brindley had no formal engineering training but was a marvel with machinery. He was obsessed with the idea of building canals. It was said that he once remarked that he believed Nature meant rivers simply to feed navigable canals.

The canal link between Manchester and Worsley was the first serious venture of its kind in England and involved tunnelling, raising great embankments and carrying the canal across the River Irwell by means of a 182.9m (600-feet) aqueduct. The canal was later extended to Liverpool, linking up with the Mersey tideway at Runcorn. The Barton Aqueduct, where the Bridgewater Canal crosses the River Irwell section of the Manchester Ship Canal, is the first navigable aqueduct ever built in England. When the ship canal was constructed it became necessary to find some way of allowing big vessels to pass under the Bridgewater Canal and a fascinating swing aqueduct was built.

When James Brindley died in 1772 he had given England 587km (365 miles) of canals, bringing life to new towns and creating burgeoning cities out of smaller ones like Manchester and Liverpool. His patron, whose genius and perseverance were vital to the success of England's Industrial Revolution, is commemorated by a memorial near Ashridge Hall, overlooking the valley through which England's Grand Union Canal runs. His first canal was always referred to as the Duke's Cut by the boatmen who worked on it.

TOWPATHS

Towpaths were originally built along the banks of canals to facilitate the horses that were used to haul boats along the waterways before the introduction of steam and diesel engines. The word itself is an English term and in Ireland the paths were more often referred to as 'the drag line', 'trackway' or 'horse walk' depending on which waterway you happened to be travelling. In cases where a waterway included a lake or a tidal section, where towpaths were not feasible, boats were required to use sails or rely on tidal flows to continue their passage.

On some canals towpaths were built on one side only. This caused difficulty where there were branches off the main canal on the side opposite to the towpath and accommodation bridges had to be built to facilitate the crossing over of the horses. In the case of the Stour Navigation in England the towpath changes from side to side so horses were trained to jump on the decks of the boats and so cross over. It was later found that when steam barges were introduced on this waterway they washed the banks away and horses were brought back.

In the time of the horse-drawn passenger boat a frequent

sight on some of the canals were liveried postilions who were armed with pistols and blunderbusses and who rode ahead of the boats as a protection against highwaymen.

Following the arrival of engine driven boats in the nineteenth century the role of the horse became redundant. However, they survived on some waterways well into the middle of the twentieth century. Hugh Malet, in his delightful book, *Voyage in a Bowler Hat,* reports an encounter with a horse-drawn narrow boat at Birmingham on his voyage through the English canals in 1958.

Today a lot of towpaths have disappeared, having succumbed to a variety of circumstances. In some cases they have been buried under the unhindered growth of many years while in others they have been subjected to poaching by local farmers. Poaching arises where the previously fenced off towpaths have been incorporated into the fields of the farmer through which the waterway passes. As you tour the waterways you will find many instances where farm animals graze right down to the water's edge.

In more recent years those charged with the maintenance and restoration of our waterways have been recovering the towpaths from the neglect and deterioration they have suffered over the years. In Europe projects are being embarked upon which will see disused towpaths brought back to life for the shared enjoyment of non-motorised users such as walkers, cyclists and even roller-bladers.

LOCKS

Locks have a very important role to play in the canal system. They are the steps that enable the water level of the canal to be changed without changing the current. For example, the Grand Canal rises 85.3m (280 feet) from its link with the River Liffey at Grand Canal Basin in Ringsend to its summit level at Lowtown in County

Kildare. About 30.5m (100 feet) of this rise takes place between Ringsend and Clondalkin. This would not be possible without locks, which effectively give the canal its constant flat appearance.

The type of lock used on Ireland's principal canals is known as a 'pound lock' or a 'chambered lock' and has its origins back in the fifteenth century. Chambered locks were invented in the tenth century by Chhaio Wei-yo who installed one on China's Grand Canal. However, invention of the modern version is credited to the Duke of Milan's engineer, Bertola da Novato, while he was building Italy's Bereguardo Canal.

Locks enable boats to pass through different water levels while remaining afloat and in a quicker and easier fashion than previous methods used, which involved much hauling and pushing. They consist of two sets of swinging gates set close to each other, forming a chamber. The more traditional locks along Ireland's waterways have balance beams which extend out over the walls of the chamber and these are used to push the gates open and shut. Leonardo da Vinci is credited with the invention of the gates used on the Irish canals. These are known as 'mitre' gates which close into a 'V' that points upstream when closed. The force of the water pressing against the gate keeps it closed. Originally the lock gates were made of oak but now the maintenance engineers use timber imported from West Africa, with central steel cores. In the case of the Shannon-Erne Waterway, which was restored and modernised in the early 1990s, the lock gates are made of steel and are fully automated. This modern waterway has changed the traditional profile of Irish locks as there are no white-ended balance beams protruding over the walls of the chambers.

In 1981 Watling St Lock Gate Factory in Dublin started to produce lock gates in premises donated by Guinness Ireland with financial help from Dublin Corporation and trainees provided by ANCO, the State training agency of the time. The primary function of this factory was to produce gates for the Royal Canal which was being actively restored by the Royal Canal Amenity Group. It did, however, produce gates for the Grand Canal also. The gates used in the restoration of the Naas Branch of the Grand Canal were made at this facility which was eventually closed in January 1990.

As you cycle along any summit canal, such as the Grand Canal, you will note that the direction of the lock gates changes once the canal hits its summit level, at Lowtown in the case of the Grand Canal. There are a total of 25 locks (7 on the Circular Line and 18 on the Main Line) on that canal bringing the water to the summit level of 85.3m (280 feet). These are known as rising locks and the gates all point westward when closed. The remaining locks on the principal lines of that canal are falling locks and all point eastward when closed. A number of the locks are double chambered. This is necessary when the desired water level change is too severe to be accommodated by a single chambered lock.

Locks can be of varying length, largely determined by the size of boats that will pass through them. The Gaujau Daugava Canal in Riga, capital of Latvia, contains the world's largest lock which is 1km long.

Bogs and Breaches

The Grand Canal is a summit level canal that courses its way through lengthy stretches of bogland, such as the environs of Edenderry and a 12.9km (eight-mile) stretch along the route from Tullamore to Shannon Harbour. Not only did the canal engineers have to deal with drainage and supply difficulties during the

13

construction, they encountered ongoing maintenance problems due to breaches caused by subsidence. Bog embankments have caused problems since they were built. The first recorded breach occurred in 1797, the year the canal was completed to Daingean.

When a breach occurs the canal quickly loses its water supply. For example, in 1989 there was a breach near Edenderry and it is estimated that the canal lost 455 million litres (100 million gallons) of its water supply as it poured into nearby rivers and drains. Despite the fact that the engineers learned from their mistakes along the way, particularly as they cut through the extensive boglands around Edenderry, the later stages of the canal have been especially susceptible to breaches. A major breach occurred near Derry Bridge (which is close to the Macartney Aqueduct – see Section A, Tour 10) in January 1954 which took four months to repair. A model of this breach and its impact is on display at the Waterways Ireland Visitor Centre at the Grand Canal Basin in Ringsend, Dublin.

Another area where the canal engineers had significant difficulties was through Ballyteigue Bog (see Section A, Tour 4). Because of severe subsidence the engineers had to construct a new stretch of canal and change one of the locks.

In the 1830s there were a number of occasions when breaches were caused by other than natural events. In some areas, during periods of severe downturns in local employment, man-made breaches clandestinely appeared in the knowledge that local labour would be required to repair them thus providing a much-needed boost for the workforce in the locality. The canal company quickly sorted this out by ruling that no local labour was to be used in the repair of breaches and this decision made the canal less vulnerable to malicious attacks.

In recent years since responsibility for the Grand Canal was transferred to the State from 1986 major repairs have been carried out to the bog embankments to safeguard vulnerable sections. The modern way of repairing breaches is to line the embankment with heavy-duty polythene which is then covered with a layer of puddle clay. Careful attention is paid throughout to the reed fringe of the canal which protects the canal banks from erosion by absorbing the wave energy created by both passing boats and the wind.

A GRAVE MISTAKE

There is story told in *The Grand Canal, Inchicore and Kilmainham*, about a body that was found floating near Sally's Bridge in Dublin. A local family was asked to identify the body and was horrified to discover that the body was that of a relative they had recently buried at Goldenbridge Cemetery near the canal. The corpse had been dug up and stolen by grave robbers who were rumbled making their getaway and the body went into the canal.

CANALSIDE 'LINGO'

Over the years the canals provided significant employment in the areas they coursed through. Apart from the boatmen there were many people involved in the maintenance and supervision of the canals. These included self-explanatory functions such as lock-keepers, weedcutters, dredgers, inspectors and toll collectors. As with other activities associated with a particular venue or area the people who worked on Ireland's inland waterways developed their own language to describe certain other people and functions specifically related to the waterways:

Greaser – pronounced as 'Grazer'. This was effectively the lowest

rank of worker on the boat and was the starting position for some-
one who wished to devote their lives to canal boats. The greaser,
who was usually aged about fourteen years old when he was first
taken on board, was responsible for greasing the engine, cooking
and whatever other duties the skipper assigned to him. An individual starting as a greaser could aspire in time to become a deck-
hand, then an engineman and, finally, a skipper.

Webs – These were casual labourers who were so called because
they tried to stick to a boat in order to get work.

Stopmen – They operated the rope used to stop the boats as they
entered locks.

Bankrangers – The responsibility of the bankranger was to moni-
tor the canal banks to ensure that they were kept in good order, to
check the drains and that nefarious activities did not feature along
the routes of the canals.

Bulker – This was a storeman who was involved in transhipping
boats.

Hackmen and Hackboats – While the majority of the trade boats
that plied their trade on the canal were company owned there were
a number of private operators. These were known as hackmen and
their boats as hackboats. They were also sometimes called bye-
traders although this term was probably more appropriate to those
boatmen who leased boats from the canal company. Boats operated by the company bore numbers with the suffix 'M' while pri-
vately-operated boats bore numbers with the suffix 'B'.

Hauler – This was the man, or in many cases boy, who walked
with the horse towing the canal boat.

Canal boatmen never referred to the port and starboard sides of
their boats in the way other boatmen do. For them the port side

was known as the 'stoprope side' while the starboard side was called the 'scuttle side', the scuttle being the companionway to the cabin.

GUINNESS ON TAP

The canal boatmen worked long hours and had a reputation of being great drinkers. They were never far from the demon drink because a lot of porter produced by Guinness at its James' Gate brewery was distributed to the regions using the Grand Canal as it was found to arrive in better condition on the calm waters of the canal then using rough roads. An unspoken tradition of tapping the porter kegs grew up among the boatmen using a gimlet and a cooper's peg. Often the keg tapping was located under the sashes so it would not be easily discovered. It was said that Guinness were well aware of this activity and it was also said that the brewers used to include that little bit extra when filling the kegs to ensure the boatmen would not be found in dire need.

COMPUTER GAMES AND THE ROYAL CANAL

A question for pub quizzes perhaps: what is the connection between computer games and the Royal Canal? The answer is the eminent Irish mathematician, Sir William Rowan Hamilton (1805-65). On 16 October 1843 Hamilton was walking with his wife near the Royal Canal when in a flash of inspiration he finally solved a problem that had been dogging him for years – the fundamental formula for quaternion multiplication. In his excitement he took out his penknife and carved the equation $i^2 = j^2 = k^2 = ijk = -1$ into one of the stones of Broome Bridge. While the formula may appear meaningless to most of us its importance in mathematical history and development is immense. Hamilton's discovery has proved vital in many scientific breakthroughs.

Quaternions were pivotal to the invention of the television and radio and most recently they have been used to develop computer games. The use of quaternions allows computer game designers to create 3D forms. Every time a computer-generated character turns a corner or rotates, quaternions come into play. Hamilton's discovery is commemorated by a plaque on the bridge.

THE SNAILS OF POLLARDSTOWN FEN

Pollardstown Fen, County Kildare, is the principal water supply for the Grand Canal. It is also home to a rare snail which gained international renown when its existence was threatened by a motorway and has since faced another threat. The following story by Liam Reid of *The Irish Times* elaborates on the snail's plight:

RARE SNAIL SURVIVES MOTORWAY BUT FALLS FOUL OF HEAVY RAINFALL

It may have fended off a motorway, but a rare snail has proved too weak for that vagary of Irish life, the rain. It has emerged that last year's unprecedented rainfall has had a significant impact on the population of the rare whorl snail (*angistora vertiego*) in Pollardstown Fen, Co. Kildare, when many of them drowned following a rise in water levels. The snail was at the centre of a major controversy after the Government was forced to delay work on the Kildare bypass for two years over environmental concerns. Conservationists complained that the water source of Pollardstown Fen would be destroyed by the road's design. Work recommenced on the bypass in 2000 after a major redesign, which added €6 million to the cost. However, despite the measures, a significant proportion of the snails died last winter. Local authority staff have been

18

monitoring four stations at the fen. A spokesman said: 'One of the ecologists noted the snails had ceased to be at one of the stations. It appears that due to excessive rainfall they drowned. This was an entirely natural occurrence and in any event we are confident the snails will recolonise. The occurrence had nothing whatsoever to do with the construction of the motorway.

23 October 2003

Ghost Stories

Ghost stories and tales of the black arts abound in Ireland and a number have connections with the inland waterways. The following are a selection:

Haunted Locks

There are a number of locks along the waterways featured in this book which have a long held reputation for being haunted. By way of pure coincidence two of these bear the number 13. The first is the 13th Lock on the Grand Canal. This is located near Lyons House and Demesne on the border between County Dublin and County Kildare. It is reported to have been built through an old graveyard, hence the reason for its haunted reputation. The other 13th Lock is on the Royal Canal and is located near Deey Bridge, marking the end of the level from Blanchardstown and is close to Carton House and Demesne, Maynooth, County Kildare. It is known officially as the 13th Lock but this discounts the tidal lock from the River Liffey at Spencer Dock. Like its Grand Canal counterpart it is a location where boatmen would never moor for the night. Canal legend has stories of strange sounds and figures associated with the area in the immediate vicinity of this lock. The reasons for the lock's sinister reputation are lost in the mists of time but its number may have something to do with it. In his book, *Irish Ghost Stories,* Patrick Byrne suggests it may have to do with a passenger boat which foundered there carrying emigrants escaping from Ireland's mid-nineteenth-century famine.

Yet another area with eerie associations is Bestfield Cut and Lock on the Barrow Navigation near Carlow. Once again the boatmen would shun this area as a mooring location. Locals say its reputation is due to several drownings that took place close to the weir at the start of the cut, which is a popular location for swimming. It is also possible that the ghost stories were dreamt up by the inhabitants of nearby Knockbeg College, a large diocesan secondary school.

On the Lagan Navigation the lock with the haunted reputation is the 5th lock at Ballydrain. While no specific cause is documented or narrated to justify its reputation other than apparitions from time to time, it is once again a location near which no boatman would moor his boat for the night. Further along the same waterway is a bridge called Lady Bridge which is said to be haunted by the ghost of Lady Moira, whose family left the area as far back as 1763. Local folklore states that she takes a midnight stroll around the area wearing a white dress and carrying a lamp.

Rialto s Black Dog

The Grand Canal had a phantom black dog with blazing eyes which was said to have been seen regularly along the banks of the Grand Canal between Rialto Bridge and Inchicore Bridge. It would disappear into the canal when spotted or pursued.

Maynooth College s Haunted Room

St Patrick's College in Maynooth, County Kildare has educated many Roman Catholic priests in Ireland and in recent years has expanded to become a flourishing third-level institution. There is a room in the college that is said to have had a chilling past. The room in question is located on the top corridor of Rhetoric House and for the past century and a half has been in use as an oratory of St Joseph. Incidents which took place prior to its use as an oratory are the reason for its eerie associations. There are many versions of the room's history but what they are all agreed on is that at least two seminarians assigned to that room committed suicide there within a short period and that a third survived another attempt. Both the seminarians who died were said to have cut their throats. Legend has it that when the survivor looked in the mirror as he was preparing to shave an unknown force was compelling him to cut his own throat and that he only survived by breaking away from his own gaze and throwing himself out the window. He ended up breaking a number of bones. After that no student would use the room. Later the front wall of the room on which the mirror was said to have been hanging was removed and the room was converted into an oratory.

The Percy Place Soldier

Patrick Byrne, in *Irish Ghost Stories,* tells a tale related to Percy Place, which is located near Mount Street Bridge and Huband Bridge on the Circular Line of the Grand Canal. It concerns a young English girl who in recent years was working in an hotel in Dublin and who used to walk past Percy Place on her way from work. She enquired from a friend why there was always a soldier stationed near Mount Street Bridge in Percy Place. Knowing that this was the scene of a battle more than half a century before, her friend asked her what kind of uniform the soldier wore and when she looked more closely on her next journey she noted that the figure was wearing the uniform of the Sherwood Foresters. She was astonished to learn that members of that regiment had fought a battle at Mount Street Bridge during the Easter 1916 rising and that several soldiers had lost their lives there.

Famine Tragedy near Killashee

The Royal Canal passes near the small village of Killashee in County Longford which lies to the west of the 43rd Lock and Aghnaskea Bridge. The village lies in the heart of an area that witnessed much emigration during the Great Famine of the 1840s. Passenger boats on the Royal Canal were regularly used to ferry emigrants on the first stage of their long and sad journey overseas. Another tale from Patrick Byrne's book centres around an intending emigrant, Sean Burke, who hailed from Rossaun in County Roscommon and was one of those making the walk to Killashee to catch a passenger boat. It was customary for those making the long voyage to bring something to eat during their journey but unfortunately Sean Burke was so poor he had nothing to bring with him. He had hoped to get some provisions at a house he knew could supply him with food. Byrne relates the tale of the unfortunate man pleading with the owner of the house. The latter refused to give him anything except in exchange for a large round flagstone that was in Burke's house and which would have been useful at that time for the grinding of corn. Despite suffering from exhaustion and hunger, Burke made the journey back to his own house, intending to return with the flagstone. However, the effort of carrying the stone on his back proved too much for him and he succumbed to its weight on the way, perishing from hunger and exhaustion on the roadside. It is said by locals that his ghost returns from time to time and can be seen walking the road, burdened by the precious flagstone. When the figure reaches a rise in the road it appears to fall to the side and disappears.

A Scary Laganside Illusionist

Pascal Downing, who lives on the banks of Lough Neagh adjacent to its junction with the Lagan Navigation, tells stories about Wanger Byrne who lived in the vicinity of Aghagallon village near Lough Neagh. He had a mysterious and dark reputation due to his frequent dabbling in the black arts.

There is a bar near Aghagallon with a private room where Wanger Byrne was said to have produced a hare and two greyhounds from a tumbler of water. A bout of coursing apparently ensued and those present swore they witnessed the animals chasing around.

Another illusion attributed to Wanger Byrne related to two men who stole some planks of wood from Byrne's yard. They were later confronted by Byrne in the pub and denied any knowledge of the missing wood. Mr. Byrne then produced a shaving mirror and when they looked into the mirror they were shocked to see themselves stealing the wood from his yard reflected in the mirror. What befell them for their thievery is not told.

CANALSIDE HUMOUR

The canal boatmen loved to play tricks on unsuspecting people they encountered on their travels. One tale relates to the time when canal boats were drawn by horses from the towpath and concerns a traveller who was passing through Graiguenamanagh on the River Barrow, apparently on his way to Dublin. Thinking it would be a pleasurable way to pass a few days and at the same time a cheap way of getting to Dublin, the cute traveller approached one of the boats on the quayside at the town and enquired whether he could hitch a ride to Dublin.

He said he was willing to work his passage. The boat's skipper was quick to see an opportunity for fun and he agreed. When the traveller asked him what he could do he was told to lead the horse along the towpath. How long he journeyed along the towpath before realising he was going to have to walk the whole way to Dublin was never revealed.

Another tale concerns a boatman who approached a farmer who had brought his cattle down to the edge of the canal so they could drink. In the argot of waterways this act is known as 'poaching'. In a bellicose tone the boatman accused the farmer of attempting to empty the canal because his cattle were so thirsty and there would not be enough water left for him to complete his journey. Whether the farmer believed him or not is not reported but the boat would have been well on its way before the farmer realised he had been the butt of a joke.

SECTION A

THE GRAND CANAL

HISTORY OF THE GRAND CANAL

It is easy to forget the two principal reasons why the Grand Canal was built, as they have been made redundant through developments in other areas over the years. Originally the canal was built to provide an efficient and comfortable transport system for trade and commerce and also to secure for the citizens of Dublin a reliable source of pure water. The Commissioners of Inland Navigation, who were established in 1751, were given the responsibility amidst controversy to forge a waterway link between Dublin and the River Shannon. They appointed an engineer called Thomas Omer to design and supervise the works. Construction of the canal started in 1756 and the early years were fraught with difficulties causing several revisions of the plans.

Omer held the position until 1763 and in that time he built just over 19km of canal, starting at Clondalkin complete with three locks, six bridges, seven aqueducts and four lock-houses. His three locks had to be rebuilt shortly afterwards as they were considered too large. In 1765 Dublin Corporation took over the completion of the canal to the River Morrell, 3.2km (two miles) short of Sallins, in order to secure a supply of drinking water which the capital badly needed.

Advance was made in 1772 with the incorporation of the Company of the Undertakers of the Grand Canal. Early directors of the company included John Binns, a merchant who later left the company to form a rival operation, the Royal Canal Company. Another director was Joseph Huband, a barrister, who served the company from 1777 up to his death in 1835 with the exception of a few years. A couple of bridges and an aqueduct were named after him.

Progress on the canal was slow and it was not until 2 February 1779 that it opened to traffic and Thomas Digby Brooke secured the honour of being the first trader on the canal. The first passenger boat started service in August 1780 between Osbertstown, near Sallins, and Dublin, a distance of 29km. The journey took nine hours to complete. The boat left Dublin at 6am every Monday and Thursday, returning every Tuesday and Friday. The service was extended to Robertstown four years later.

Over the next couple of years a number of important works were completed. In 1780 work started on the construction of an aqueduct over the River Liffey just west of Sallins. To augment the canal's water supply two feeders were installed. The most important of these is the Milltown Feeder (see Tour 7) which enters the summit level near Lowtown and is the main source of water for the canal. It extends for 12.9km (8 miles) and commences at a pool in Pollardstown Fen that is fed by an area abundant with natural springs. There are at least 36 known springs at this location. The second was the Blackwood Feeder which linked into the canal at Bonynge or Healy's Bridge about 2km east of Robertstown. This was 6.4km (4 miles) long with a reservoir at Foranfan. It was closed in 1952 and is now mostly filled in.

While work continued on the Main Line the network was extended in other directions as well. In 1789 the Kildare Canal Company completed a 4km branch to Naas. The branch was subsequently bought over by the Grand Canal Company when its Kildare counterpart ran into financial difficulties a number of years later. In 1790 work started on the Circular Line which was to link the Main Line to the Liffey at Ringsend. This line was completed in 1796.

The Barrow and Shannon Lines of the Grand Canal were completed over the late 1790s and early 1800s but not without considerable difficulties encountered on the way. The stretch across the marshlands in the environs of the Bog of Allen leading to Edenderry witnessed major subsidence problems necessitating the canal to be carried on high embankments across the bog. This stretch alone took ten years to complete.

When the canal reached Tullamore in 1798 further delays were caused by disputes over the remaining course it should take to the Shannon. Thomas Omer, the canal's first engineer, had planned to use the River Brosna. This was rejected in favour of a still-water navigation that in fact followed closely the course of the Brosna. Once again the canal had to make its way across a lengthy stretch of bog. Despite learning from the experiences near Edenderry and allowing longer drainage times, there were still difficulties staunching subsidences with the result that the first trade boat did not pass through the canal to the Shannon until 1804.

In the following 30 years the network was expanded with the

addition of branches to Edenderry, Ballinasloe, Mountmellick and Kilbeggan. The Edenderry Branch was financed by local landlord Lord Downshire and despite being only 1.5km long it took five years to complete. With the exception of the Naas Branch, it is the only branch to remain intact to this day, all others having been closed to navigation and either fully or partially filled in.

In 1834, in an effort to reduce travelling times, the Grand Canal Company introduced, 'fly' or 'Scotch' boats to the canal. These were narrower and lighter boats pulled by four horses and could achieve speeds of 14.5km (9 miles) per hour, double the speed of existing boats. However, as the years passed, the company faced increasing competition from the coming of the railway and all passenger traffic on the canal ceased in 1852. Trade boats continued in service for over a century more, largely due to the carriage of Guinness. However, in 1960 Coras Iompair Éireann, which was responsible for Irish railways and had merged with the Grand Canal Company a decade earlier, withdrew the last of the trade boats and so ended the canal's life as a transport system.

In November 1963 the Grand Canal's existence came under further threat when Dublin Corporation formally requested the then Minister for Local Government to close the canal. The Corporation had designs on the use of the bed of the Circular Line that traverses the south of Dublin city as a surface water sewer. The new surface would then have been concreted over for use as a roadway. Thanks to a strong publicity campaign launched by the Inland Waterways Association of Ireland, the Corporation was thwarted in its efforts and in 1969 it agreed instead to place the sewer in a tunnel beneath the canal.

In recent years responsibility for the Grand Canal has passed through the hands of a number of Government departments and agencies. It now lies with Waterways Ireland, a 32-county body established under the British-Irish Agreement in 1999. Its brief is to manage, maintain, develop and restore inland navigable waterways, principally for recreational purposes.

GRAND CANAL ROUTE OVERVIEW

The Grand Canal cuts a line westward through the province of Leinster, reaching the River Shannon in County Offaly with a southward branch linking it to the River Barrow. It has four principal components:

Circular Line: This runs from Ringsend in the south east of Dublin city, where it has a link to the River Liffey and to Suir Road Bridge in Dublin 8, where it connects to the Main Line. Covering a distance of 6km, it has seven locks.

Main Line: This line runs for a total of 40km from Dublin to Lowtown in County Kildare. It passes through eighteen locks and rises to a summit level of 85.3m (280 feet) at Robertstown and Lowtown. There is a 4km branch to Naas which enters the Main Line near Sallins.

Shannon Line: Running westward for 85km, this line courses from the summit at Lowtown, through the Offaly towns of Daingean and Tullamore, to join the River Shannon at Shannon Harbour near Banagher. The line has eighteen falling locks and branches at Edenderry and Kilbeggan. The Kilbeggan Branch was closed to navigation in 1961. A branch to Ballinasloe at the end of the line is also closed.

Barrow Line: From Lowtown this line turns south through the County Kildare towns of Rathangan and Monasterevin to join the River Barrow at Athy, a distance of 46km. It has nine falling locks and a branch leading to Mountmellick from Monasterevin which was closed in 1960. The Milltown Feeder, which is the canal's principal water supply, flows into the Barrow Line close to Lowtown.

Tour 1
Ringsend to Hazelhatch
Grand Canal Basin
(21 Kilometres)

This tour starts at Ringsend in the south east of Dublin city and embraces all the Grand Canal's Circular Line, which extends for 6.5km to Inchicore, and then moves on to the Main Line, the first lock of which is located at Suir Road. For all the Circular Line and the first three locks of the Main Line, cyclists have to use the roads which run parallel to the canal before embarking on the towpath at Suir Road in Drimnagh. You can stay on the left towpath right up to the Lucan Road Bridge which is the 16km mark for this tour. You should then switch to the right hand towpath for the remainder of the journey.

Maps
Ordnance Survey of Ireland Discovery Series:
Map 50 Dublin City and District (ISBN 1-901496-64-3).

Tour 1 - Grand Canal
Basin to Hazelhatch
Circular Line

Key

∨ Lock

♦♦ Bridge

Grand Canal Basin

Ringsend

Ballsbridge

Ranelagh

Rathmines

St Stephen's Green

Luas Bridge

Portobello Hotel

Harold's Cross

Dolphin's Barn

Former James' Street Branch

Suir Road Bridge

Luas Bridge

Main Line

Circular Line

1. Macquay Bridge and 1st lock, Lower Grand Canal Street
2. Mc Kenny Bridge and 2nd Lock, Lower Mount Street
3. Huband Bridge and 3rd Lock, Upper Mount Street
4. Macartney Bridge and 4th Lock, Baggot Street
5. Eustace Bridge and 5th Lock, Leeson Street
6. Charlemont Bridge and 6th Lock, Charlemont Street
7. La Touche Bridge and 7th Lock, Portobello Hotel, Rathmines

CIRCULAR LINE

While work on the Main Line was started in 1756, the Circular Line was started later as a link to the River Liffey and was opened in 1796. Access to the tidal Liffey is by means of three sea locks that are located in one corner of the basin. This area has been the subject of recent and ongoing extensive redevelopment which makes it an attractive starting point for this tour.

Located at the Grand Canal Basin is the attractively constructed Waterways Ireland Visitor Centre, an exhibition centre devoted entirely to Ireland's inland waterways. Fittingly, the Centre is actually built on the water with access via a walkway and is a must see for those interested in learning more about Ireland's canals. To some Dubliners it is affectionately known as 'the box in the docks'. For details of opening hours please see Appendix I.

Going west the canal courses through an area that is dominated by offices and provides an attractive amenity for those workers on their lunchbreaks as it is tree-lined and well cared for. Cyclists should not use the towpaths as these are reserved for pedestrians. There are seven locks and seven bridges along the Circular Line stretch between Lower Grand Canal Street and Portobello, beside Rathmines. Most Dubliners do not know the names of these bridges as they are normally called after the adjacent streets. You will impress the locals with the following knowledge:

Lower Grand Canal Street	Macquay Bridge and 1st Lock
Lower Mount Street	Mc Kenny Bridge and 2nd Lock
Upper Mount Street	Huband Bridge and 3rd Lock
Baggot Street	Macartney Bridge and 4th Lock
Leeson Street	Eustace Bridge and 5th Lock

| Charlemont Street | Charlemont Bridge and 6th Lock |
| Portobello/Rathmines | La Touche Bridge and 7th Lock |

McKenny Bridge at Lower Mount Street was the location of some of the most intensive fighting during the Easter Rising in 1916, where some of the insurgents were holed up in the building that is now the Schoolhouse Hotel.

Keeping to the left of the canal you pass Herbert Place. Elizabeth Bowen (1899-1973), Anglo-Irish novelist and short story writer, was born at number fifteen on this street.

Just past Macartney Bridge and 4th Lock at Baggot Street two notable figures from Ireland's cultural past who had close associations with the canal are commemorated. On the Mespil Road side there is a seat, erected in 1968, in memory of Patrick Kavanagh (1904-1967), a Monaghan-born poet who was regularly seen by the banks of the canal in the mid-twentieth century. Kavanagh lived much of his adult life in houses close to the canal and it is said he secured his rebirth as a poet by its banks.

On Pembroke Road look out for my ghost
Dishevelled with shoes untied.

The Grand Canal regularly features in his poetry. He said that it was while he was lying between Macartney Bridge at Baggot Street and Eustace Bridge at Leeson Street that he composed the poem, 'Lines written on a seat on the Grand Canal', which is engraved on the seat and which starts as follows:

O Commemorate me where there is water, canal water,
preferably, so stilly

Greeny at the heart of summer.

On the opposite side is a life-size seated bronze of the poet by sculptor, John Coll, which was unveiled by the then President of Ireland, Mary Robinson in June 1991. Engraved on this seat are the following lines from his poem 'Canal Bank Walk':

Leafy-with-love banks and the green waters of the canal
Pouring redemption for me.

Beside the lock is also a seat commemorating Percy French (1854-1920), poet, painter, artist and engineer. Ironically the seat is on the site where Kavanagh is said to have written his poem. French lived at 35 Mespil Road, the street that borders the canal to Leeson Street.

One final item of interest at the 4th Lock is a stone plinth erected in 1995 in recognition of the link between the Grand Canal and the Grand Union Canal which runs through the midlands in England. There is an iron plate nearby with the name Braunston and the distance '296 miles' noted on it. Braunston Marina is twinned with Shannon Harbour (see Tour 10) where the Grand Canal completes its journey to the Shannon. Another notice at Shannon Harbour mentions '377 miles' which included the 130km (81 miles) that the Grand Canal has coursed on its way through Ireland to reach that point.

As you pass Leeson Street you are close to St Stephen's Green, which has a little-known association with the Grand Canal. The large lake in the centre of this park is fed with water from the canal. Just below Charlemont Bridge and 6th Lock a new bridge traverses the canal to facilitate the passing of the Luas trams.

The imposing building at the recently refurbished La Touche

Bridge at Portobello is one of the five hotels that were built by the Grand Canal Company to facilitate travellers using the canal system. The others were located at Sallins, Robertstown, Tullamore and Shannon Harbour. The Portobello Hotel was opened in July 1807 and operated as such until 1855 when it closed and was converted into an asylum for blind people until 1868. In 1896, Miss Hampson took over the building for use as a private hospital and it survived as a nursing home until 1971. It was later converted to offices and today exists as a thriving college run by the Institute of Education.

When it was a nursing home the building boasted literary and artistic connections. It features in the poem 'Enueg' by renowned playwright, Samuel Beckett (1906-1989). Furthermore, artist Jack Butler Yeats (1871-1957) periodically used to take a room at the top of the house and enjoyed frequent walks on the banks of the canal to see the swans and ducks.

The 7th Lock at Portobello has an unfortunate history in being the Grand Canal lock that has claimed the greatest number of victims. In 1824 a soldier from the nearby barracks was drowned when the lock-keeper refused to lend his drag to rescue him. Later that century, on 6 April 1861, a horse-drawn bus bound for the city from Rathmines mounted the bridge and rolled backwards into the lock, resulting in the deaths of six people. In 1940 four occupants of a car drowned when the driver accidentally drove into the lock.

Stretching southwards from Portobello Bridge is the Dublin suburb of Rathmines which was originally known as Meone's Rath (*rath* means fort in Irish) after the De Meones family who lived nearby. It is famous for a battle that took place in the summer of 1649 which was the last battle to be fought in Dublin until the Easter Rising of 1916. The Battle of Rathmines saw the final defeat of the Marquis of Ormonde's Royalists by the Parliamentarian forces commanded by Colonel Michael Jones, Governor of Dublin. Ormonde barely escaped himself and only did so by jumping a ditch on his horse.

MAIN LINE

The canal takes a distinct change in direction to the left at Suir Road Bridge as we change from the Circular Line to the Main Line, and in terms of lock numbers we now start at number 1 again. A newly-constructed bridge to take the Luas trams over the canal has meant a complete overhaul of this junction. At the junction you will see the small linear park which now occupies the space previously used by the James' Street Branch of the canal before it was filled in during the early 1970s at the behest of local action groups. This park now accommodates the track for the Luas line to Tallaght. The original small canal branch was used to link the Main Line to the canal's original terminus at James' Street Harbour and was a key connection to the Guinness Brewery at St James' Gate. Guinness used the Grand Canal system extensively from the 1790s right up to 1960, both for the transport of grain to the brewery and the distribution of its internationally renowned produce to its native customers. The last barge to officially carry freight on the Grand Canal set off on 27 May 1960 from James' Street Harbour with a cargo of Guinness on a four-day trip to Limerick.

You can now finally leave the road and mount the cycle path, sandwiched between the recently installed Luas line and the canal, and running the full length of Davitt Road. The official opening of the 1st Lock, which is located at Suir Road Bridge, took place in 1770. It is double-chambered as is the 3rd Lock 1.5km further on at Blackhorse Bridge. This facilitates a greater

Tour 1 - Grand Canal
Basin to Hazelhatch
Main Line

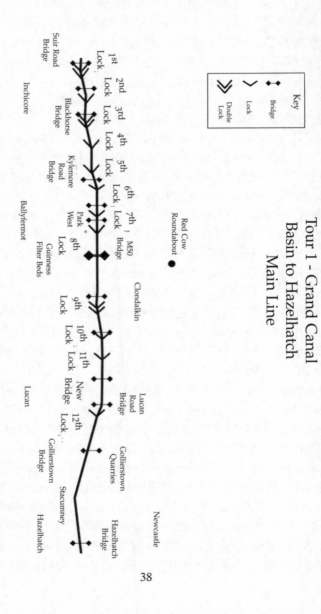

Key

Double
Lock

Lock

Bridge

1st
Lock

2nd
Lock

3rd
Lock

4th
Lock

5th
Lock

6th
Lock

7th
Lock

8th
Lock

9th
Lock

10th
Lock

11th
Lock

12th
Lock

M50
Bridge

New
Bridge

Suir Road
Bridge

Blackhorse
Bridge

Kylemore
Road
Bridge

Park
West

Guinness
Filter Beds

Lucan
Road
Bridge

Gollierstown
Quarries

Gollierstown
Bridge

Hazelhatch
Bridge

Inchicore

Ballyfermot

Red Cow
Roundabout

Clondalkin

Lucan

Newcastle

Stacumney

Hazelhatch

rise in the level of the water. It is interesting to note that the canal rises 30.5m (100 feet) between the Grand Canal Basin and Clondalkin, a distance of only 13km.

Follow the path past the 2nd Lock to Blackhorse Bridge where there is a pub called the Blackhorse Inn. If you take a look down the embankment behind this pub you will be able to see the aqueduct that was built over the River Camac.

Crossing the road at Blackhorse Bridge you get the first opportunity to leave the road. Keeping to the left-hand side the 4th, 5th ,6th, 7th and 8th Locks come in quick succession as you pass an area that has become built up with industrial buildings. A new bridge has been constructed just before the 7th Lock to take the traffic once carried by the small humpbacked bridge that struggled to accommodate modern transport needs and has now been pedestrianised. The stretch between the 7th and 8th Locks was the scene of one of the canal's saddest historical events. Just before Christmas 1792 a passenger boat sank with the loss of eleven lives, five men, four women and two children. It is said that the boat, which was the early Athy service, was overloaded with upwards of 150 passengers, some of whom had become unruly in the minutes leading up to the tragedy, partly due to the amount of drink that had been consumed.

Just beyond the 8th Lock, on the far side and beside the recently-built Park West development, are the filter beds that used to supply the water Guinness used for brewing. These beds are still in use today but not for brewing. Treated canal water is still used by Guinness for washing and cleaning machinery but water for brewing has been drawn since the mid-1980s from the Vartry Reservoir.

A striking new sculpture was installed as part of the Park West Development and adds to the passing sights to be enjoyed by users of this amenity.

Passing under the M50 the towpath has recently been much improved up to the double-chambered 9th Lock at Clondalkin. During April you may be lucky enough to see some nesting swans on this stretch. They seem to return regularly to the same spot year after year. As you cross the road at the 9th Lock it is better to change to the right or north side. From this Lock on, the path changes to grass and rough track, getting rougher, but quite passable even following bad weather.

The 11th Lock is worthy of closer inspection. Along with the 12th and 13th Locks, these were the first three locks built on the Grand Canal by its first engineer, Thomas Omer. They are unusual, because when they were first built they measured 41.8m (137 feet) long by 6.1m (20 feet) wide and were planned to accommodate vessels of 70 tons, much like those in use on some English canals. However, a report prepared by John Smeaton recommended smaller chambers designed to accommodate vessels carrying about 40 tons. A new engineer, John Trail, was appointed to succeed Thomas Omer and he reduced the size of the original locks by shortening them to 18.3m (60 feet) long with a width of 4.3m (14 feet) and by narrowing the entrances and exits. The original lower or tail-gate recesses are still visible today below the 11th and 12th Locks while at the 13th Lock the stone facing was used for the lower gates when it was converted to a double lock in 1783.

Just past the 11th Lock you will see the ivy-clad ruins of one of the three lock-houses built by Omer. If you look back in a southeasterly direction you will see the conical cap and upper part of the round tower at Clondalkin which is worth an off-route excursion. Towers such as this served as bell towers in monastic settlements and also as places of refuge. There are 65 surviving round towers in

Ireland and the one at Clondalkin is the only one in the Greater Dublin Area and one of the best preserved in the country. Its conical cap was left untouched in the rash of restoration that was carried out on round towers in the late nineteenth century. The tower stands on the site of a monastery founded by St Crohan or Mochua in the seventh century that was plundered by the Vikings in 832 and burned in 1071. Dating from between 950 and 1200, its slender structure rises to a height of 27m (88 feet). Its base has a circumference of 13.7m (45 feet) and its walls are just under one metre (three feet) thick. It has an unusual bulge at its base with an open staircase leading to a door opening 4.6m (15 feet) above ground. The eighteenth-century Dutch Huguenot artist, Thomas Beranger, who created a huge body of topographical drawings of Irish antiquities, stated on a drawing executed in 1767 that the bulge was a later addition designed to strengthen the tower, having been damaged at that point. Twenty years after this drawing was made there was a massive gunpowder explosion involving 260 barrels of powder stored at the nearby Corkagh Powder Mills, which is said to have damaged buildings over a wide area including some close to the tower. Fortunately the tower survived unscathed.

The pleasure of the 3km journey between the 11th and 12th Locks has diminished in recent years with the construction of houses and industrial parks on the south side of the canal. On the north side, open fields remain but for how long? A new road crosses the canal at the midway point between the two locks. To the left on the southern side is a housing estate called Deansrath. The land on which the estate stands was once bog and was given to the Dean of St Patrick's Cathedral by Archbishop Henry de Loundres in 1220 when he established that office. The Dean was

41

required to pay the Archbishop one pound of frankincense every Easter as nominal rent for the land.

At the Lucan Road Bridge, just before the 12th Lock, you can only proceed on the right-hand side of the canal. You are now entering one of the more delightful stretches of the canal, although the encroaching population is beginning to take its toll. At the 12th Lock is another of Thomas Omer's lock-houses in a considerably better state of preservation. The stone building alongside the lock was formerly a mill, the only one of several between here and the city to have survived.

The path from here to Hazelhatch is grass covered but in good condition, although there is increasing evidence of use by motorbike scramblers over the past few years. Just over a kilometre from the 12th Lock you will find an accommodation bridge called Gollierstown Bridge and a little bit further on, Gollierstown Quarries. These quarries provided the supply of the limestone used in the construction of the canal's locks and bridges and Thomas Omer purposely trailed his canal through these quarries to avail of the supply. Locals now refer to the quarries as 'the three lakes'. Two of the lakes are located on the south side while one is on the north side and are the result of the stone excavation carried on at this site.

About 1.5km further on the canal takes a slight turn to the left at Stacumney where you will see the ruins of another of Thomas Omer's lock-houses. The last 2km to Hazelhatch will give you a true appreciation of the delights of cycling alongside the Grand Canal. Soak in the views southwards to the Dublin Mountains and glory in the singing of the birds and scents of a rich and varied habitat before visiting the pub in Hazelhatch for well-deserved refreshment in advance of the return journey.

Tour 2
Hazelhatch to Naas via Sallins
Main Line and Naas Branch
(17 Kilometres)

Moving from Dublin through the eastern region of County Kildare and into one of Kildare's principal towns, this tour tracks the main line to Sallins and then diverts south to take in the Naas Branch. The route offers a range of cycling surfaces with a good deal of tarred roads and paths. However, the section approaching Sallins can be quite muddy, even in good weather.

How to Get There
Hazelhatch is situated to the extreme west of Dublin county and is approximately 22km from Dublin city centre. It can be accessed using the M4/N4 and taking the R403 exit for Celbridge, just past Lucan. As you reach Celbridge take a left turn in the direction of Newcastle on the R405 which will bring you to Hazelhatch. Hazelhatch Bridge is located on the south side of the village. For those located near the N7 (Naas Road), take the Newcastle exit (R120) at Rathcoole and the R405 in the direction of Celbridge just after the village.

Tour 2 - Grand Canal
Hazelhatch to Naas via Sallins
Main Line

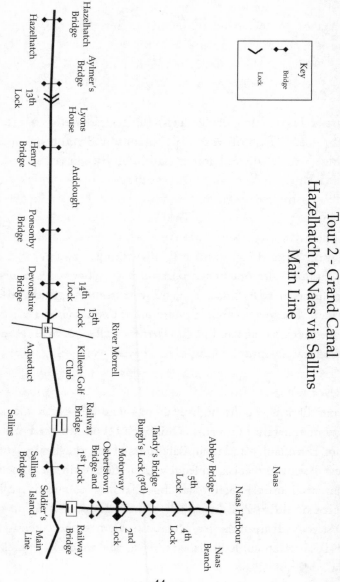

Key
Bridge
Lock

44

MAPS

Ordnance Survey of Ireland Discovery Series:

Map 50 Dublin City and District (ISBN 1-901496-64-3)

Map 49 Kildare, Meath, Offaly and Westmeath (ISBN 1-901496-16-3)

Map 55 Kildare, Laois, Offaly and Wicklow (ISBN 0-904996-67-0)

Start at Hazelhatch Bridge and keep to the south, or left, tow-path. After 1.6km of reasonably solid ground you reach Aylmer's Bridge which you can either pass under or use the road. The stretch you have just passed was the location of a lock that was initially constructed and then quickly removed. The engineers decided instead to convert the 13th Lock further on into a double chambered lock. The road at Aylmer's Bridge leads on the south side to Newcastle, just under 3km (two miles) away.

Aylmer's Bridge is named after the Aylmers of Lyons who were prominent landowners in the area from around the fifteenth century. There is no visual record of the castle they once occupied nearby which was sited at the bottom of Lyons Hill, close to a place now occupied by Lyons House which you will pass by shortly. The castle was destroyed in the 1641 Irish rebellion.

As you make your way to the 13th Lock you pass along the Lyons Demesne. The high walls of this estate partly block your view of the Hill of Lyons, an historic hill which takes its name from Liamhain, one of four daughters of the ancient Irish king of Desi Bregia who was killed by their father for disobeying his injunction against them marrying. Liamhain is said to have been buried on the Hill of Lyons whose Irish name is *Cnoc Liamhna*.

Lyons House at the centre of Lyons Demesne is presently owned by Tony Ryan of Ryanair fame and he has been painstakingly restoring it and filling it with suitable treasures. The house and estate were formerly the home of the Lawless family who used the title of Lord Cloncurry. Nicholas Lawless, son of a rich Dublin draper of humble origin, acquired the estate in 1796 from Michael Aylmer who had run up substantial gambling debts. By this stage Lawless had risen to the peerage, having converted from Catholicism to the established church. As a Catholic he had been prevented by the penal laws from buying land. Construction of Lyons House was started in 1797 to the design of architect Oliver Grace. Later remodelling work and enlargement of the original structure was carried out by another architect Richard Morrison, at the behest of the 2nd Lord Cloncurry, Valentine Lawless, who led an interesting life.

Valentine Lawless was an active member of the Society of United Irishmen, which was founded in 1791, while he was an undergraduate in Trinity College Dublin. He was twice committed to the Tower of London on suspicion of treason as a result of his political allegiances. While on travels around Europe he met and married Georgina Morgan and on their return to Ireland in 1805 Lady Cloncurry had a liaison with her husband's old school friend, Sir John Piers bt. who had gained infamy as a duellist and gambler. A court case ensued in which Lord Cloncurry sought damages of £100,000 against Piers for 'criminal conversation'. He won the case but obtained only £20,000, a massive amount of money in those times. He later married Emily, widow of John Leeson, heir to the 3rd Earl of Milltown, with whom he had a much happier life. He was also one of the directors of the Grand Canal Company of Ireland in the early parts of the nineteenth century.

The next Lord Cloncurry, the 3rd, had an unfortunate end. He threw himself out a window of Lyons House in 1869, dying from his injuries. His daughter, Emily, was a poet of renown and a prominent figure of the Irish revival in the early twentieth century. Her niece, Kathleen, inherited the property in 1929 from the 5th and last Lord Cloncurry. The property finally moved out of the hands of the Lawless family in 1958 when Kathleen's cousin, Mark Wing, sold the estate to University College Dublin. Tony Ryan acquired the house and estate in the 1990s and apart from restoring the house to its original splendour he also runs a stud farm on the estate.

Returning to the canal, the 13th Lock has the reputation of being haunted. It was said to have gone through the site of a graveyard. Drivers of the horses that used to pull the boats in the early life of the canal often reported being accompanied by a mysterious companion along the towpath near this lock. In addition, canal boatmen would never moor their boats near this lock.

Leaving the 13th Lock behind the path blends with one of the rear access roads to the Lyons estate and for the next 2.5km there is a good road running next to the canal, giving you a comfortable ride past Henry Bridge and the townland of Ardclough to reach Ponsonby Bridge. A short distance to the south is Oughterard Hill where there is the ruin of a sixth-century round tower rising to a height of 9m. This can be accessed taking the road south from Henry Bridge. In a cemetery at the foot of the tower is the grave of Arthur Guinness who died in 1803 and whose brewery has a lengthy association with the canal.

The stretch of the canal from Ponsonby Bridge is embanked and the towpath is low-lying, often becoming quite marshy. It is less frequented than other stretches of the canal and at times the grass can become high, making your cycle a little difficult.

The next landmark you reach is Devonshire Bridge. You have

just entered one of the most important areas for the canal in terms of its water supply. Just beyond the bridge are two locks in quick succession, the 14th and the 15th. Alongside these is a feeder channel that carries water from the nearby River Morrell to supply the canal and is controlled by a sluice near the old lockhouse beside the 15th Lock. It is interesting to note that this relatively small river, which is a tributary of the River Liffey, was an important source of drinking water for Dublin via the canal until the Vartry Reservoir system started to supply the capital's drinking water in 1869.

The canal crosses the River Morrell by a small aqueduct and immediately to the south is Killeen Golf Club, whose grounds run alongside the canal for just under a kilometre.

After 1km the canal courses through a long, winding section which is heavily wooded and in some places quite dark. From a cyclist's viewpoint the path can be muddy and difficult at times as it is shaded from the drying of the sun. About 1km from Sallins the canal passes under the main railway line from Dublin to Cork. In the 1840s this railway bridge was the subject of a prolonged dispute between the Grand Canal Company and the competing railway company. Recognising the threat presented by the faster speeds of the rail network, the canal company tried to frustrate the rail company by refusing to grant permission to bridge the canal. Permission was only granted when the dispute was referred to the highest levels of government.

At Sallins there is the chance to take on board some refreshment, perhaps at the Bridgewater Inn. Sallins was the location of the second of the five hotels that were built along the route of the canal. The Sallins hotel was built in 1784 on the north side of the canal close to the bridge. It was never very successful, due perhaps to its proximity to Dublin. It was eventually used as a meat packing factory and was demolished in the late 1990s.

NAAS BRANCH

As the intention of this tour is to go to Naas you are going to have to leave the canal banks briefly in order to access the towpath on the south side because buildings at Sallins Bridge have been erected right up to the canal bank. To ensure you miss the least amount of the canal's banks you can resume the path by going through the recently built Sallins Wharf estate. You will come out opposite Soldier's Island, a small, heavily wooded triangular island in the middle of the canal, which marks where the Naas Branch leaves the Main Line. Almost immediately you pass under the Dublin-Cork rail line and you will see Osbertstown Bridge ahead and just past that the 1st Lock of this branch. (An alternative route is to use the north towpath and after the Leinster Aqueduct (see Tour 3 Map) you find an underground tunnel that allows access to the south towpath from which you can backtrack to Osbertstown Bridge.)

The Naas Branch had its origins in an Act of Parliament passed in 1786 that established the County of Kildare Canal Company, allowing local landowners to build a canal to Naas. By 1789 the canal reached Naas, a distance of 4km. The company got into financial difficulties and was eventually picked up in 1808 by the Grand Canal Company of Ireland through the Court of Chancery for £2,250 (€2,857), a quarter of the costs incurred in constructing the canal. It was later extended to Corbally, a distance of 8.5km, without a lock. All work was completed by 1810. It was intended to continue the line through Kilcullen and Baltinglass, into County Wicklow, but nothing came of this. The canal was officially closed to navigation in

1961 but was re-opened in 1987 following restoration undertaken by the Office of Public Works.

At Osbertstown Bridge take the opportunity to cross to the road which tracks the canal all the way into Naas. A short cycle on you will pass under the motorway which bypasses Naas and arrive at the 2nd Lock and Odlum's Mills. These mills date back to 1790 and had their own fleet of boats on the canal until 1940.

The ride through to Naas Harbour is very pleasant, with the canal bounded by the estates of Oldtown, the Knocks and Keredern and mature beech trees. The tarred surface provides good cycling comfort. You pass by three further locks and two bridges, firstly Tandy's Bridge and then Abbey Bridge, before entering the Harbour. Abbey Bridge is so called because it is said it was built using recycled stone from a monastic settlement. A short cycle from the Harbour up Basin Street will take you to the town centre where there are a number of coffee shops and hostelries nearby to provide much needed sustenance.

Note: The towpath along the Corbally extension is overgrown and poorly defined and the canal itself has become full of weeds. There are a lot of fences and barriers along the 8km route and it is not an attractive touring proposition for even the most determined cyclists. Perhaps in future years attention will be paid to the restoration of the towpaths at least.

Tour 3
Sallins to Lowtown
Main Line
(13 Kilometres)

This tour tracks the progress of the canal as it passes over the River Liffey and moves through the last four rising locks towards its summit level at Lowtown. The surrounding countryside is flat and open, and the first stretch of bogland is encountered close to Robertstown. The paths are generally good with the exception of the stretch between Cock Bridge and Bonynge Bridge which at times can become quite overgrown in places.

How to get there
Sallins is about 33km from Dublin and is located 4km to the north of Naas. Take the Naas exit on the N7 at the Maudlings Interchange and immediately take the first turn right. Follow this access road for about 2km to a roundabout that marks the junction with the R407. Taking the exit which leads over the M7 motorway will lead you to Sallins.

Tour 3 - Grand Canal
Sallins to Lowtown
Main Line

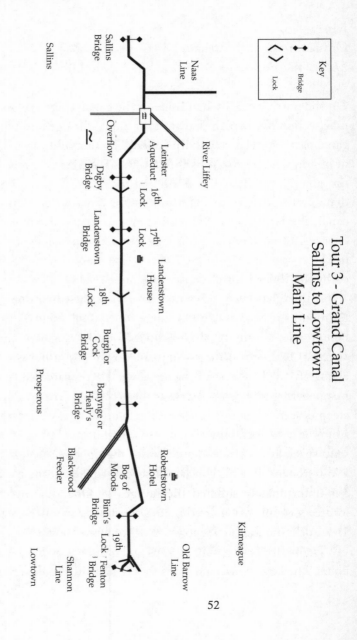

Key

Bridge

Lock

Naas
Line

Sallins
Bridge

Sallins

Overflow

River Liffey

Leinster
Aqueduct

16th
Lock

Digby
Bridge

17th
Lock

Landenstown
Bridge

Landenstown
House

18th
Lock

Burgh or
Cock
Bridge

Prosperous

Bonynge or
Healy's
Bridge

Robertstown
Hotel

Bog of
Moods

Blackwood
Feeder

Binn's
Bridge

19th
Lock ' Fenton
' Bridge

Old Barrow
Line

Kilmeague

Shannon
Line

Lowtown

Maps
Ordnance Survey of Ireland Discovery Series:
Map 49 Kildare, Meath, Offaly and Westmeath (ISBN 1-901496-16-3)

On the north, or right-hand side of the canal, there is a good tarmac section of towpath that starts at Sallins Bridge and tracks the canal past two relatively sharp bends. The first of these is a couple of hundred metres from Sallins and the second at Soldier's Island, the junction of the Main Line and the Naas Branch. The path deteriorates as it approaches one of the finest aqueducts on the canal, the Leinster Aqueduct, which carries the canal across the River Liffey. There is a pumping station at the aqueduct which is used to raise water from the Liffey to augment the supply provided by the River Morrell feeder (see Tour 2).

If there has been heavy rain or you are travelling during winter months it is advisable to change to the south side of the canal here to take advantage of a road which tracks alongside the canal right up to Digby Bridge. You can do this by using the tunnel about fifty metres west of the aqueduct. Be prepared to do a little manoeuvring with your bicycle as the access off the path involves a steep descent. The north towpath gets quite boggy a little further from the aqueduct. However, it is worthwhile persisting in order to see a specially constructed overflow to the right of the path behind a low stone wall. This consists of several circular stone basins and has unfortunately suffered the ravages of time. The overflow is located a couple of hundred metres short of Digby Bridge and the 16th Lock, the first lock encountered for almost 9km.

Digby Bridge was built in 1794 and has some interesting neighbours. The large house and lands that border the canal on the north side just before the bridge belong to Ronnie Wood of the Rolling Stones fame. Politician and current EU Commissioner Charlie McCreevy, lives around the corner on the same side. Staying with politics, the bridge is named after Simon Digby MP who was one of the early directors of the Grand Canal Company and whose family occupied the nearby Queen Anne mansion, Landenstown House.

Keeping to the south side of the canal for the next kilometre, there is the choice of using the path, which at times can be somewhat overgrown, or alternatively, taking the first turn right on the road running from Digby Bridge and then right again 100m further up that road. This will lead you to Landenstown Bridge, the 17th Lock and the gates to Landenstown House. Crossing the bridge to the north side the road runs parallel to the canal for over a kilometre up to the 18th Lock, the last rising lock. The road continues sharply right and leads to the village of Prosperous 3km away.

The towpath between the 18th Lock and Cock Bridge, and onwards to Bonynge or Healy's Bridge, a distance of 2km, can get very muddy after rain and often the grass is high, making cycling difficult. However, this is a scenic and very quiet stretch of the canal, with a lot of overhanging trees, and is well worth persisting.

At Bonynge or Healy's Bridge the canal used to receive supply from the Blackwood Feeder, located to the north side, which was eventually closed in 1952 and is now partly filled in. Crossing once more to the south side there is a good grassy towpath which runs in a straight line the remaining 2.2km to Robertstown, passing through the Bog of Moods.

Robertstown marks the summit of the canal, reaching 80.3m (280 feet) above the level of the city basin at Ringsend. It is the location of the third of the hotels built by the Grand Canal Company. Originally planned for Lowtown, 1.5km further on, the hotel opened in October 1801 and was extended in 1804. The information panel outside the hotel provides details of its rather chequered history, including use by both the Royal Irish Constabulary and Bord na Móna. Since the 1970s it has been used once again for tourism. The panel draws attention to the fine Crosthwaite clock situated on the top storey of the building.

Trips from Robertstown along the canal used to be available up to the summer of 2003 on a converted canal boat which was originally built in 1928 and was one of the boats that used to carry supplies of Guinness to the provinces. Alas this facility no longer exists.

One interesting feature you may notice is that there are no overhead wires in Robertstown. This is thanks to a local priest, Fr P.J. Murphy, who in an effort to improve the visual impact of the surroundings arranged for all utilities to be supplied through underground channels. It is probably the only town in Ireland where this has been achieved.

Crossing at Binns Bridge, take the road which runs parallel to the canal for the last 1.4km to the 19th Lock and Lowtown where the Barrow Line joins the Main Line. To confuse things, for a short stretch of about 1.3km there are two Barrow Lines leading away from Lowtown. The new Barrow Line was constructed to save water and for a while both routes were used. The Old Barrow Line was closed in the 1860s and was sometimes used up to then to avoid tolls levied at the 19th Lock. It is now navigable again.

There is a marina and boatyard at Lowtown on the site of a coalyard constructed by the Grand Canal Company in 1808. On the opposite side is an extensive parking area. Despite often frenetic activity in the area there is unfortunately nowhere to get refreshments at Lowtown so a quick retrace to Robertstown will have to suffice.

TOUR 4
LOWTOWN TO MONASTEREVIN
BARROW LINE
(23.5 Kilometres)

This is one of three tours that have Lowtown as their starting point. The good thing about starting at Lowtown is that there is ample secure parking. The gate to the parking area never appears to close. Along this route you will encounter contrasting scenery as the canal winds its way through a mixture of bogland, forest and quality farmland.

HOW TO GET THERE

Lowtown is about 40km from Dublin. Take the Naas exit on the N7 at the Maudlings Interchange and proceed through Naas. At the traffic lights at the end of the Main Street turn right in the direction of Newbridge on to the R445. Take a right turn less than 1km on to the R409 in the direction of Prosperous. This long straight road passes through Carragh village. After a further 3km, watch out for the signposted left turn to Robertstown. Crossing the canal at Binn's Bridge in Robertstown, keep to the road that runs parallel to the canal and leads to Lowtown.

Tour 4 - Grand Canal
Lowtown to Monasterevin
Barrow Line

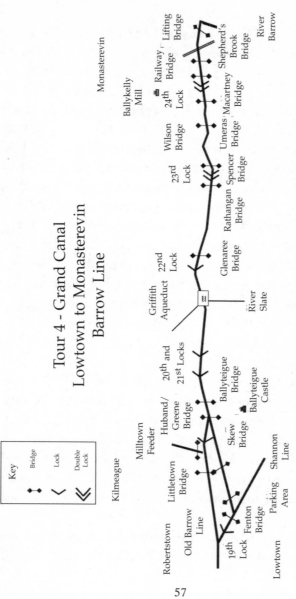

Key
- ◆ Bridge
- ⌄ Lock
- ⟨⟨ Double Lock

Kilmeague

Robertstown

Old Barrow Line

Littletown Bridge

Milltown Feeder

Huband / Greene Bridge

20th and 21st Locks

Griffith Aqueduct

22nd Lock

Glenaree Bridge

23rd Lock

Wilson Bridge

Rathangan Bridge

Spencer Bridge

Umeras Bridge

Macartney Bridge

24th Lock

Ballykelly Mill

Railway Bridge

Shepherd's Brook Bridge

Lifting Bridge

Monasterevin

River Barrow

Rathangan

River Slate

Ballyteigue Bridge

Ballyteigue Castle

Skew Bridge

Shannon Line

Parking Area

Fenton Bridge

19th Lock

Lowtown

57

Maps

Ordnance Survey of Ireland Discovery Series:

Map 49 Kildare, Meath, Offaly and Westmeath (ISBN 1-901496-16-3)

Map 55 Kildare, Laois, Offaly and Wicklow (ISBN 0-904996-67-0)

To access the Barrow Line you have a choice of routes for the first 1.3km. Crossing the bridge at the 19th Lock you can use the north towpath of the Old Barrow Line passing under Littletown Bridge until you come to Skew Bridge where the old and the new lines meet again. The old 19th Lock is located just before this bridge. Just back from the old 19th Lock is the entrance to the Milltown Feeder (see Tour 7). Alternatively, seek permission to go through the boatyard and carry your bicycle over the footbridge to access the towpath along the new line. There is a good path all the way to Skew Bridge and then a short way on to Ballyteigue Bridge.

Ballyteigue Castle occupies a prominent position close to the canal. There is an information panel at the bridge with the following explanatory inscription:

> Ballyteigue Castle is a typical example of an Irish fortified house of the fourteenth to sixteenth centuries. It is thought to have been a Geraldine Castle and Silken Thomas is said to have taken refuge here after the Battle of Allen in 1535.
>
> To the east is the Hill of Allen where Finn McCool is reported to have lived. The tower is a folly erected around 1860 by one of the Aylmer family on the site of a prehistoric tumulus.

An interesting feature of the tower is that the names of locals who worked on its construction are inscribed on the 83 steps to the viewing platform.

At Ballyteigue Bridge you should switch to the left towpath for the journey through Ballyteigue Bog as the right-hand side of the canal is very difficult to negotiate. This is an open part of the canal and there are fine views on both sides. Two locks are passed in quick succession, the 20th and 21st. The next landmark is Griffith Aqueduct which carries the canal across a tributary to the Slate River which runs parallel to the canal to the west.

At about 14km out from Lowtown you pass the 22nd Lock and Glenaree Bridge. A short ride on and the scenery changes as you approach Inchaneart Forest which is divided by the canal. On a windy day the shelter provided by the forest is in stark contrast to the exposed path through Ballyteigue Bog. There is a strange but not unwelcome silence along this section until the surroundings open out again as you approach Rathangan. The local community have done much to improve the area around the canal, making it into a linear park with information panels describing the flora and fauna to be seen along its banks.

Notable literary associations with Rathangan include the poet William A. Byrne who is commemorated by a plaque near Rathangan Bridge, and also Maura Laverty, the twentieth-century novelist. There is a road running parallel to the canal from the bridge to the 23rd Lock (another of the canal's double chambered locks) and Spencer Bridge. The lock has a 5.2km (17.2 foot) fall which is necessary as the canal has been carried through Rathangan on a high embankment. The canal widens out to an old harbour after the bridge where there is now a hire-boat base run by Canalways Ireland.

Spencer Bridge was built in 1784 and was paid for by the local landlord, Lord Spencer, said to be a distant relative of Lady Diana

Spencer who became Princess of Wales. Unfortunately he came to a sorry end, being piked to death during the 1798 Irish rebellion.

Keeping to the left towpath there is a fine, grassy path all the way to Wilson's Bridge and then on to Umeras Bridge, a distance of 4.6km. However, looks can be deceptive as the surface is in parts very uncomfortable for cyclists due to the impact of heavily ridged tractor tyres which when dried out is like cycling on a corrugated tin roof. A peat factory at Umeras used to make horse-bedding in the 1880s for the British Cavalry's Irish stables. There is an old mile marker about 200m back from Wilson's Bridge. The inscription has almost worn away but the words Monasterevin and Dublin are still visible.

The path over the following 3km to the next significant landmarks, the 24th Lock and Macartney Bridge, is a mixture of rough grass and worn tracks but generally comfortable. The scene at the 24th Lock is very pleasing as the lock-house and the double-chambered lock are well maintained. The large building on the left-hand side just up from the bridge is Ballykelly Mill, which dates back to 1801. A little further on is Shepherd's Brook Bridge where the towpath ends. You can continue to track the canal using the road that passes Ballykelly Gaelic Football Grounds towards the railway line that passes overhead and an old lifting bridge. This bridge used to be lifted by hand and it usually took two men to do so, although there are stories about one or two powerful boatmen who managed to lift the bridge on their own. Today it is lifted by an electric motor. Barrow Aqueduct, which took two years to build starting in 1829, carries the canal over the River Barrow at Monasterevin.

To a lot of passing motorists Monasterevin was regarded as 'a horrid little hole' to quote Frank O' Connor the renowned short story writer who was also an avid cyclist. The town occupied a pivotal place on the main routes from Dublin to Cork and Limerick and up to 2004 was regularly subjected to sardine factor traffic jams of the highest levels that would try even the patience of St Evin, the man who gave his name to the town. The new motorway, bypassing the town itself, enables visitors to properly appreciate Monasterevin for its interesting history, its people and its privileged position of having two waterways flowing through it.

Monasterevin is the original spaghetti junction with four different transport arteries, roads, railway, canal and river all crisscrossing each other at some point in the town. To confuse things further there are the remains of another branch of the canal at the southern end of the Barrow Aqueduct. This was the Mountmellick Branch, constructed in the 1820s with the original intention to provide transport to the Castlecomer coalfields. However, it only reached Mountmellick, a distance of 18km. It fell into disuse and was closed to navigation in 1961. Many stretches have since been filled in with some of the land sold off. As a result attempts to track it using the old towpaths are futile as there are now barricades and fences along its route.

A monastery founded in the sixth century by St Evin of Cashel is responsible for the town's name. St Evin was one of the authors of the *Tripartite Life of St Patrick*. The town's religious associations continued in the twelfth century with the establishment of a Cistercian abbey on the banks of the River Barrow on the site where Moore Abbey now stands. With the lands having been forcibly passed out of religious hands, they descended by marriage to the Moores, Earls of Drogheda, who had come to Ireland in Elizabethan times and who had been granted extensive tracts of church lands. The first Earl of Drogheda, Henry Moore, was a prolific developer, not only in Monasterevin but also in Dublin, and to this day his associations with Dublin's city centre are enduring with no fewer than three well known streets still bearing parts of his name: Henry Street, Moore Street and Earl Street. Moore Abbey was built in 1607 and in more modern times has returned to religious hands. It is presently occupied by the Sisters of Charity. One famous former occupant was the great Irish tenor, John Count McCormack who, in 1924, leased it for a number of years from Lord Drogheda.

English poet and Jesuit priest, Gerard Manley Hopkins (1844-1889), also had an association with the town, where he lived for several years. There is a monument and garden in his memory on the street leading to the town centre from the Barrow Aqueduct. One of the town's principal hostelries is also named after him. Every July there is an international poetry festival held in the town in his memory.

No visit to Monasterevin would be complete without a visit to the friendly Country Kitchen Coffee Shop on the Main Street for well-deserved refreshment.

TOUR 5
MONASTEREVIN TO ATHY
BARROW LINE
(22.6 Kilometres)

From a cycling perspective this is one of the easiest tours, as there is a tarmacadam path or road alongside the canal for over 60 per cent of the journey. To avail of the road to the maximum you will need to keep to the right towpath for 8km from the 25th Lock to Courtwood Bridge and then switch to the left towpath. With the exception of a short stretch of rough terrain there is a surfaced path all the way to Athy on this side.

HOW TO GET THERE
Monasterevin is 64km from Dublin. Follow the N7 (Naas Road) out of Dublin and remain on the M7 motorway, passing through the Curragh and the Kildare bypass, and straight on to Monasterevin, where you will need to follow signs to take the turning off the motorway into the town.

Tour 5 - Grand Canal
Monasterevin to Athy
Barrow Line

Monasterevin

Moore
Abbey

Moore's
Bridge

25th
Lock

Cloheen
Bridge

Barrow
Aqueduct

River
Barrow

Mountmellick
Branch

Wooden
Bridge

Fisherstown
Bridge

Courtwood
Bridge

Key

Bridge

Lock

Glasha
River

Gratton
Aqueduct

Vicarstown
Bridge

Stradbally
River

Camac
Aqueduct

Ballymanus
Bridge

Vicarstown

Stradbally

Milltown
Bridge

Bert
House

26th
Lock

Lennon's
Bridge

Cardington
Bridge

27th
Lock

Augustus
Bridge

28th
Lock

Athy

River
Barrow

MAPS
Ordnance Survey of Ireland Discovery Series:
Map 55 Kildare, Laois, Offaly and Wicklow (ISBN 0-904996-67-0)

Starting at the Barrow Aqueduct the canal swings slowly left as it passes the blocked entrance to the now-defunct Mountmellick Branch until it reaches the 25th Lock and Moore's Bridge. The Mountmellick Branch was part of a plan to connect the Grand Canal to the coal-mining town of Castlecomer, a distance of almost 50km. Work was started in 1827 but the plan was curtailed and instead was confined to a 18km stretch to Mountmellick. This branch was opened to traffic in 1831 and was officially closed to navigation in 1961 when, in common with a number of other branches, its entrance was sealed off.

At Moore's Bridge the canal takes a sharp turn right. You will not see another lock for 21km as the canal enters a long stretch, maintaining its level through cuttings and embankments while it follows the course of the Barrow Valley. You should cross the bridge and keep to the right towpath. Half a kilometre further on is Clogheen Bridge which carries the main Dublin-Limerick road over the canal. The path beneath this bridge is very narrow and can sometimes get overgrown. The alternative is to cross over the main Dublin-Limerick road and resume the path via a small slip road 50m on.

There is a wooden bridge about 3km further on where you can take the opportunity to make an early switch to the left towpath. The earthen path on this side is used by local farmers and their stock. While it has many potholes it usually offers a more comfortable ride during periods when the mainly grassy path on the right side has become overgrown or you grow tired of the constant shudder caused by the aftermath of the heavily-ridged tyres of the tractors used to cut the grass. Whichever side is chosen the canal carries on through rather featureless countryside to Fisherstown Bridge and then to Courtwood Bridge.

The next landmark is Gratton Aqueduct, which crosses the Glasha River as it makes its way to the Barrow. This was built in 1790 by Richard Evans, an engineer who was closely involved in the construction of the Royal Canal. The aqueduct is said to be named after the eighteenth-century parliamentarian, Henry Grattan. Curiously, however, the stoneworker who inscribed the name on the plaques on both sides of the aqueduct spelled the surname as 'Gratton'. This is almost as confusing as the fact that during the parliamentary period known in Irish history as 'Grattan's Parliament', Grattan himself was not part of the governing party but always remained as a member of the opposition.

A couple of hundred metres from Gratton Aqueduct there is a welcome change in the path to a tarmacadam surface as you near Vicarstown in County Laois. There you will find two pubs, one on either side of the canal: Turley's on the left and Crean's on the right, and the depot for another canal boat hire company. If you are interested, leave the canal at this point, cross the bridge and pass Crean's pub to make the 5km journey to Stradbally to visit the renowned steam museum, run by the Irish Steam Preservation Society. The museum displays include a range of agricultural steam engines such as binders, reapers and cornmills, as well as a steam locomotive from Guinness' Brewery. Ireland's glorious steam age is celebrated by a rally held in the village every August bank holiday weekend.

For the next 10km there is a road which tracks the canal

almost all the way to Athy. Along the route you will first encounter the Camac Aqueduct which carries the canal across another of the Barrow's tributaries, the River Stradbally. This is followed after another 0.5km by Ballymanus Bridge which is heavily marked on its rising sides by the ropes used by horse-drawn boats as they negotiated the canal's turn at this point.

As you approach Milltown Bridge 4km further on you will be able to catch glimpses of the Barrow as the two waterways converge quite closely. The imposing Georgian house to the east is Bert House which was once owned by the Geoghegan family who were significant landowners in the area. It has changed hands a number of times in recent years and most of the land has been sold off.

Continuing to follow the road you pass by Cuan Mhuire, a charitable institution founded and run by Sister Consilio for people with addictions. If you cannot wait to reach Athy there is a small restaurant at this centre where you can avail of refreshments. The 26th Lock, the first for 21km, and Cardington Bridge quickly follow as does Lennon's Bridge before you reach Athy at the 27th Lock and Augustus Bridge. A short step further on is the 28th Lock and the junction with the River Barrow. At the time of writing there was a new marina under construction to the east of the canal, close to this junction.

Athy is one of Ireland's designated heritage towns. To learn more about its fascinating history from its Anglo Norman foundation to modern times you can visit the town's Heritage Centre which is located in a former eighteenth-century market house and assembly hall situated in the centre of the town, close to the river. The town was the location of a ford across the River Barrow and was named after Ae, the King of Leinster who died in a battle in the town in the eleventh century. The Irish word for ford is *Ath* hence the name Athy (*Ath-Ae*). The river divides the town and the imposing Crom-a-boo Bridge provides the link between both sides. The unusual name of the bridge comes from the town's association with the Fitzgeralds, once the Earls of Kildare. Crom-a-boo was the war cry of the Fitzgeralds as they went into battle. Guarding one end of the bridge is a fine, sixteenth-century castle that is known as White's Castle. Built by the Earl of Kildare in 1506 it is believed to have been named after a family called White who enlarged and extended it in 1575. The coat of arms of the Fitzgeralds can be clearly seen on the streetside wall of the building. If you examine this closely you can make out the figure of a monkey in the coat of arms. Local legend has it that a pet monkey rescued the infant heir of the Earls of Kildare when a fire broke out at Woodstown Castle on the western outskirts of Athy. The deed was thereafter commemorated by the inclusion of a monkey in the Fitzgerald coat of arms. This legend has also been attributed to other Fitzgerald castles, including the one at Maynooth.

The polar explorer, Ernest Shackleton, originally hailed from Athy and the Heritage Centre celebrates this with a permanent exhibition which includes an original sledge and harness from one of his Antarctic expeditions, a 4.5m (15 feet) model of his ship, *Endurance*, and an audio visual display featuring original film footage of his 1914-1916 expedition.

The Heritage Centre also celebrates the 4th Gordon Bennett Motor Race which took place on the 2 July 1903. This race is famous for being the first to take place on a closed circuit and was the forerunner of today's Formula One Grand Prix races. The race started at Ballyshannon, County Kildare, midway between Athy and Kilcullen, with Athy being one of the control points on two loop circuits that provided a race distance of 527km (327.5 miles).

It is interesting to note that the winning driver, a Belgian called Jenazy, driving a 60 hp Mercedes, managed an average speed of 79.2km (49.2 miles) per hour.

Finally, there is an excellent coffee shop and restaurant on the square in front of the Heritage Centre called J-1 should you be in need of refreshment.

TOUR 6
LOWTOWN TO EDENDERRY,
INCLUDING EDENDERRY BRANCH
SHANNON LINE
(19.5 Kilometres)

In this tour careful attention has to be paid to locations where it is recommended to change sides or you will find yourself either doubling back with your path blocked or dismounting due to difficult terrain. Overall there are four locations where you should change – Shee Bridge, Hamilton Bridge, the 20th Lock and, finally, the Blundell Aqueduct, so keep these in mind. Once again you can avail of the secure parking at Lowtown for the start of your journey.

HOW TO GET THERE
Lowtown is about 40km from Dublin. Take the Naas exit on the N7 at the Maudlings Interchange and proceed through Naas. At the traffic lights at the end of the Main Street turn right in the direction of Newbridge on to the R445. Take a right turn less than 1km on to the R409 in the direction of Prosperous. This long

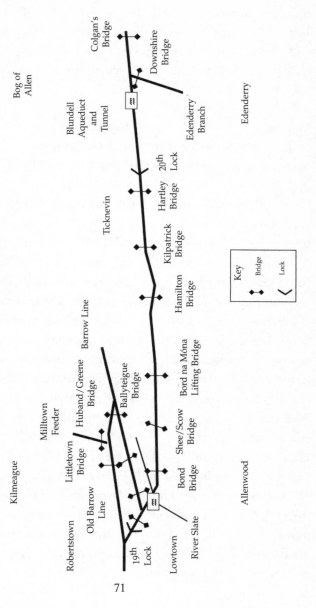

Tour 6 - Grand Canal
Lowtown to Edenderry
Shannon Line

straight road passes through the village of Carragh. After a further 3km, you will need to watch closely for the signpost and a left turn to Robertstown. Crossing over the canal at Binn's Bridge in Robertstown, keep to the road that runs parallel to the canal and leads to Lowtown.

MAPS

Ordnance Survey of Ireland Discovery Series:

Map 49 Kildare, Meath, Offaly and Westmeath (ISBN 1-901496-16-3)

Head to the end of the car park on to the towpath and you will quickly encounter the aqueduct that carries the canal over the River Slate. Continue to Bond Bridge, which is adjacent to Allenwood, and then to Shee or Scow Bridge where you cross sides. The Allenwood Power Station, which was the second of the turf-burning stations to be built in Ireland, was commissioned in 1952 and is visible about 1km to the north. Shee Bridge is the only oblique-arched bridge on the canal apart from the later railway arch at Ringsend. The construction of a skewed bridge is something of a rarity as the engineers preferred to re-align the roads so they crossed the canal at right angles rather than involve themselves in the engineering complexities of a skewed bridge. There are two more examples on the Royal Canal system, both in Westmeath, one near the Hill of Down called Ballasport Bridge and the other at Ballinea.

You now have the choice of immediately resuming the towpath via the small Millennium Park which the Allenwood community have installed along the canal just after the bridge or use the R414 road for a couple of hundred metres, taking the first turn right which leads down to the canal. This road runs alongside the canal for the next 3km, passing a now disused Bord na Móna lifting bridge at 1.5km and eventually reaching Hamilton Bridge after a comfortable ride, given the surface. At this point it is important to change sides once again as the left towpath only continues for a few hundred metres before fences block the way.

The road alongside the canal continues for another 1.2 km up to Kilpatrick Bridge which was built by Bord na Móna in 1949 to provide access to the Lullymore peat briquette factory which is now closed. At this point the path changes to a hardcore track which is not too bad as a cycling surface but beware of the large potholes. The track leads to Hartley Bridge at Ticknevin, a distance of just over 10km from Lowtown.

You are now entering a long stretch of the canal where the scenery is dominated by its bog surroundings. The canal runs through the Bog of Allen, which was once Ireland's greatest raised bog but is now considerably smaller due to drainage and the commercial extraction of turf. The bog originally developed from the lakes that dominated Ireland's central areas at the end of the last Ice Age. Vegetation growing around the lakeshore took over, turning the lakes firstly into fens and then subsequently into great mossy domes of raised bog. The Grand Canal was instrumental in opening up the Bog of Allen as a commercial resource.

The 20th Lock, which is just under 1km from Ticknevin, gets my vote for the best kept lock on the Grand Canal system, despite its isolation. All credit to the lock-keeper who lives alongside the lock in a beautifully maintained cottage fringed with manicured grass and an abundance of flowers and shrubs. It is the only lock where the base stones at the bottom of the chamber are often clearly visible, even when the chamber is full.

At this point you should change to the south or left side of the canal where the path is considerably better, all the way past the unmarked Kildare/Offaly border to Edenderry. On the north side the path has been churned up, probably due to the considerable restorative work which has been undertaken in recent years on this problematic stretch of the canal.

With only patches of afforestation to break the vista of water, bog and sky the canal is carried on a high embankment for another 4.6km before reaching the Blundell Aqueduct which carries the canal across the Edenderry-Rathangan road. At this point, using the tunnel underneath the aqueduct, change to the north side of the canal, otherwise you will miss the junction of the Shannon Line and the Edenderry Branch and will have to cycle on to Colgan's Bridge at the far end of Edenderry and double back.

The original construction of the canal across this area of bog by means of high embankments took nearly ten years to complete and was a significant engineering achievement due to regular subsidence difficulties. Breaches causing loss of water were a regular feature. It was along the stretch between Blundell Aqueduct and the Edenderry Branch that the canal suffered one of its most serious breaches when in 1989 it lost more than 100 million gallons of water after the embankment gave way. It took over a year to repair this breach. For this reason a lot of attention has been paid in recent years to reconstructing the embankments to prevent such incidents from recurring.

Construction of the short, curving branch canal to Edenderry, which is 1.5km long, was commenced in 1797 but was not completed until 1802. It was financed by local landlord, Lord Downshire, in whose honour is named the quaint pedestrian bridge at the entrance to the branch. The narrow entrance to the branch contrasts with the generous width of the channel which is significantly more expansive than the main line. Its easy access from the town means you will see many fishermen along its banks. The branch leads right into the town where there is a well-maintained harbour immediately adjacent to the town's main street. Close to the harbour are the ruins of Blundell Castle which are surrounded by a public park.

TOUR 7
LOWTOWN TO THE MILLTOWN FEEDER
AND POLLARDSTOWN FEN
(14.5 Kilometres)

The Milltown Feeder is the main source of water supply for the Grand Canal and for the cyclist it presents one of the most pleasant and interesting tours along the entire canal system. It is a waterway that very few boats now enter because of clearance restrictions at Pluckerstown Bridge located approximately 5km along the route. However, in earlier years it saw a lot of traffic because of its proximity to the Curragh Military Camp. A lot of the bricks used in the construction of the camp were imported from England and were transported from Dublin to Milltown on the canal. One thing you will note all along the length of the feeder is the clarity of the water.

HOW TO GET THERE
Lowtown is about 40km from Dublin. Take the Naas exit on the N7 at the Maudlings Interchange and proceed through Naas. At the traffic lights at the end of the Main Street turn right in the direction of Newbridge on to the R445. Take a right turn less than 1km on to

Tour 7 - Grand Canal
Lowtown to the Milltown Feeder
and Pollardstown Fen

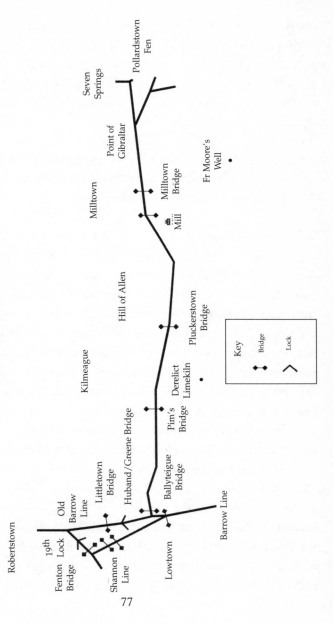

the R409 in the direction of Prosperous. This long straight road passes through the village of Carragh. After a further 3km you will need
to watch closely for the signpost and a left turn to Robertstown.
Crossing over the canal at Binn's Bridge in Robertstown, keep to the
road that runs parallel to the canal and leads to Lowtown.

MAPS
Ordnance Survey of Ireland Discovery Series:
Map 49 Kildare, Meath, Offaly and Westmeath (ISBN 1-901496-16-3)
Map 55 Kildare, Laois, Offaly and Wicklow (ISBN 0-904996-67-0)

To access the feeder from Lowtown progress along the left path
of the Old Barrow Line until you come to Littletown Bridge, a
distance of about 1.5km. Cross the bridge and follow the road for
about 1km to a bridge that is doubly named. On the south side of
the bridge facing the Old Barrow Line the inscription says that it
is Greene Bridge while on the Milltown Feeder side there is a
plaque that describes it as Huband Bridge. The bridge crosses the
feeder at its point of entry to the canal. Turn left before the bridge,
follow the road for about 300m and access the towpath where the
road turns sharply right.

You are now in the heart of quality farmland and the earthen
path for the next 2km to a stone bridge called Pim's Bridge is used
a lot by local farmers and their stock. In wet weather it can be
quite muddy but overall presents a reasonable cycling surface. You
should be mindful of the plentiful potholes. Cross to the left towpath at the bridge, passing by the ruins of a building that house a
derelict lime-kiln furnace, which looks like a very large deep-
water well. Such kilns were a common sight in the eighteenth and
early nineteenth centuries and were used to produce quick or

dehydrated lime that was put to use in making mortar for building purposes or whitewash. The addition of water produced slaked lime that was used by farmers as fertiliser. To make the lime, the stone kiln was loaded with alternating layers of firewood, turf and limestone under which a fire was lit. It was left for a few days and then sealed to burn for a further week without oxygen. In some areas coal was used to fuel the lime-kilns. You will encounter other lime-kilns on later tours, a notable example being on the banks of the River Barrow, north of St Mullins.

A few hundred metres further on the path joins a narrow road that is well surfaced and you will have a comfortable ride for the next kilometre to Pluckerstown Bridge. You will note that this bridge, which was built in more modern times, is a low bridge and it differs from a lot of other canal bridges in this respect. It is said that the bridge was built low to provide a flat surface for the lorries servicing the basalt rock quarry which you will see to the side of the Hill of Allen. This has displeased a lot of boatowners because its limited clearance of only 1.83m (6 feet) prevents many boats progressing from this point. Most of the narrow canal boats, which have a shallow draught and low cabins, have no difficulty at this bridge.

Once again you will need to change sides to the right-hand towpath which skirts the base of the Hill of Allen which is 206m (676 feet) high. About 0.5km on there is a marked deterioration in the quality of the path, where work has been done on dredging the feeder. Unfortunately, from a cyclist's viewpoint, the dredged material has been dumped on the side in large clumps with no effort made to make the surface even. This lasts for over 1.5 bumpy and uncomfortable kilometres before the path reverts to a smooth and grassy surface as it approaches a stone bridge which in bygone times provided access to the picturesque mill now standing ivy clad and in ruins on the opposite side.

Less than 500m further on is a delightful pub and restaurant at Milltown Bridge called the 'Hanged Man'. The now-restored premises were previously used as a canal house and stores and at one time were occupied as a barracks by the Royal Irish Constabulary. For many years afterwards they were used as a bar/grocery and were purchased in the late 1990s by the present owner who has sympathetically restored the building maintaining a lot of the original features. It gets its unusual name from a tragic story of unrequited love that resulted in a canal worker taking his own life in the basement of the pub in the middle of the last century. Despite its name the pub is very welcoming and is an ideal place for refreshments either on the outward journey or on the return leg.

Taking a small detour off the canal, a visit to Fr Moore's Well is worthwhile. It is located just over 1km from Milltown Bridge and can be accessed by crossing the bridge and heading westward until you see the sign on the left of the road indicating its location. Pollardstown Fen can be clearly seen to the left along this route. The well is named after a Catholic priest who lived from 1779 to 1826 and was Curate of the parish of Allen. The well was restored and enclosed by the local community in 1952 and is regularly visited by those seeking cures for ailments.

Continuing the detour from the canal, it is worthwhile following the road to the next turn left at the signpost indicating the directions for the Pollardstown Fen. This narrow road leads, after a cycle of about 2km, to a raised viewing area for the Pollardstown Fen.

Back to the canal route, there is a good path that leads into the Fen on the right side of the canal from Milltown Bridge. Cycling just under 2km on a good surface, you reach a fork in the canal known as the Point of Gibraltar. Continuing by the gently curving right channel you will notice that the canal slowly narrows until it dissipates into several smaller channels and streams which draw their water from the myriad of springs present in this area. These date back to the late eighteenth century and were constructed to augment the supply generated from the eastern side of the Fen from which the original water supply came.

To witness the true source you can cycle up the left bank, although there is no defined path and you will have to cross a few barriers. It is worthwhile as you will have the chance to take the left channel at the Point of Gibraltar to an area known as the Seven Springs, the true origin of the water that feeds the Grand Canal. Once again the canal narrows, reaching a small pool known as James' Well.

Pollardstown Fen is an officially designated nature reserve extending to 130 hectares and is renowned for botanical richness, possessing rare plants and vegetation and a small, rare snail whose Latin name is *Angistora vertiego*. A fen is a transitional phase in the conversion of a freshwater lake into a bog. You will see many different types of aquatic plants such as pondweed and duckweed, as well as sedges, reeds and orchids. There are also a lot of airborne insects, particularly in the summer months. It is an area to be respected and savoured yet it was nearly lost in the 1960s when attempts were made to drain it so as to reclaim it for farming. Fortunately, however, it was acquired by the State in 1983 and the drains were blocked so it could revert to wetlands. It also survived another threat in 1999, when concern was expressed that the new Kildare bypass would cut it off from its water sources. Special drains were incorporated into the roadway construction to prevent this from happening. It should be noted that the removal of any living or non-living thing from the Fen is illegal.

Tour 8
Edenderry to Tullamore
Shannon Line
(33 Kilometres)

This tour brings you through the very heart of Ireland, where you will encounter extensive peatlands. While this is one of the longest tours in this guide it is not that arduous as almost 40 per cent of the route is cycled on tarred surfaces. In addition, from a practical viewpoint you can remain on one side for the entire journey. The north, or right-hand, path will carry you all the way to Tullamore.

How to get there
Edenderry is in County Offaly and is about 62km from Dublin. Take the N4/M4 out of Dublin to Enfield. Using the bypass, turn left at the traffic lights that are about halfway on the bypass and take the R402 which takes you all the way to Edenderry. Take care because the R402 is a very windy road, with some sharp bends. There is plenty of safe parking in Edenderry close to the Edenderry Branch Harbour.

Tour 8 - Grand Canal
Edenderry to Tullamore
Shannon Line

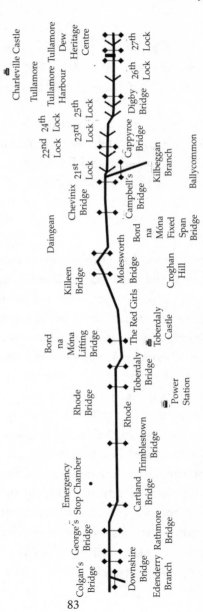

83

MAPS

Ordnance Survey of Ireland Discovery Series:

Map 48 Offaly and Westmeath (ISBN 1-901496-45-7)

Map 49 Kildare, Meath, Offaly and Westmeath (ISBN 1-901496-16-3)

Starting from the harbour of the Edenderry Branch, keep to the left towpath for the 1.5km to Downshire Bridge, where the branch meets the Shannon Line. The bridge has a high arch and is suitable only for pedestrians and cyclists. The relatively narrow entrance to the Edenderry Branch contrasts sharply with the width of the channel which is at least 1.5 times the width of the main canal.

Turning right over the bridge, you will quickly encounter two more bridges on the outskirts of Edenderry: Colgan's Bridge and George's Bridge. A short ride further on is Rathmore Bridge and the location of a recently constructed emergency stop chamber whose purpose is to prevent large-scale loss of water supply in the event of a canal bank breach in the area. Learning from the experience of major breaches which occurred in the vicinity over the years, the canal's maintenance engineers have installed stop-gates, designed to shut automatically when a breach occurs, thereby saving water and protecting the canal's fragile banks.

The next landmark is Cartland Bridge after which there is a very lengthy stretch of some 7km of grassy towpath, interrupted midway by Trimblestown Bridge. It is stretches like this that reaffirm the value and benefit of the Grand Canal as a unique amenity and a delight for those that choose to enjoy it. Roads are distant so there are no sounds of traffic. Evidence of human habitation is sparse and the litter-free paths point to the route being seldom used. You will come across two milestones along the route but their inscriptions have long since faded.

Having savoured the peace and tranquillity of the past few kilometres, you approach two bridges in quick succession. The first of these is Rhode Bridge which leads to the village of Rhode 1.5km to the north. In the same direction used to be the twin peat burning towers of the closed Rhode Power Station. These striking landmarks were demolished in 2004. Also to the north, Croghan Hill is prominent in the distance. This hill is significant for a number of reasons. On the hillside can be found a graveyard and the remains of a small abbey where St Brigid was said to have become a nun in the fifth century. Later it was the home of the Moores, who were Elizabethan settlers coming from England in the 1600s and were the founders of the town of Tullamore. On the top of the hill is a cairn and according to local legend this caps an extinct volcano. It is said that you can be sucked down the hole under the cairn if you are not careful. The hill also has literary associations as it is mentioned in Spenser's *Faerie Queene*.

At Toberdaly Bridge you will catch sight of the ruins of Toberdaly Castle which are only a short ride from the canal and worthy of a visit.

There is a good grassy surface and plenty of tree protection for the next kilometre until the route opens out on to more bogland. Restorative work is ongoing on the towpath leading to Bord na Móna's light railway lifting bridge which is in regular use. Despite this, going can be slow after damp weather. Once past the railway bridge the canal passes by an area known locally as 'The Red Girls'. It is said that the farmhouse on the north side of the canal was occupied at one time by a family whose daughters all had red hair, hence the name.

The next bridge you encounter is Killeen Bridge, where the towpath can be quite soft and muddy but not for long. The golf course to your right is Castle Barna Golf Club. Fortunately, there is a good tree line along this stretch so you will not have to worry about errant golf balls. At the entrance to the golf club the path changes to a tarred surface for the short ride to Molesworth Bridge and the town of Daingean.

Daingean was known for a time as Philipstown, having been renamed in 1557 during the reign of Philip and Mary at the time when King's and Queen's Counties were being formed. These counties are now called Offaly and Laois, respectively. Its original Irish name was restored in 1920 and means 'fort'. In the immediate vicinity of the canal is an old store house on the south side and the imposing Molesworth House. On the north side, high dark grey walls surround a building that once put the fear of God into the young people of Ireland as it was a reform school. It is now used as a store for the National Museum. An attractive new mooring quay was constructed in 2000 just past the bridge on the south side.

Keeping to the north side of the canal there is an excellent tarred roadway running parallel to the canal from Daingean. This, in fact, stretches for the next 12km almost all the way to Tullamore, with some limited interruption around Ballycommon. As you leave Daingean you will see a magnificent garden built by one of its residents. Moving onwards the route opens out to a mixture of scrubland and bog. After 3km you reach a modern, arched, fixed-span concrete bridge that was constructed by Bord na Móna to accommodate its light railway system. As you progress the further 2km to Ballycommon and Chevinix Bridge you will notice the telecommunications mast which reaches over 300m (1,000 feet) into the sky and is clearly visible for miles around. The mast is located close to the 21st Lock.

Just past the bridge is the sealed junction of the Kilbeggan Branch that linked the Shannon Line to the town of Kilbeggan, 13km to the north (see Tour 9). Campbell's Bridge spans the sealed junction. A little further on is the 21st Lock, the first lock for almost 30km, and this is quickly followed by the 22nd and 23rd Locks. There is a small accommodation bridge, Cappyroe Bridge, located just beside the 22nd Lock.

The easy ride on the tarred surface continues as you pass the 24th Lock and the nearby base for Celtic Canal Cruisers until you reach the 25th Lock and Digby Bridge. The tall spire of the church in Tullamore can now be seen prominently in the distance. After this bridge the path reverts to a combination of grass and hardcore until you reach the 26th Lock, which is known as Boland's Lock. The lock-house, which has an unusual bay-fronted entrance, has recently been restored as a heritage building and is open to the public during the months of July and August each year. The final kilometre into Tullamore from this point is once again on a tarred surface.

The Grand Canal reached Tullamore in 1798 and was a major boost to what was then little more than a village. The canal's arrival was timely as Tullamore was still recovering from a major fire which took place on 12 May 1785 destroying about 100 houses. The fire was started by a hot air balloon that failed to gain height and hit the chimney of a house, causing its roof to catch fire, quickly spreading to neighbouring houses.

For some time Tullamore was the end of the line for the canal while the directors of the Grand Canal Company of Ireland deliberated on the best route to take to reach the Shannon. The town flourished and built a harbour to accommodate the growing canal trade. It was also the location for one of the five hotels built along the route of the Grand Canal but this building was demolished several years ago. Among the first people to take the canal to Tullamore in 1798 were British troops on their way to fight a French force that landed in Killala, County Mayo, to support an Irish rising.

Now a thriving and modern town, Tullamore is famous worldwide for its Tullamore Dew brand of Irish whiskey and for its Irish Mist Liqueur. A visit to the Tullamore Dew Heritage Centre, located in a former bonded warehouse bordering the canal, not far east from the 27th lock, is a must. You will even get the chance to sample some of the famous produce, and there is also a coffee shop.

Another highlight of Tullamore is Charleville Castle, which is considered to be the finest Gothic house in Ireland. It is located on the outskirts of Tullamore, to the south of the canal, and can be reached by taking the N52 in the direction of Birr. It was designed in 1798 by Francis Johnston for the 1st Earl of Charleville, Charles Moore. The King tree standing on the avenue to the castle is reputed to be the biggest oak tree in Europe.

TOUR 9
THE KILBEGGAN BRANCH
(13 Kilometres)

The Kilbeggan Branch was started in 1830 and it took four and a half years to complete the 13km from the junction with the Shannon Line at Ballycommon to Kilbeggan Harbour. It was closed along with a number of other branches in 1961 and allowed to dry up. As boats can no longer navigate this part of the canal the bicycle comes into its own for exploring its hidden treasures.

If there is any one section of the canal that fully encapsulates its value as an amenity worth savouring this is it. With the exception of locks the Kilbeggan Branch has everything bar, strangely enough, a lot of water. However, it makes up for this deficiency with its offerings of tranquillity, remoteness, variety of scenery, abundant wildlife and a cacophony of nature's most beautiful sound effects.

Be warned, the journey is not easy. In places the path is arduous and you will encounter impediments along the way but it is worth persevering. While the towpath on at least one side of the canal is regularly maintained by Waterways Ireland there are, however, stretches where the regular passage of farm animals has

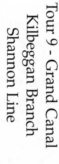

Key

Bridge ◆◆

Lock ⋁

Tour 9 - Grand Canal
Kilbeggan Branch
Shannon Line

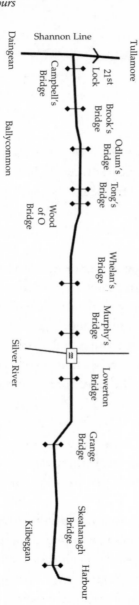

Shannon Line

Daingean

Tullamore

21st Lock

Campbell's Bridge

Brook's Bridge

Odlum's Bridge

Ballycommon

Tong's Bridge

Wood of O Bridge

Whelan's Bridge

Murphy's Bridge

Silver River

Lowerton Bridge

Grange Bridge

Skeahanagh Bridge

Kilbeggan

Harbour

rendered the path difficult for cyclists and you will have to dismount frequently, particularly after damp weather. You will also encounter a number of farm gates – at least twenty along the route. Please ensure you shut each gate after you pass through.

How to get there
The start of the Kilbeggan Branch lies just west of Ballycommon, County Offaly, about 9km east of Tullamore. The best route to get to Ballycommon is firstly to go to Edenderry, also in County Offaly, and about 62km from Dublin. Take the N4/M4 out of Dublin to Enfield. Using the bypass, turn left at the traffic lights that are about halfway on the bypass and take the R402 which takes you all the way to Edenderry. Take care because the R402 is a very windy road, with some sharp bends. Continue along the R402 to Daingean. At Daingean cross the canal by turning right over Molesworth Bridge and then immediately left to gain access to the road that runs alongside the canal. Ballycommon is 5km from Daingean using this road. There is ample space to park a car along the canal close to the 21st Lock near the entrance to the Kilbeggan Branch.

Maps
Ordnance Survey of Ireland Discovery Series:
Map 48 Offaly and Westmeath (ISBN 1-901496-45-7)

At Campbell's Bridge take the grassy towpath to the right which is well defined and clear. Almost immediately you find yourself in a leafy and sheltered corridor which leads all the way to the first landmark, Brook's Bridge, an accommodation bridge for local farmers. Along this stretch the canal has almost completely disappeared under a cloak of reeds, bushes and trees and in some places the local farmers have created pathways right through the canal, leaving the bridge redundant.

Several hundred metres further on the path comes to a halt and you can continue by road for about 200m until you reach Odlum's Bridge. Cross over at this point and use the road that runs parallel to the canal for the next 1.5km. Ballycommon Roman Catholic Church, which dates back to 1841 and is dedicated to both St Francis of Assisi and St Brigid, is on the left. The church bell is unusually located in the graveyard to the left of the church and is an attractive structure in itself. Just after the Church is the unusually named Tong's Bridge. Despite its oriental sounding title it is in fact named after a local family.

A short ride further on is the Wood of O Bridge, named after the woodland that you can see 500m to the left. Despite the fact that all the maps and guides indicate that the path continues to the right of the canal you will need to go through the gate on the left after you cross the road. After about 100m the path moves across the canal bed to the right-hand side where you will stay almost until you reach Kilbeggan.

For the next 2km or so you will cross a raised bog where your senses will be fully entertained. It is one of the highlights of this tour and is worthwhile stopping midway just to look and listen. Very few people pass this way and nature has reclaimed the canal bed in an appealing way. There is a gate at the end of the bog section where the path starts to rise gently to Whelan's Bridge that once again was built as an accommodation bridge for local farmers. It now stands isolated and redundant, with only sheep for company.

Continuing on the right towpath the canal bends first gently right and then more pronounced to the left, proceeding to

Murphy's Bridge. From this bridge there is a well-defined track which leads across the Silver River and the county border between Offaly and Westmeath to Lowertown Bridge. After this bridge the track becomes considerably more difficult as it passes through several farms where the farmers avail of the path to lead their animals to various fields. The result is that the surface for the next 2km is very challenging even in dry conditions. To add to your discomfort is the proliferation of electric fences installed by the farmers, particularly along the route of the canal. Some have become hidden in foliage and you may get the odd shock as you brush pass them. In one area the farmer has draped the electric fence right across the path so be careful.

The route slowly improves as you make your way towards Grange Bridge, which follows a sharp turn to the right in the canal's direction. You will have to endure the opening and closing of numerous gates along the way. This trend continues until you reach Skeahanagh Bridge. Curiously this bridge bears an inscription stating that it is Mann Bridge with the date 1831 indicated. This was a mistake that was never rectified and even locals are unaware of the inscription.

The Ordnance Survey maps and other guides suggest you can continue by the right towpath at Skeahanagh Bridge. In fact you will need to change to the left towpath for the short journey to Kilbeggan, otherwise you will end up in the front yard of a delightfully presented thatched cottage. The towpath from this point to the harbour at Kilbeggan has been resurfaced and provides welcome relief. At Kilbeggan Harbour the buildings were tastefully and painstakingly restored a number of years ago and are now occupied as offices. One of the companies using these premises is aptly called The Water Store. The harbour was dredged a number of years ago but with no water supply feeding into it the bed has become a field of grass.

Kilbeggan is renowned for the whiskey produced by Locke's Distillery which is located close to the centre of the town beside the Brosna River. The distillery is believed to be the oldest licensed pot distillery in the world, having been licensed in 1757. The distillery closed in 1957 but there is a visitor's centre and museum at the distillery that are worth a visit and there is also a very good coffee shop and restaurant at the same location.

Tour 10
Tullamore to Shannon Harbour
Shannon Line
(34 Kilometres)

This tour encompasses one of the most pleasant and least peopled stretches of the entire Grand Canal Line particularly the stretch from Pollagh Village to Belmont, a distance of about 13.7km. The stretch to the east and west of Macartney Aqueduct is mainly grass and gets very boggy in winter and after prolonged periods of rainfall.

The towpath is well defined along the entire route, with a combination of tarmacadam changing to rough path, in turn changing to grass. This tour covers a stretch of the canal that was constructed in the very early years of the nineteenth century. While the canal was completed in 1803 there were early difficulties in making it passable due to regular breaches in the bogland areas it traversed and it was not until 1805 that it was permanently secured after almost two years of work staunching its weaker parts.

The route passes through a lengthy stretch of bogland traversing the Brosna Valley and keeping close to the course of the River Brosna. Thomas Omer, the canal's first engineer, originally planned to make this river navigable when he set out his early

Tour 10 - Grand Canal
Tullamore to Shannon Harbour
Shannon Line

Key

Bridge

Lock

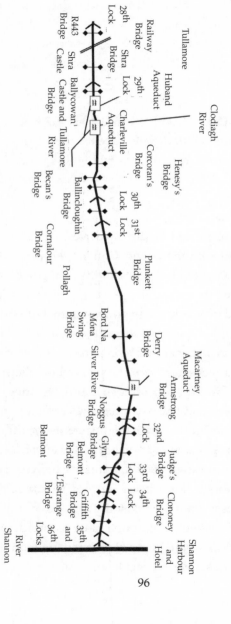

plans for the canal but it was subsequently decided to pursue a separate still-water navigation.

Start at the 28th Lock. Keep to right towpath until Becan's Bridge and then switch to the left towpath until Shannon Harbour.

How to get there

Tullamore, in County Offaly, is located in the heart of Ireland, approximately 96km by road from Dublin. Take the M4/N4 to Kinnegad, then the N6 to Kilbeggan and the N52 to Tullamore.

Maps

Ordnance Survey of Ireland Discovery Series:
Map 47 Offaly, Westmeath and Galway (ISBN 1-901496 – 40-6)
Map 48 Offaly and Westmeath (ISBN 1-901496-45-7)

Leaving the 28th Lock behind, pass under the Dublin-Athlone railway bridge. Almost immediately on the right are the ruins of Shra Castle which date back to 1588 when it was built by an officer in Queen Elizabeth's army, John Briscoe. In earlier times the full name of the castle was Shrahikerne Castle signifying *Kearney of the Shragh*. Briscoe had married a lady whose family name was Kearney who came from the townland of Scraghe near Tullamore. The ruins are presently used as a shelter for farm animals.

Much more impressive are the ruins of Ballycowan Castle which is located about 3km further on, just past the 29th Lock. The castle occupies a prominent position in a local farmer's farmyard so permission should be sought before wandering in to inspect it. It was built by Sir Jasper Herbert in 1626 on the site of an earlier castle. Some of the thick walls of the earlier castle, known locally as Molloy's Castle, can still be seen. The castle was burnt in Cromwell's time and has remained in its present condition ever since. The family crest can still be seen above the entrance door, bearing the motto, *By God of Might I hold my Right.*

Just past Ballycowan Castle is Huband Aqueduct which is dated 1803 and crosses the Tullamore River. It is named after one of the longest-serving directors of the Grand Canal Company, Joseph Huband, who served the company for over 50 years and also had bridges named in his honour located at the 3rd Lock on the Circular Line at Percy Place in Dublin and at Lowtown. It is said locally that when construction started on the aqueduct the workers started to raid some of the stone from the burnt out ruins of Ballycowan Castle before they were stopped by concerned locals.

A short ride on, following the gentle bend of the canal, lies the Charleville Aqueduct named after a prominent local landowner, Lord Charleville, whose castle lies to the south of the canal.

Over the next couple of miles the canal is crossed by the following bridges in quick succession:

Corcoran's Bridge: It is a very short cycle to Rahan village should refreshments be needed.

Becan's Bridge: It is advisable to change towpaths at either this bridge or at the next one.

Henesy's Bridge: From this bridge on, the left towpath going westward is the better preserved all the way to Shannon Harbour.

Ballincloughin Bridge: This lies west of the 30th Lock. Note the lock-keeper's cottage which is superbly maintained.

Cornalour Bridge: This lies just west of the 31st Lock.

Plunkett Bridge: Located at Pollagh Village.

After Pollagh village the canal closely follows the path of the Brosna River to your right and enters a lengthy stretch bounded by scrub and bogland. Extensive bog workings are noticeable and the prominent towers of Ferbane power station are clearly visible looking westwards. Bord na Móna constructed a swing bridge to facilitate its small peat-bearing trains. Just past the swing bridge the towpath forms part of the Offaly Way so expect to see a number of walkers in this area.

The Bord na Móna bridge is followed a couple of hundred metres later by Derry Bridge. If you wish to slip off the towpath for a while, the ruins of Kilcolgan Castle are located about 2km to the north of the bridge. This was owned by the MacCoughlan family but little remains of the original building and it is said locally that its stonework was used for road building.

Resuming the towpath you will quickly encounter the very fine Macartney Aqueduct, constructed in 1803 and named after Sir John Macartney, a former Chairman of the Grand Canal Company. It crosses the Silver River, a tributary of the River Brosna.

The Macartney Aqueduct is approximately 13km from Shannon Harbour. For the first six of these kilometres the canal courses through a very quiet and relatively uninhabited area. Two bridges are encountered in quick succession just before the 32nd Lock. The first of these is Armstrong Bridge, also known as Gallen Bridge, named after a local family who were the previous occupants of the Gallen Priory, a convent to be found close by. The second bridge is called Noggus Bridge. The lock-keeper's cottage at the 32nd Lock is sadly derelict.

Glyn Bridge and an accommodation bridge known as Judge's Bridge, are both encountered before reaching the 33rd Lock. This lock, which is to be found close to Belmont village, is interesting as it is double chambered and can be problematic for boatowners to navigate as Belmont Bridge is built across one of the two chambers. Keeping to the left side, the towpath is grassy for about three-quarters of the remaining journey. In wet weather passage can be tough as the grass is fairly long in some parts. The next landmark encountered is L'Estrange Bridge which bears the date 1800 and where the ruins of a former inn can be seen. Just under a kilometre further on is the 34th Lock and Clononey Bridge.

You are now nearing the end of your journey as you see Griffith Bridge, which is at the entrance of Shannon Harbour. This bridge was named in honour of Richard Griffith, the engineer who supervised the construction of this part of the canal and who used to spend five days each month on this task. It was he who, in 1802, laid the foundation stone of the last lock, the 36th. There is a guide to the harbour on display and you will note that some of its imposing buildings such as the hotel (which was completed in 1806 but was never a success), the stables and the police barracks are now in ruins. The agent's house is now a Bed & Breakfast. Shannon Harbour is twinned with the English Midlands' town, Braunston Marina on the Grand Union Canal.

At the end of the journey are two locks in close proximity, the 35th and the 36th. These are the final two locks on the main line before the canal makes its way through to the River Shannon which is navigable for boats. These two locks are of different dimensions to the canal's other locks. They measure 24.4m x 4.9m x 1.8m (80 feet x 16 feet x 6 feet) to conform with the locks on the Shannon navigation, so that riverboats can reach the harbour. Unfortunately from a cyclist's viewpoint, this is where the journey ends as the towpath beside the Shannon from this point onwards is variable, with lots of barriers.

SECTION B

THE RIVER BARROW

HISTORY OF THE BARROW NAVIGATION

'Sweet Barrow'; 'Fair Barrow'; 'Goodly Barrow'. When people speak of or write about the River Barrow they do so with reverence and enchantment. This is understandable given its captivating beauty and scenic abundance. It is truly a jewel among the many sparkling rivers of Ireland and it is difficult to do it justice with the written word. It is a river that has to be experienced at first hand.

The source of the River Barrow can be found at Barna Mountain in the Slieve Bloom range. Celtic legend states that the river has its source in a sacred well there which has magic properties. According to the legend if one were to gaze upon the sacred waters of the well, or to be so daring as to touch them, there is an immediate volcanic-type eruption creating a powerful flow of water. Celebration of mass is reported to be the only way to set the disturbed waters of the well at rest, thus saving the surrounding areas from flooding.

From Barna Mountain the infant Barrow first streams in a northerly direction across the bogs of Offaly before meandering eastwards across County Laois towards Portarlington and onwards into County Kildare. Gathering strength and bulk from tributaries like the Black River, it continues its eastward drift before embarking on a course to the south just north of Monasterevin that will ultimately lead it to the sea. Monasterevin marks the first contact with the Grand Canal and it was originally thought that the Barrow could be made navigable for commercial traffic from this point onwards. However, different counsel prevailed and the river was not canalised until further down its course at the town of Athy. From there the river channel was made navigable via a system of locks, weirs and lateral canals up to Scar Rock near St Mullins in County Carlow where it becomes tidal. During its passage to St Mullins the Barrow passes through a number of large and medium-sized towns, including Carlow, Leighlinbridge, Bagenalstown and Graiguenamanagh, all of which have contributed to the rich tapestry of history associated with this great river.

Whatever the nature of its source the River Barrow develops into Ireland's second longest natural waterway stretching 192km from its rise in the Slieve Blooms to the sea. Prior to flowing into the sea it joins up, firstly with the River Nore several kilometres north of New Ross and then further south with the River Suir at Waterford Harbour. Collectively the three rivers are known as 'The Three Sisters'.

Efforts to make the Barrow navigable date back to the early eighteenth century but it was not until 1759 that any real work started, when Thomas Omer was appointed to oversee the project.

Omer was closely involved with the early construction of the Grand Canal, which began three years earlier. Progress was slow and by 1790 only seven locks had been built. In that year the Barrow Navigation Company was incorporated and took over the works. They appointed William Chapman, an engineer, to supervise the works and the company made the surprising decision to redesign the navigation system so as to accommodate 80-ton boats. The rationale behind this is unclear given that the Grand Canal locks above Athy could not accommodate boats of this size, making seamless passage of traffic between the two systems unworkable. A total of fourteen of these locks were built including the reworking of four of Omer's original locks.

By 1812 the navigation was still unfinished and there were frequent complaints about the depth of the river. Even after its completion it was not possible to accommodate fully-laden boats during the summer months and complaints about navigability persisted throughout the nineteenth century. In 1894 the Barrow Navigation Company was sold to the Grand Canal Company.

In subsequent years the Grand Canal Company sought to improve navigation by deepening the river. In the 1930s, a drainage scheme in the upper reaches of the river led to increased silting in the lateral canals on the navigable section and the Company was eventually paid the sum of £18,000 in compensation. Commercial traffic on the Barrow ceased in 1959 and it is now used exclusively for leisure boating.

THE RIVER BARROW – ROUTE OVERVIEW

This book deals only with that part of the River Barrow along which there is a towpath or 'trackway' bordering the navigable stretch of the river. The towpath stretches 69km from Athy to

Scar Rock near St Mullins in the southern reaches of County Carlow. In his book, *Goodly Barrow,* Tadhg O' Sullivan describes how, on a walk along the towpath to St Mullins, you 'encounter, not roses or lilies or daffy-down-dillies, but a dense jungle of thistles and briers and neck-high nettles. Perhaps one day the responsible authority may restore this amenity for those of us who prefer grass and water to asphalt and fumes.' O'Sullivan's words appear to have been listened to for nowadays the towpath is clear and open, with a firm grassy surface that is well maintained particularly below Carlow. For cyclists it is certainly the best surface adjacent to any waterway in the 26 counties.

The towpath, or trackway, commences at Athy and passes unhindered through Carlow, Leighlinbridge, Bagenalstown Goresbridge and Graiguenamanagh before terminating adjacent to St Mullins. For much of its course along the towpath the Barrow marks county boundaries, firstly between Carlow and Laois and later between Carlow and Kilkenny. Beyond the range of the towpath it also provides the county boundary between Kilkenny and Wexford. The Blackstairs Mountains with their highest peak, Mount Leinster, are a dominant feature to the east while Brandon Hill, with a peak of 515m (1,690 feet), commands the skyline near Graiguenamanagh.

The distance from Athy to Scar Rock is 69km, with a fall of 51.5m (169 feet), overcome by 23 locks one of which, at Ballykennan, near Graiguenamanagh, is a double lock. In total there are 17.7km of lateral canals along the route to overcome the shallow stretches of the river.

If you wish to track the River Barrow beyond St Mullins you will have to do so by road as no towpath exists from where the river becomes tidal.

Tour 1
Athy to Carlow
(19 Kilometres)

The town of Athy marks the end of the Grand Canal's Barrow Line and the beginning of the Barrow Navigation. It also marks a move into the northern reaches of County Carlow. For much of this tour the Barrow forms the county boundary between Carlow and Laois. As the southerly descent continues there is a noticeable improvement in terrain, with plenty to interest the eye. The eddies, swirls and rocky shallows of the free-flowing river contrast sharply with the still and placid waters of the lateral canals built to bypass shallow sections. Along the Barrow the towpath is usually referred to as the trackway and the further you progress on the improving track the more the beauty of the river and its historic surroundings enchant you.

How to get there
Athy is approximately 70km from Dublin. Departing Dublin via the N7/M7 road network, turn right at the M9 motorway junction in the direction of Kilkenny. Approaching the end of that motorway turn right on to the N78 which will lead all the way to Athy.

Tour 1 - Barrow Navigation
Athy to Carlow

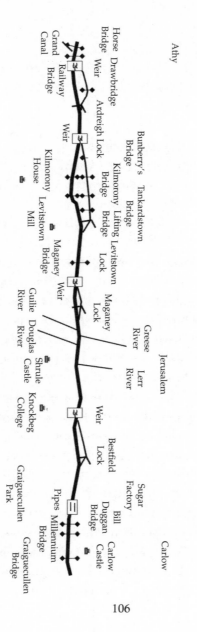

MAPS

Ordnance Survey of Ireland Discovery Series:

Map 55 Kildare, Laois, Offaly and Wicklow (ISBN 0-904996-67-0)

Map 61 Carlow, Kildare, Kilkenny, Laois and Wicklow (ISBN 1-901496-31-7)

The starting point of this tour is the east side of the horse bridge adjacent to the junction of the Grand Canal and the River Barrow, just below the 28th Lock. This can be accessed from the town using the path that runs from Crom-a-Boo Bridge past the new marina that is being constructed on the east bank of the river. The horse bridge is an interesting structure with four arches of diminishing size moving from west to east and was used to bring the towing horses across the river in the era when canal boats had no engines.

Just past the now disused railway bridge is the first of the lateral canals of the Barrow Navigation system. At the start of each canal cutting is a weir which tends to be a popular place for herons and other birdlife. Further on, away from the noises associated with townlife, the roar of water cascading over a weir can be heard for some distance and will herald an upcoming canal cut. The towpath along this initial stretch from Athy is firm and is a popular walk for locals as far as Ardreigh Lock. The former lockhouse at Ardreigh has been extended and is now a B & B facility.

Beyond Ardreigh the path is rougher but still passable as it is frequented by fishermen. The start of the longest lateral canal along the river, the Levitstown Cut is a little further on. The canal along this cut extends for over 3km. The path deteriorates but not dramatically so as you pass two accommodation bridges in quick succession. The first is Bunberry's Bridge and the second is

Kilmorony Bridge, which allowed access to Kilmorony House, the ivy-clad remains of which can be seen to the west. Between the two bridges, and almost hidden by heavy growth, is one of the last remaining milestones along the navigation. The inscription is almost totally faded and is impossible to read.

Kilmorony Bridge is in poor condition with the parapets gone on one side. Unusually for bridges along this waterway it has railings instead of stone work. Perhaps the stone walls were too low and railings were added later as a safety feature to prevent livestock from falling into the water.

After Kilmorony Bridge the river narrows towards the canal but then turns away so that it can no longer be seen from the towpath. The next sight of the river is at Levitstown Lock. Just before Levitstown is Tankardstown Bridge followed by a small lifting bridge to access the island between the cut and the river. At Levitstown is an imposing castellated building once used as a maltings until 1943 when it was destroyed by a fire. Malt was transported by canal boat from here to the Guinness Breweries in Dublin where it was used to make the world famous stout. Nowadays Levitstown continues to be a busy place, with a number of river related activities such as eel trapping and electricity generation. It is also the base for Leisure Afloat, a boat-hire company.

For the next 3km to Maganey Bridge the path is bounded on the eastern side by trees, offering good shelter, and by the broad river on the western side. In the distance you can make out the hills of south-eastern Laois which form part of the Castlecomer Plateau. It is a quiet and peaceful stretch, much loved by local and visiting fishermen. The Castlecomer Plateau is the centre of the Leinster Coalfields and is bounded on its east side by the Barrow Valley and on its west by the Nore Valley.

Close to Maganey Bridge, a fine seven-arched structure built in 1790, the three counties of Laois, Carlow and Kildare meet. To the left of the bridge are Harris' pub, aptly called The Three Counties, and an adjacent shop. The bridge marks the intersection of two official way-marked trails, the Barrow Way and the Slieve Margy Way. The Barrow Way follows the path of the River Barrow while the Slieve Margy Way is a network of walking routes in south-east County Laois. The two also intersect on the southern side of Carlow town at Graiguecullen.

From Maganey Bridge to Maganey Lock, a distance of 1.4km, there is a well used and firm hardcore surface which services the restored lock-house at the Maganey cut, one of the shortest on the navigation. Just beyond the cut the towpath reverts to grass and is relatively smooth. This is an extremely attractive part of the river. From time to time trees line the path on both sides creating a verdant corridor which, while restricting the view, generates a soothing atmosphere. Along this stretch a number of smaller rivers flow into the Barrow from both sides in fairly quick succession. From the west come the Giulie and Douglas Rivers while on the eastern bank two small humpbacked bridges mark the entrance of the Greese and Lerr rivers.

Looking at the map you will note some strangely named townlands in the vicinity of this stretch. Firstly, Jerusalem lies between the Greese and Lerr Rivers and south of the Lerr River is Gotham, a name familiar to fans of Batman.

The Elizabethan Shrule Castle lies on the west bank almost directly opposite where the River Lerr streams into the Barrow. It is well hidden amongst dense woodland and is almost impossible to see from the eastern bank during the summer months. You will be able to get glimpses of the castle through a small clearing on the west bank about 200m downriver. A little further south of Shrule is the more visible Knockbeg College, a large diocesan secondary college dating back to 1793. The weir near the college marking the start of the Bestfield Cut is a popular location for local swimmers and there is even a diving board 200m upriver from the weir.

Bestfield Lock is said to be haunted and like the 13th Locks on both the Grand and Royal Canals is a place where boatmen would not moor their boats. Just past Bestfield Lock there is another of the rare surviving granite milestones. On this occasion it is possible to read the faint inscription which states 'St Mullins 33 miles'.

Approaching Carlow town it is hard to ignore Ireland's first and largest sugar factory which comes down to the path on the east side. The factory was established in 1926 by a Belgian company with state funding, was later bought by the Irish Government and was then privatised in the 1980s. Sugar is made at the factory by evaporating and crystallising the juice from beet, grown throughout the region. The company made good use of the river when commercial traffic was operating on the Barrow and the extensive quays used by the boats remain. Sadly this piece of Carlow's history will soon disappear as it has recently been decided that the factory will close.

Beyond the factory you pass under the Bill Duggan Bridge, named after a noted local solicitor. You then pass Braganza, formerly the location of a bishop's residence, followed by a graveyard, known locally as the 'old graves'.

The approach to Carlow has changed much in recent years with the development of Graiguecullen Park on the west bank, where the river curves gently to the right. Access to the park from the east side is by the recently constructed footbridge called

Millennium Bridge. The eastern skyline is dominated by the spire of St Mary's Church of Ireland church, reaching 59.4m (195 feet). Further east, you will be able to make out the top of the tower and lantern of the nineteenth-century Carlow Cathedral which rises to 45.7m (150 feet). Looking ahead and slightly eastwards as you pass the Millennium Bridge you will just be able to see the top of one of the two remaining towers of Carlow Castle, although continued building in the area is rapidly concealing the view of the castle from this approach. Up ahead Graiguecullen Bridge, which dates back to 1569, marks the end of the tour.

Carlow is a prosperous town with a history as the focus of several struggles caused by its Barrowside location and its erstwhile importance as a strong military fortress. The castle at Graiguecullen Bridge is the remnant of previous structures which occupied its site. The first, a timber structure, was built by Hugh de Lacy around 1180 for a Norman knight called John de Clahull who had been granted title to the lands around Carlow. The choice of site was significant, being located on a hill at the confluence of the Barrow and Burrin rivers. A bog separated the castle from the town on its east side thus assisting its natural defences.

The timber castle was replaced by a stone structure in the early thirteenth century by William Marshall, who married Strongbow's daughter, Isabella. The castle has an important place in Irish history. In the early part of the fourteenth century it came under the direct control of the English Crown. Between 1361 and 1394 it became the new seat of government in Ireland and the Exchequer was located at the castle for those years.

Having survived many attacks in the following centuries it eventually fell to the guns of Oliver Cromwell's army in 1650, like so many of Ireland's castles. Further ruin was caused in 1814 by a

Dr Middleton who planned to use the castle as a lunatic asylum. He managed to create structural havoc with gunpowder in a futile effort to reduce the thickness of the walls and to enlarge the windows. Two battered towers and part of an intervening wall are all that now remain.

George Bernard Shaw (1856-1950) had a proprietorial association with Carlow, though he is said to have visited the town only once in his adult years. He inherited property in the town from his mother's family which he eventually gifted to the Local Authority. The main property is a building on Dublin Street lying between Mc Hugh's Hotel and Cox's Lane. Following the gift it was used initially as a technical school and then subsequently as the town library. A number of years ago the town library was relocated to the former Presentation Convent on Tullow Street and Shaw's gift now lies in a dilapidated state.

Not far from Shaw's building is the imposing Carlow Courthouse which is said to have been based on the Temple of Lissus in Athens and was designed by William Vitruvius Morrison in 1830. Local history suggests it was originally intended for Cork but due to a mix up in plans ended up in Carlow.

Not far from Carlow is one of Ireland's best known dolmens, Browne's Hill Dolmen, whose cap-stone is said to weigh at least 100 tonnes and is reputed to be the largest in Europe. There are three 1.8m (six-foot) uprights and two recumbent stones at the other end. To see the dolmen take the R276 east out of Carlow for approximately 3km (two miles). There is a sign on the road indicating its location.

Carlow boasts many fine hostelries and restaurants and for those in need of refreshment Brooks Café at Óstan Dinn Rí on Tullow Street is well worth a visit before heading off on the return journey.

TOUR 2
CARLOW TO GORESBRIDGE
(25.2 Kilometres)

Flanked initially on the western side by the Castlecomer Plateau and later on the eastern side by the Blackstairs Mountains this tour gracefully descends deeper into the western reaches of County Carlow, passing by the historic towns of Leighlinbridge and Bagenalstown. There are long stretches of uncrowded trackway bounded by either tilled fields or rich pastureland. The trackway is in good condition throughout, with one change required at Leighlinbridge.

HOW TO GET THERE
Carlow town is approximately 90km from Dublin and can be reached via Athy. Departing Dublin via the N7/M7 road network, turn right at the M9 motorway junction in the direction of Kilkenny. Approaching the end of that motorway turn right on to the N78 which will lead all the way to Athy. From Athy, take the R417 for the 18km journey to Carlow. Alternatively, you can remain on the N9 for the entire journey to Carlow. There is less traffic via Athy.

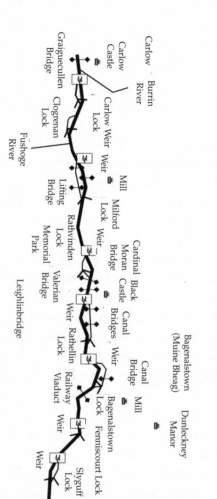

Tour 2 - Barrow Navigation
Carlow to Goresbridge

Key

Bridge

Lock

MAPS

Ordnance Survey of Ireland Discovery Series:

Map 61 Carlow, Kildare, Kilkenny, Laois and Wicklow (ISBN 1-901496-31-7)

Map 68 Carlow, Kilkenny and Wexford (ISBN 1-901496-95-3)

Starting at the western end of Graiguecullen Bridge follow the path past Carlow Lock and the marina entrance for Ceatharlach Moorings. A well-trodden path yields to a grass track as the hustle and bustle of Carlow town is left behind. The river broadens and the western bank of the Castlecomer Plateau provides a pleasant vista to the west. Once again the Slieve Margy Way shares the path for the short journey to Clogrenan Lock which was the last to be constructed on the River Barrow. The weir at Clogrenan is unique in that it is the only naturally occurring one on the Barrow Navigation. A couple of hundred metres below the lock the path crosses the Fushoge River as it contributes its waters to a broadening and faster flowing Barrow. To the west are the ruins of Clogrenan Castle, at the gateway to Clogrenan House.

The next stretch of trackway to the stone bridge which marks the arrival at Milford is quiet with a good grassy surface. Milford features a complex array of water channels and a number of small islands, and at one time had a thriving milling industry. When the milling industry declined the mills were used to generate electricity and Carlow became the first town in Ireland to have a public lighting system, with power generated from this source. Electricity is still generated at Milford. A private dwelling has now been built on the island between the lateral canal and the river. The swing bridge close to Milford Lock has been temporarily replaced by a footbridge.

After Milford the quality of the towpath is excellent. For boatmen, it must have been idyllic here on balmy summer days, with inspirational surroundings guaranteed to soothe the nerves of even the most stressed out individual. There were also tougher winter days when the boatmen had to even contend with ice in the slower moving lateral canals. Canal boatmen I have spoken with and those I have read about appear to remember with equanimity the good and bad days and are almost unanimous in their affection and respect for the waterways.

At Rathvinden Lock a relatively modern bridge carries the N9 over the river. The bridge is named after Cardinal Patrick Moran (1830-1911), Bishop of Ossory, before being appointed Archbishop of Sydney in Australia. In 1885 he became the first cardinal to represent the Australian Catholic Church. Born in nearby Leighlinbridge, Cardinal Moran was only the second Irishman to rise to the highest levels in the Church and was the first ecclesiastic to become a Freeman of Dublin.

A short ride further on brings you to the attractive town of Leighlinbridge, with its fine stone bridge spanning the wide river. The town's name is derived from the Irish words *leath ghleann,* the 'one-sided valley'. The bridge is the oldest on the river and is reputed to be one of the oldest functioning bridges in Europe. It dates back to 1320 and was built by an ecclesiastic, Canon Maurice Jakis of Kildare Cathedral, to allow him speedier access around his diocese. The bridge is known as Valerian Bridge, perhaps because of the red valerian that festoons its parapets during the summer.

A ruined castle lies at the eastern end of the bridge. This is known as Black Castle and was originally built in 1181 by Hugh de Lacy for John de Clahull, the same Normans who built Carlow Castle upriver a year earlier. All that remains of this original structure is the western half of the tower rising to about 15.2m (50 feet) and part of the bawn wall. The castle was built to defend a strategic crossing point on the river and later offered protection to a Carmelite Friary founded close by in the late 1260s. In 1547 after the friary succumbed to Henry Vlll's suppression, the English Lord Deputy Sir Edward Bellingham rebuilt it and added a circular gun turret. A local Irish chieftain, Rory Óg O'More captured and destroyed the castle in 1577. It was partly rebuilt but attacked again later by Cromwell's forces. Half of the tower collapsed in 1888.

Apart from the aforementioned Cardinal Moran a number of other famous people have associations with Leighlinbridge and are commemorated in a Memorial Garden and a Sculptured Garden located on the west bank as you approach the bridge. Among these are Colonel Myles Walter Keogh (1840-1876) who died fighting alongside Custer against Sitting Bull and the Sioux tribe of Indians at the Battle of the Little Big Horn on 25 June 1876. Also remembered is John Tyndall (1820-1893), a world acclaimed scientist and climber. He worked on solar chemistry and invented the light pipe, a forerunner to today's fibre optics technology. He is best remembered for providing the first explanation for why the sky is blue. According to Tyndall, the reason is that dust in the air scatters much of the short-wavelength blue light. Apart from his scientific studies he also found time for mountaineering and was the first person to climb the Weisshorn in the Alps. The circumstances of his death were unfortunate. His wife mistakenly gave him an overdose of sleeping draught after mixing it up with medicine he took for indigestion. The

Memorial Garden also contains a tree planted by Brian Mulroney, former Prime Minister of Canada, on the occasion of his visit to his ancestral home at Leighlinbridge on 12 July 1991.

Another interesting artefact on display in the garden is a culm crusher. This is a grinding stone once numerous in the Carlow/Kilkenny area in the nineteenth and early twentieth centuries but particularly around Castlecomer. It was used for tempering culm and also for grinding corn, bones and chalk, as well as making mortar and rendering for building purposes. The term culm refers to poor quality coal dust that was the primary fuel for poor local farmers. The manner in which the grinding stone was used is unusual. Instead of lying flat on the ground, like other millstones, culm crushers were positioned upright on their rim. A horse was used to walk the stone around in a tight circle crushing the culm underneath.

In more recent times Leighlinbridge became the focus for meteorologists having gained the distinction of being the location for the world's last recorded fall of a meteorite in the last millennium. This happened on 28 November 1999 and fragments of the disintegrated meteorite were found on the Bagenalstown Road. Small parts of the meteorite are held by the Geology Department of Trinity College Dublin and London's Natural History Museum. It was the first recorded fall of a meteorite in Ireland since the Bovedy meteorite of 1969.

Proceeding from Leighlinbridge it is necessary to cross to the east bank where the trackway continues to be of good quality. Another of those rare milestones can be seen on the fringes of the path about 300m from Black Castle. On this occasion you will barely be able to make out the name of St Mullins on the face of the stone but the distance is faded. Not too far ahead is the start of the lateral canal for the Rathellin Cut. The path is tree lined restricting views of the hinterland but with its own tranquil appeal. Along the path are two small accommodation bridges which allow access to the sizeable landbank between the canal cut and the river. Rathellin Lock marks the end of the cut and it is good to see that the lock is identified by a plaque mounted on one of the lock gates' balance beams. This is repeated on nearly all the locks from here to the end of the navigation at St Mullins.

A couple of hundred metres past Rathellin Lock the trackway passes an outdoor swimming pool as you approach a town with two names, Muine Bheag or Bagenalstown. The official name is Muine Bheag but you are more likely to hear the town referred to by its older name, related to the Bagenal family who settled in the town in the sixteenth century. The town was an important milling centre and the canal cut, which curves significantly to the right as it passes through the town, predates the development of the navigation proper. In fact ownership of the cut and Bagenalstown Lock, which is beside the extensive Brown's Mills at the south of the town, did not pass into public ownership until as recently as 1988.

While the Bagenal (sometimes listed as Bagnall) dynasty in Ireland was founded in the sixteenth century the town and its streetscape owe most to Walter Bagenal, who in the eighteenth century developed plans for the town that were inspired by Versailles in northern France. He made a bright start with a courthouse modelled on a Greek temple, much like the one seen earlier in Carlow. You will have seen this building on your approach to the town. Unfortunately circumstances conspired against his building ambitions and his plans were frustrated. The courthouse remains the only monument to his grandiose vision.

About 2km north east of Bagenalstown is Dunleckney

Manor, home to the Bagenal family for almost three centuries and worthy of an off-route visit. The present structure was built in 1850 for Walter Newton, heir to the Bagenal line through his mother Sarah Bagenal, although parts of the house date back to the seventeenth century. It was designed in Tudor Gothic style by architect Daniel Robertson and remained in the Bagenal family until 1941. It is open to the public in the afternoons from April to September.

As you leave Bagenalstown by the track on the east side and travel towards Royal Oak Bridge, the Blackstairs Mountains to the east become more prominent. Royal Oak was originally an inn at the junction of two roads. Nowadays it is a small village on the principal road to Kilkenny. Beyond the bridge the Barrow begins a long winding curve to the right amidst what are now familiar rich pasturelands. The trackway is generally in good condition although the lack of regular traffic can often result in the grass growing thickly in stretches. A railway line passing over the river via a five arched limestone bridge provides interest as you make your way to Fenniscourt Lock, at the end of a small canal cutting. The track-way in this vicinity is a little rougher but still easy to negotiate.

While the scenery along this stretch is attractive you may become impatient for the next of the river's architectural land-marks. These are well interspersed and the first comes after over 2km at Slyguff, which translates as 'the black way'. The weir at Slyguff is the oldest on the navigation and is fairly extensive even though the cut is small by comparison with some of the other lateral canals already encountered.

As you gaze upon Mount Leinster, the highest point of the Blackstairs Mountains, it is interesting to note that the last wolf to be killed in Ireland was found on the north slope of this mountain in 1786.

Moving further down the track you come to another weir and the start of a canal cut which is much longer than Slyguff. This is the Upper Ballyellin Cut and there is increased evidence of human activity and industry here. Halfway down the cut is a sharp twist in the canal and the track. Cross a small bridge here, spanning the water intake for the mill race of the large mill on the east bank. There are lime works close to Upper Ballyellin Lock and the bank immediately south of the lock has been developed to provide easy access to the river.

After Upper Ballyellin Lock Goresbridge comes quickly into view. To access the village pass underneath the bridge to a path on the left that leads to the road crossing the bridge. The village is in County Kilkenny and its name is derived from a local family, the Gores, who lived in Barrowmount House a short distance to the south of the village. In the centre of the village is a small day-time restaurant called Pauline's Coffee Dock that is worthy of a visit. Do not be put off by the narrow entrance as the restaurant expands at the back and even has a small garden where you can dine al fresco. The food is good and is excellent value. There is little alternative in Goresbridge for hungry cyclists or trekkers.

TOUR 3
GORESBRIDGE TO ST MULLINS
(25 Kilometres)

The final stages of an edifying relationship with an enchanting river are arguably the most rewarding. Squeezed by hilly and mountainous terrain on both sides the Barrow meanders its way through a land which has been host to a vast array of ecclesiastical and political history, some of it extremely violent. The joy of being so close to the river as it continues southwards turns to sadness that this proximity cannot be maintained all the way to the sea. You are, however, left with mesmerising memories and a desire to repeat the experience frequently.

How to get there
Goresbridge, County Kilkenny, is approximately 120km from Dublin. There are two ways to reach the village. You can travel to Carlow town, approximately 90km from Dublin via Athy using the N7/M7 road network. From Carlow, take the N9, in the direction of Kilkenny until you reach the outskirts of the village of Gowran. Turn left just before the village on to the R702 which will lead you eastwards to Goresbridge. The alternative route is to

Tour 3 - Barrow Navigation
Goresbridge to St Mullins

Key

Bridge ◆—◆

Lock ⋁

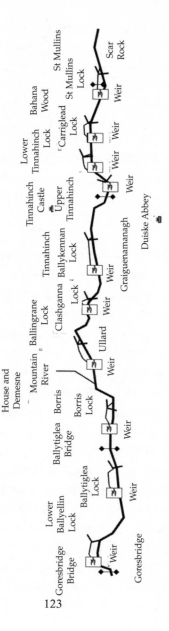

123

turn off the N9 at Leighlinbridge and follow the R705 through Bagenalstown (Muine Bheag) until you come to Kilcumney cross-roads where you turn right for the short journey to Goresbridge. There are a number of turns before Kilcumney where you will see signposts for Goresbridge. These will lead you down some winding secondary roads and are not recommended.

MAPS
Ordnance Survey of Ireland Discovery Series :
Map 68 Carlow, Kilkenny and Wexford (ISBN 1-901496-95-3)

There is plenty of car parking at the new quay on the western bank of the Barrow south of the bridge. For this tour you will need to access the trackway on the east bank of the river via the small lane off the road at the eastern end of the bridge. The trackway all the way to St Mullins provides an excellent surface for cyclists allowing you to devote your full concentration on the scenery and historic settings.

From Goresbridge the trackway brings you firstly on a south-easterly tack towards the Blackstairs Mountains passing by a weir which marks the start of the Lower Ballyellin Cut. The lateral canal gently curves to the right leading to the lock at the end of the cut where the river continues in a south-westerly direction. These shifts in course are typical of what you will encounter along this tour as the river meanders its way through a fertile valley at the foothills of the Blackstairs Mountains. Despite its well kept appearance there is no great evidence that the trackway is used much in this area and you can cycle a long way without encountering anyone. This is part of its appeal yet there is a tinge of sadness that so few bother to avail of this natural amenity, with its

124

glorious scenery.

The sound of cascading water heralds yet another weir and lateral canal. This is unusual because the canal runs past a number of islands with weirs running between them before reaching Ballytiglea Lock. Approximately 1.5km further on is the five-arched Ballytiglea Bridge over which the Borris/Graiguenamanagh road passes. Almost immediately after the bridge the east bank becomes densely wooded marking the outer fringes of Borris Demesne the ancestral home of the MacMurrough Kavanagh family, descendants of the former Celtic kings of Leinster. The family is still in residence in Borris House which cannot be seen from the trackway but whose entrance and gate lodge dominate the centre of the nearby town of Borris.

With a dynasty going back to at least the thirteenth century in this locality it is not surprising there have been some notable members of the MacMurrough Kavanagh family. One such was Art Óg MacMurrough Kavanagh who from a relatively young age tested his mettle against Richard II and his English armies. Initially he was forced into submission but eventually, through a combination of early guerilla warfare and Richard II's urgent return to England to defend his throne, Art became one of the most powerful chieftains in Ireland. He met with an unfortunate end though, being poisoned in New Ross in 1417. He is buried in the churchyard at St Mullins.

Another prominent MacMurrough was Arthur, born in 1831 with only short stumps for both legs and arms. Despite this, and mainly due to the promptings of his mother, he became a noted outdoor sportsman becoming proficient in horseriding, shooting, sailing and fishing. He travelled extensively and became a Member of Parliament. He was a benevolent landlord who devoted a good deal of his time to improving the lot of his tenants. He developed a sawmill and helped to found the Borris lace industry. He was also instrumental in bringing the railway to the town in the 1850s. The rail line was part of the Great Southern and Western route from Bagenalstown to Wexford and is no longer in use.

There is a magnificent sixteen-arch stone viaduct taking the railway over the Mountain River, a tributary of the Barrow, which to this day dominates the eastern skyline of the town. This was built over four years and was completed in 1862 at a cost of £20,000. Affectionately known to this day in the local folklore as 'the crippled Kavanagh' there is a monument to Arthur's memory close to the main gate of Borris House.

The town of Borris, which lies approximately 2.5km from Ballytiglea Bridge, is worth an off-route excursion. Apart from its splendid viaduct it boasts an undulating streetscape proudly retaining cut stone clad dwellings, commercial premises and public buildings with intricate and ornate stonework. Most of these date back to the nineteenth century and are an enduring legacy enjoyed by both residents and visitors. The gate and lodge of Borris House were built in 1813 to a design by William Morrison. The house itself, which was redecorated in Tudor style in the nineteenth century, can be seen from a distance at the southern end of the town beyond the entrance to the golf club.

Returning to the trackway the densely wooded boundary on the east side features intermittently almost all the way to Graiguenamanagh. The appeal of this stretch varies across the seasons. In the height of summer, when most people will see it, the full trees provide a lush green curtain that affords shelter. In autumn there is a rage of colour as the trees begin to shed their leaves. This is perhaps the best time to explore the waterway. In the winter and early spring the bare trees reveal a hidden hinterland, allowing you to discover buildings and other objects of interest that are concealed when the trees have their full growth.

A short ride from Borris Lock the trackway passes over a humpbacked bridge spanning Mountain River as it flows into the Barrow, followed by Ballingrane Cut and Lock. This is a popular location for swimming. The ruined lock-house is ripe for restoration and would yield an idyllic residence given its location. On the west bank is the townland of Ullard where there are the ruins of a monastery dedicated to St Fiacre (or Fiachra), the patron saint of both taxi-drivers and gardeners. St Fiacre spent much of his life in France where he founded hermitages at both Meaux and Brie. He died in 670 AD and is commemorated in a fine stained-glass window by Patrick Pollins at the east end of Duiske Abbey in Graiguenamanagh where he is depicted holding a spade and watering can. Among the ruins at Ullard are a twelfth-century nave, a Romanesque doorway and a granite high cross believed to be dated back to the ninth or tenth century. There is also a holy well dedicated to St Fiacre at the site and near the well are two large smooth sided stones called *bullauns*.

The most photographed lock on the Barrow is Clashganna (sometimes spelt as Clashganny) Lock. It is perhaps the most visited lock on the navigation outside those located in towns and villages. This is because it is accessible by a short laneway off the R729 and is a popular location for swimming, canoe training and casual boating. There is a small inlet behind the restored lock-house where a number of small craft are moored. A little further downriver is Ballykennan Cut and Lock, the only double-chambered lock on the navigation.

The approach to Graiguenamanagh is very appealing. The

precipitously rising Brandon Hill dominates the skyline to the west while the eastern slopes are blanketed by trees. Because of the raised ground to the east the trackway can be quite wet in the early mornings until the sun rises high enough to dry the heavy dew. On the final approach into Graiguenamanagh the trackway sweeps around a prominent outcrop of land known locally as 'the devil's eyebrow' before passing the marina for Valley Boats and onwards towards the splendid seven-arched bridge that splits the twin towns of Tinnahinch to the east and Graiguenamanagh to the west.

Graiguenamanagh is a captivating town with a history dominated by religion and the river. The long quays on its western bank are indicative of a once bustling commercial river trade and you can still find men who in their formative years were proud to become boatmen, following in the footsteps of their fathers and uncles. Its name is an anglicised version of the Irish for 'hamlet of the monks' and is derived from a monastic settlement founded in 1204. Previously the town was known as Duiske after the river which flows from Brandon Hill into the Barrow at the town. Duiske is an abbreviation of the Irish term *Dubh Uisce* meaning 'black water' and the name lives on through Duiske Abbey.

The abbey is located a short distance to the west of the bridge and is worth a visit. It was founded by English Cistercian monks from Stanley in Wiltshire and took 40 years to complete. It was the largest Cistercian abbey in Ireland and at its height accommodated 60 monks, and several hundred lay brothers. It occupied over five acres of land and also served as a hospital, hospice, school and farm. There is a model of the abbey as it was in the thirteenth century on display in the present restored building. As will be seen the church was cruciform with an aisled nave, transepts with side chapels, a crossing tower and a vaulted chancel. The tower, south aisle and part of the side chapel to the south have all disappeared as well as part of the north aisle.

The monastery was suppressed at the time of the Reformation in 1536, its community dispersed and ownership transferred to the Butler (Ormonde) family. It fell into disrepair and in 1774 its great tower fell bringing down the chancel roof and covering over the medieval tiled floor with 1.5m (five feet) of masonry. In 1812 the church portion of what remained was handed over to the Catholic authorities who began a partial restoration. Unfortunately they built over the buried floor. A number of the tiles are displayed on the wall at the entrance to the church. In 1974 major restoration was undertaken lasting over six years and the church is now a proud centrepiece in the town.

There are several pubs in Graiguenamanagh but the one which is most closely related to the river and the boatmen is The Anchor on the west bank, immediately south of the bridge. Famous for its breakfasts, a pictorial record of the town's association with the Barrow Navigation is proudly displayed on the lounge walls. You might also be fortunate to bump into men like Eamon Hoare who with his father, Jimmy, sailed the *34M* and who will regale you with songs and poems associated with the canals, such as the 40-versed 'The Fighting Calibar' or 'The Ghost of the 13th Lock'.

Resuming the journey on the east bank, it is a short ride by a quayside lined with leisure craft and the ruin of Tinnahinch Castle to Upper Tinnahinch Lock. The castle dates back to 1615 and was built by James Butler who subsequently lost his lands when he became involved in the Confederate War of 1641. It protected a wooden bridge that spanned the river prior to the construction of the stone bridge upriver in 1767. The castle was destroyed by fire around 1700 and has been left untouched ever since.

Just past Upper Tinnahinch Lock the trackway reverts to a comfortable grass covering and accompanies the river in a prolonged curve to the south east in a course dictated by the proximity of Brandon Hill. Almost at the end of this curve is Lower Tinnahinch Lock after which dense woodland once more shelters the path, and the river's tortuous course takes a sharp turn directly south. You will encounter Carriglead Cut and Lock, the oldest on the Navigation, soon after. The lock-house has been tastefully extended and restored and the owners are blessed with being able to regularly look out on one of the most scenic stretches of the river.

About 0.5km south of Carriglead Lock is a seat hewn out of hard granite in the shape of a throne. It is positioned so that if you sit on it you are looking directly upriver towards Carriglead Lock. Some refer to it as the Giant's Chair while to others it is known as Freney's Chair, commemorating the eighteenth-century local highwayman who was said to have used the chair to keep an eye on his hidden loot and to watch out for pursuers. Not too far south from the chair is a disused lime-kiln.

Bahana Wood rises above you as you approach St Mullins Cut and Lock. Several boats appear to be permanently moored along this cut, particularly close to the lock itself.

The lock-house at St Mullins is another fine example of these structures designed by Thomas Omer and first built by the banks of the Grand Canal and on the Lagan Navigation. It has been said that the lock-house at Drumbridge on the Lagan Navigation is the only one of Omer's houses still lived in, although a number have survived. This is disputed by Michael Higgins, the present owner of the St Mullins' lock-house. He states that his family has been in continuous occupation of the lock-house since 1849 and at present he is modernising it. His mother's family, the Websters, were the lock-keepers at St Mullins. Having reared a large family, his mother lived in the house until her death, when it passed to him. Michael has been extremely sensitive to retaining key features, such as the tight stone spiral staircase.

The trackway after the lock has been resurfaced with a dusty hardcore providing an uncomfortable short ride to St Mullins where a well-kept quayside and a quaint terrace of houses makes for a picturesque setting. This is where the trackway ends although you can cycle a further 200m or 300m down by the side of a rocky shelf known as the Scar, marking where the river becomes tidal. There are a number of old buildings along the east bank, one of which has been restored to provide a private residence.

St Mullins is a fascinating place that seeks to emulate Clonmacnoise for ecclesiastic provenance but also possesses an interesting secular history. There is a steep road at the end of the trackway that leads up to the village where you will find monastic ruins as well as the remains of a motte and bailey. The locality takes its name from St Moling who was born of royal blood in 614 and went on to become Archbishop of Ferns. St Moling features in much local folklore and legends. One of the stories told about him relates to the time before he settled at St Mullins. He had previously lived as a hermit at Mullenakill, County Kilkenny, about 20km to the west. He was badly afflicted by sores on his legs and a local widow's cows used to lick the sores to aid the healing process. The milk yield of the cows fell as a result which caused the widow to give offence to the saint after which he moved to St Mullins.

St Moling is said to have been instrumental in the abolition of the *borumha* capital tribute, an ancient form of central taxation, levied by the High King of Ireland. A small pocket gospel book, known as the Book of Moling, is preserved in Trinity College Dublin. The saint is named as a scribe but it is thought more likely that it was written after his death by one of his followers. There is a stained-glass window by Patrick Pollins in Duiske Abbey depicting the saint with the head of an ox. St Molling died on 17 June 696 and is buried in the graveyard of the monastic settlement.

The remains of the settlement include a medieval church ruin, the base of a round tower, a high cross dating back to the ninth or tenth century and a former Church of Ireland church built in 1811, which is now in use as a heritage centre. There is also a graveyard in which are buried various participants in the ill-fated 1798 rising. These are identified with green plaques. Some were beheaded merely for making pikes while others were killed in action at Calvary Hill.

Because of its location, and the presence of the monastic settlement, the Anglo-Normans found the area attractive. Around 1170 Strongbow (Earl Richard de Clare) granted St Mullins to Peter Giffard and it passed to various other Anglo-Normans. Despite its attractions, however, it never developed into a large and prosperous town.

Close to the settlement is a motte and bailey stronghold, a fortification introduced to Ireland by the Normans in the late twelfth century. This consisted of a mound (motte) raised by excavating ground from a deep surrounding ditch, and an attached lower and larger area that was also ditched (bailey). A castle would be built on top of the mound surrounded by a palisade where the lord or marshal would have his headquarters. Because the early motte castles were fabricated from wood they were vulnerable to fire and to counter this risk it was the custom to drape wet hides around the buildings as protection. In later mottes wood gave way to stone. The castle's garrison and its household would have lived in the bailey which was also palisaded. Because they were relatively cheap and quick to raise mottes were a popular defensive structure among the early Normans and others can be found elsewhere in Ireland. Two of the largest examples rise to a height of 16.8m (55 feet). One of these is at Knockgraffon, County Tipperary, built beside the River Suir by the Normans in 1192 when they were on a raid against Donal Mór O'Brien, King of Thomond. The other is at Ardschull, County Kildare not far from Athy which is of a similar vintage. The example at St Mullins is smaller and in the long and narrow embanked enclosure running northwards from the motte it is still possible to make out the outline of some of the buildings enclosed within the bailey.

There is a small coffee shop on the quayside close to the Scar (the rocky formation that marks the start of the tidal element of the river) where you will find a warm welcome and a pot of tea that eschews the modern style, since it is made with loose tea leaves – and all the better for it. While acknowledging that hunger is good sauce and that exercise is good for the appetite Maggie O'Dwyer's freshly made sandwiches, on granary bread, are worth the journey in themselves and will set you up for the return journey.

St Mullins is where the trackway finishes and so ends our journey on this waterway. It is possible to track the Barrow to its confluence, firstly, with the Nore and then with the Suir and all the way to the sea. However, to do so you will have to use the road network and be satisfied with only occasional glimpses of the river from a distance. Having been no more than a few feet from its glistening waters for almost 70km the attractions of pursuing the river further are moderate.

SECTION C

THE ROYAL CANAL

HISTORY OF THE ROYAL CANAL

Much like Mark Twain, rumours of the demise of the Royal Canal have in the past been greatly exaggerated. When writing a foreword to the second printing of his book, *Green and Silver*, first published in 1949, L.T.C. Rolt commented that the Royal Canal was little more than a memory by 1968. He added that he was unaware when he made his journey in 1946, through the Royal from Dublin to the Shannon, that he was writing its epitaph. He also described the canal as a lost waterway.

Happily Mr Rolt was to be proven wrong and the Royal Canal has made a phoenix-like recovery from the threats to its existence. This is thanks largely to Dr Ian Bath, who founded the Royal Canal Amenity Group in April 1974 and who has inspired many volunteers and ultimately state agencies to save the waterway from the fate foretold by Rolt in 1968. The restoration efforts are thankfully ongoing.

To some, the Royal Canal is a poor relation of its larger counterpart. Given the neglect it suffered over many years I was concerned that the towpaths would have deteriorated to such an extent that cycling along them would not be feasible. I am pleased to report that my concerns were misplaced. The towpaths presented a more onerous challenge than the Grand Canal or River Barrow and progress in parts was slow due to the poor quality of the surface. The rewards, however, made it worthwhile, not least an introduction to parts of the Irish landscape which probably have changed little in the two centuries since construction of the canal began.

The towpaths of the Royal Canal offer cyclists an off-road cycling experience that is hard to match. Untouched for years except by farm stock and wildlife, some stretches have benefited from a return to nature and the restoration work that is being done appears to be sympathetic to these changes. Watching the restoration in progress gives an appreciation for the huge effort required two centuries ago to construct this waterway in the first place without the benefits of today's earthmoving machinery. Some stretches cut through lengthy rock formations while others cross peatlands and bogs which presented huge drainage and bank reinforcement problems. Yet all these were surmounted to present a navigable waterway which, while having lost its original raison d'être can now offer an amenity to be enjoyed by boatowners, trekkers and cyclists alike.

As a cycling route one is drawn to make comparisons between the Grand and the Royal. The Royal Canal has had a more chequered history than the Grand and its neglect over a longer period has taken its toll on the infrastructure that surrounds it. There are a lot more derelict buildings along the route but their ivy-clad façades provide their own character and are testimony to the remoteness and serenity to be found on its banks. The Grand Canal appears to offer more in the way of engineering achievements although the Royal's Boyne Aqueduct near Longwood in County Meath rivals anything the Grand Canal can produce. The shorter Royal limits the number of tours that can be undertaken but this is a physical fact and does not place any limitation on the variety of scenery and sensations to be enjoyed, which match those of the Grand Canal. They are both marvels of engineering and we should give thanks to those whose brainchildren they were, and those like Ian Bath whose commitment to a cause has ensured that we have an amenity that can be savoured.

From the outset the Royal Canal has had a colourful history. It is said to have had its origins in the disenchantment of one of the directors of the Grand Canal Company of Ireland, John Binns, who believed he was not being sufficiently listened to in relation to plans for the Grand Canal. Instead, in 1789, he persuaded a combination of businessmen and landlords to come together to form the Royal Canal Company to take advantage of a debenture scheme introduced by Parliament the previous year which was designed to help finance private companies to build canals. This company shook the cobwebs from the discarded plans of one of two schemes that were considered as far back as 1755 to make an inland navigation from Dublin to the River Shannon. The other scheme went on to become the Grand Canal, which was chosen as a more viable option at the time.

The original plans for the Royal Canal were to be a blend of canal and river navigations beginning at the north-west end of Dublin city and linking up with the River Shannon in County

Longford. It was to be 175.4km (109 miles) in length, with 76 locks and branches off the main line going near Trim to Navan, Kells, Athboy and Delvin.

Works on the canal started in 1790 and the first lock to be built was at Cross Guns Bridge, which is now the 5th Lock. The ceremony for the laying of the first stone was performed on 12 November 1790 by John Fane, Earl of Westmoreland. However, problems quickly set in so for the following five years the company only managed to build 24km (fifteen miles) of canal before it had spent all the shareholders' money plus the Parliamentary grants. These problems were largely self made. Firstly, the canal was run through a limestone rock quarry at Carpenterstown near Castleknock, which involved blasting a channel through 2.4km (1.5 miles) of rock instead of going round it. Secondly, a decision was made in dubious circumstances to pass the canal through the village of Maynooth, which was a diversion from the original plans and required the construction of a costly aqueduct over the Ryewater River near Leixlip. This decision was probably prompted by the Duke of Leinster who owned the village and was also a director of the canal company. Furthermore, poor standards of workmanship were a feature of the early construction, mainly because the work progressed without the direction of a full-time engineer.

In the following years work on the canal continued as the company accumulated mounting debts. By 1800 the canal had reached Newcastle, County Meath, 45km (28 miles) west of Dublin at a cost of £350,000. Two years later the death of Richard Evans, who had assumed the position of principal canal engineer, caused further delays and it was not until the end of 1806 that it arrived at Mullingar. In the meantime a passenger service had commenced on 2 December 1796 between Dublin and Kilcock with an intermediate stop at Leixlip. The Leixlip stop became a popular one due to the attractions of the spa there, discovered by workmen digging the canal in 1791. The passenger service was extended as sections of the canal were commissioned.

By 1809 the canal had been completed as far as Coolnahay, 10km (seven miles) west of Mullingar. This was the end of its summit level. Over the next four years the company struggled to make any headway against the background of increasing debts and disputes about the remaining course of the canal to the River Shannon. The Grand Canal Company made repeated attempts to frustrate their Royal counterpart's desire to extend the canal to Ballymahon as they feared loss of trade from Athlone, given that the Royal had lower tolls. Finally, in 1813, the Royal Canal Company was dissolved and the canal fell under the jurisdiction of the Commissioners of Inland Navigation who were delegated to complete the canal using public funds. This they did and by 1817 they finished the canal reaching Termonbarry via the River Camlin. Total cost of the completed canal was over £1.42million which was more expensive than the longer Grand Canal. Following completion the canal was handed over to a new Royal Canal Company. The 8.4km branch to Longford was subsequently added in 1830 having taken three years to build at a cost of £12,651.

Like the Grand Canal the Royal Canal faced increased competition from expanding and improving road networks and the coming of railway. In 1833 the Royal Canal introduced 'fly boats' which were capable of speeds of around 16km (10 miles) per hour and could take 110 passengers. These reduced the travelling time between Dublin and Mullingar from twelve to eight hours. They were six months ahead of the Grand Canal with this development.

Notwithstanding the reduced journey times the company's passenger service did not prove enduring, as indeed was the case with the company itself. In 1844 the Midland Great Western Railway Company made a successful bid for the company at a price of just under £319,000, a considerable discount on the construction costs. The intention of the railway company was to build a railway line on the bed of the canal but they were frustrated from doing so by the authorities. Instead they built a parallel line on canal property alongside the canal all the way from Dublin to just over 6.4km (four miles) beyond Mullingar.

Trade boats first appeared on the Royal Canal in 1796 but their growth in numbers was impeded by the delays in construction both of the canal itself and the necessary infrastructure to support enhancement of trade, such as harbours and access transport to and from the canal. After the takeover by the railway company canal trade went into rapid decline due to a combination of increased tolls and lacklustre maintenance. After many years of constant decline there was a revival of trade during the 'emergency years' of the Second World War. However, once the war was over the declining pattern was resumed and eventually trading on the canal ceased completely in July 1951, with the last boat being operated by a Mr Leech of Killucan, County Westmeath.

In the meantime the Royal Canal changed ownership once again. In 1925 the 26 separate railway companies that were operating in Ireland were amalgamated to form the Great Southern Railway Company. The Royal Canal thus became part of this operation. In 1944 legislation was passed providing for the merger of the Great Southern Railway Company with the Dublin United Tramway Corporation to form Córas Iompair Éireann (CIE). This meant yet another new owner, and darker days for the canal. The 1960 Transport Act gave CIE the power to close the canal to navigation. In subsequent years a dam was placed across the canal at Ballinea, 4.8km (three miles) west of Mullingar, effectively cutting off water supply to all points beyond. This was followed by the construction of a number of low-level bridges across the canal to the west of Mullingar. A further threat to the canal's future was the recommendation in 1971 by the Dublin Transportation Study Group to build a road along the canal line from Castleknock to North Strand in Dublin.

Brighter days were coming. In 1974 a campaign to save the Royal Canal was launched with the formation of the Royal Canal Amenity Group by Ian Bath whose objective was to make the canal a fully navigable waterway once again. Early work on restoration was carried out by volunteers but as the canal changed hands once again in 1986, this time to the Office of Public Works, there was increased state-sponsored involvement. By 1990 the canal was completely restored from Blanchardstown to Mullingar. Further changes in ownership, firstly to the Department of Arts Culture and the Gaeltacht in 1996 and subsequently, in 1999, to Waterways Ireland have not diminished restoration efforts and the canal is now fully navigable from Dublin to Abbeyshrule. Considerable work has already been completed in restoring the canal banks beyond Abbeyshrule and from a cyclist's viewpoint the towpaths remain passable all the way to the River Shannon.

Royal Canal Route Overview

The Royal Canal provides a waterway connection between the north of Dublin city to the River Shannon at Cloondara, County Longford. The main line of the waterway is 145.6km long and begins at Spencer Dock on the north bank of the River Liffey, not far from the Custom House. It passes through the north of Dublin, and the counties of Kildare, Meath, Westmeath and Longford. There is also a branch measuring 8.4km linking it directly to the town of Longford. Previously there was a branch link to Broadstone on the north side of Dublin measuring 1.2 km but in 1956 the final part of this link was filled in and converted to a linear park.

There are a total of 46 locks on the canal, ten of which are double chambered. Its summit level is 98.6m (323.5 feet) which it reaches at the 25th Lock near Footy's Bridge after a journey of 71.5km. The level continues for 24.6km before the canal starts its descent towards the River Shannon at Coolnahay Harbour, 10km west of Mullingar.

The canal's main water supply comes from Lough Owel near Mullingar by means of a feeder canal stretching 3.6km. While the feeder is much narrower and shallower than the canal itself and never formed part of the navigation, it nevertheless presents an attractive short cycle route almost right up to the lake.

The canal's towpaths have, over the years, suffered the neglect endured by the waterway itself. Farm animals grazing along the paths in some of the more neglected areas have, however, ensured that the paths still exist. This is a double-edged sword as their presence has rendered the surfaces of the path difficult to negotiate over some stretches. In the ongoing restoration the paths have not been ignored and in some areas present a good cycling surface. I am pleased to report that the entire stretch of the canal, including the Longford branch, presents a viable cycling route, albeit with a higher degree of difficulty in some locations than a cyclist would encounter along the more favoured Grand Canal.

TOUR 1
SPENCER DOCK TO LEIXLIP
(20.7 Kilometres)

This tour has an inauspicious start but fairly quickly leaves the hustle and bustle of city life behind. The canal courses in a relatively straight line through the northside of Dublin city where the towpath has been much improved before hiding behind the industrial estates of Glasnevin and Finglas. The waterway temporarily adopts a tree-lined rural atmosphere before passing by the complexities of the M50 motorway junction with the Navan Road and then onwards to the Dublin-Kildare county boundary before arriving at Leixlip.

MAPS
Ordnance Survey of Ireland Discovery Series:
Map 50 Dublin City and District (ISBN 1-901496-64-3)

The Royal Canal's link to the River Liffey is located on Dublin's North Wall adjacent to the International Financial Services Centre. Much new development has taken place in this area over the past decade and is ongoing, with both new apartment and commercial buildings under construction near the banks of the

Tour 1 - Royal Canal
Spencer Dock to Leixlip

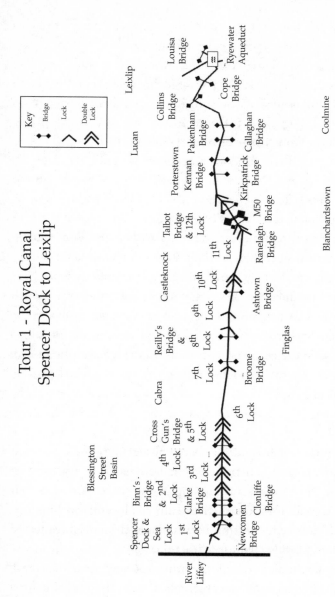

143

canal. This will help improve the surroundings at the start of this tour as they had been quite neglected previously.

There is a redundant sea lock here where the canal links to the River Liffey, located under the pair of lifting bridges on the North Wall Road. Boats now wishing to enter the canal must rely on tidal flows to negotiate the low headroom under the lifting bridges and the drawbridge at Sheriff Street.

There is no towpath alongside the canal until the 1st lock, located just beyond Newcomen Bridge on the North Strand Road. You can follow the canal at a slight distance, however, by using Guild Street and Sheriff Street and turning right at the Five Lamps junction with the North Strand Road for the short ride up to Newcomen Bridge. Prior to the redevelopment, this was a very unattractive portion of the canal and for a large part remains bordered by railway lines. Looking back from Newcomen Bridge you will see the new lifting bridge that was installed to allow a single track railway line cross the canal. The style is unusual as it lifts vertically, like the lock gates that predated the apex-shaped mitre or pound lock gates which are in use on Irish canals. Vertical gates were found to be inefficient due to the water displacement problems. The new bridge virtually touches the canal water when it is in place.

One of the canal's earliest known tragedies took place at Newcomen Bridge. The bridge collapsed when it was almost complete due to insufficient bonding of the stone work and four workmen tragically lost their lives in the incident. It was symptomatic of the poor standards of workmanship that was a feature of the early days of the canal's construction.

Passing by the well-kept lock-keeper's cottage at the 1st Lock you will now be able to access the towpath on the south side for a short while as you approach the imposing Croke Park, headquarters for Ireland's national games, Gaelic Football and Hurling. Just beyond Croke Park you pass under Clarke Bridge, bearing a plaque indicating its construction date of 1794. In recent years the path has been blocked from Clonliffe Bridge on Jones' Road to Binn's Bridge, owing to construction activity, but it is passable in normal circumstances.

Binn's Bridge marks the first of the more serious upward shifts in the canal's level as there are five locks in quick succession, four of them being double chambered. These help the canal to rise over 28m (92 feet) in 1.2km.

A recently erected sculpture of the Irish writer, Brendan Behan stands at Binn's Bridge and was created by John Coll, the same sculptor responsible for the Kavanagh sculpture on the Grand Canal.

You should now switch to the north towpath on which you will be able to remain for the next 5.2km. The towpath to Cross Gun's Bridge has recently been restored and provides an excellent cycling surface as you pass the rear of Mountjoy Prison and the junction with the former Broadstone Branch, just to the right of the prison. It is worthwhile making a small diversion to inspect the now filled-in branch that has been converted to a linear park off which is Blessington Street Basin, one of Dublin's hidden treasures. Even long-term Dublin residents have never seen it or are even aware of its existence.

Blessington Street Basin was originally built as a reservoir for drinking water and was fed from the Royal Canal via the Broadstone Branch. It was commissioned in 1810 and was originally named the Royal George Reservoir to commemorate the golden jubilee of King George III. Measuring 123.1m (404 feet) long by 57.3m (188 feet) wide the basin occupies 1.76 acres of ground and varies in depth from 2.4m to 3.7m (8 to 12 feet). In 1868 the Vartry Reservoir replaced it as a source of drinking water for the people of Dublin. However, the basin was not rendered redundant as it was then used exclusively to supply the Jameson Distillery at Bow Street and the Power's Distillery at John's Lane, where the water was used for both malting and cooling. This continued until 1970 in the case of Jameson's and 1976 in the case of Power's. After a period of neglect it was refurbished in 1994 and opened as a public park with cobbled seating bays and flower-fringed walkways. It still receives its water supply from the Royal Canal by a cast iron subterranean pipe and is now home to great variety of birdlife.

The 5th Lock at Cross Gun's Bridge was the first lock built by the canal's engineers. The ceremony for the laying of the first stone was performed on 12 November,1790 by John Fane, Earl of Westmoreland. The canal widens as it passes a former mill building that has been converted into modern canalside apartments. After the 6th Lock the canal begins to shed its concrete surroundings as it passes close to Glasnevin Cemetery to the north, with its round tower providing a distinctive landmark. Over the next couple of kilometres you will be aware of a variety of aromas emanating from the factories which closely bound the canal to the north as it passes under the combined railway and canal bridge known as Broome Bridge (named after one of the directors of the Royal Canal Company). You may note the difference in brickwork where the railway bridge was added at a later date to the original canal bridge.

There is an interesting connection between Broome Bridge and William Rowan Hamilton (1805-1865), one of Dublin's most learned men, who is best remembered as a mathematician of considerable renown. He was also Professor of Astronomy at Dunsink Observatory. Hamilton was born in 1805 at 36 Lower Dominick Street. He possessed a prodigious talent for languages and is said to have been able to read Hebrew at the age of seven and speak thirteen languages by the time he was fourteen. There is a memorial on the bridge unveiled by Eamon de Valera in 1943 which records that on 16 October 1843 Hamilton was crossing the bridge with his wife when he was hit by a flash of inspiration which led him to discover the fundamental formula for quaternion multiplication. In his joy he took out his penknife and carved the formula on the stone wall of the bridge. Sadly it is no longer there.

The canal emerges into clearer terrain after Reilly's Bridge and the 8th Lock which are dated 1792. A one-time resident of the area near Reilly's Bridge was Lord Norbury, better known as the 'Hanging Judge', who eventually rose to the high office of Chief Justice. His family name was Toler and he was a descendant of Nicholas Toler who served as Quarter Master General in Oliver Cromwell's army. Among those Lord Norbury sentenced to death by being hanged, drawn and quartered was Robert Emmet, whom he tried in September 1803 after Emmet's unsuccessful insurrection earlier that year.

Emmet was a member of the Society of United Irishmen who staged a failed rebellion in 1798. Having risen to national prominence, he travelled to Europe seeking support for another French-backed revolution in Ireland. In 1802 he returned to Ireland, gathering together the remnants of the United Irishmen for another rebellion. However, an explosion in an arms depot forced him to act in Dublin without French support on 23 July 1803. The rebellion failed and Emmet was forced into hiding, eventually being captured in Harold's Cross on 20 August. At his trial for treason,

Emmet made a speech from the dock that has become famous in the annals of Irish history and won him the praise of his enemies. He was only 25 years old when he was executed. Despite a reputation for being a brutish man Lord Norbury is said to have broken down in tears after passing sentence on Emmet. During his career on the bench Norbury had many legal encounters with an eminent barrister of the period, John Philpott Curran, whose daughter, Sarah was engaged to Robert Emmet at the time of his execution. There was no love lost between Norbury and Curran. On one occasion when Curran was making a speech in court an ass started to bray on the street outside. The judge was heard to remark to the court, 'One at a time, please, Mr Curran'. It was not all one-way traffic. Another tale of their frequent verbal spats related to a time when they were dining on circuit in a country hotel and complaints were made about the toughness of the meat. Curran was heard to remark to Norbury, 'You try it, then it will surely be well hung'. According to local legend children who ventured into the orchard of Lord Norbury's estate at Segrave House in later years encountered a headless ghost carrying the head under his arm. And another ghostly tale tells of how Norbury turned into a phantom dog at death and began to prowl the area, dragging a chain behind him.

The ability to look north after Reilly's Bridge across a wide expanse of land, towards and beyond Dunsink has been largely curtailed by major residential developments along the canal up to Longford Bridge at Ashtown. (For those interested in stargazing, Dunsink is the location of an observatory which has limited public opening hours during the winter evenings.) Looking to the left across the railway line at Longford Bridge you will see a former mill building that has been converted into an enterprise centre.

The large clock on the front is said to have come from Newgate Prison in England.

A change to the left-hand towpath is necessary at Longford Bridge as you enter a quiet, scenic, tree-lined stretch, on a good grass path, leading to the 11th Lock. A short ride further leads to a sequence of bridges and a modern aqueduct, as the canal passes the junction of the M50 motorway and the N3 Navan Road to reach the 12th Lock and Castleknock. Beyond Castleknock train station the towpath starts to rise gently and takes on a rougher quality with small rocks protruding. This signals the start of what is referred to as the 'Deep Sinking', where the canal was cut at great expense through Carpenterstown Quarries for about 3km. This is an area where cyclists should take great care due to a combination of the rugged quality of the towpath and a steep fall to the canal. In some spots the towpath rises some 9m (30 feet) above the water.

You will note that the canal is very narrow through the 'Deep Sinking' and this caused considerable difficulty for the boatmen when navigating this stretch of the waterway. It was not possible for two boats to pass each other through the restricted channel. In order to avoid one boat having to reverse for a long period it became the custom for boats to carry a trumpet which they used to signal their arrival at either end of the sinking. If there was no response to their signal they knew they could progress unhindered.

This stretch of the canal was the setting for the greatest tragedy to take place on Ireland's inland waterways. On 25 November 1845 a night passenger boat capsized after hitting the rocky bank of the canal, causing the loss of fifteen lives. At the time of the accident the boat was being steered by an employee of the Canal Company who was not a regular boatman while the usual helmsman was said to be having his dinner. The employee was later found guilty of manslaughter while the helmsman was dismissed. There is a plaque mounted on the side of Kennan Bridge at Porterstown in memory of those who perished.

At Kennan Bridge you should change to the right-hand towpath which courses its way through a tunnel of trees and shrubs for several hundred metres. As you make your way through this tunnel it is easy to miss an unusual building with an interesting history. The three-storey structure has a high apex roof and was built by the local parish priest, Father Dungan, in 1852 as a national school for the local community. Its architecture differs sharply from that of other such schools of the same period which were usually single-storey structures. Local folklore relates that in the nineteenth century the parish priest approached the local landlord, whose demesne included Luttrelstown Castle, for a parcel of land on which to build a national school. The landlord refused and was said to have commented that he did not want the children of the local riff-raff sullying his land. Following this refusal the priest bought a narrow stretch of land extending to five acres from the Royal Canal Company and erected the school here. Popular folklore relates how the priest returned to the landlord to say that every time the latter looked out the windows of his castle he could not avoid being reminded of the priest's original request and the landlord's offhand refusal.

After Callaghan Bridge at Clonsilla the path opens up and there is a good grassy surface which lasts almost to Leixlip, with the last few kilometres being a combination of rough path and grass. You will pass the imposing stone structures that once provided the base for the Dublin and Meath Railway line to Navan and then an amenity area with a building which prominently displays the name of the Royal Canal Amenity Group. About 0.5km after Cope Bridge, at Confey, the canal turns sharply to the left where it is carried across the Ryewater River by an extensive earth embankment, controversially built at great cost to facilitate the diversion of the canal to allow it to pass through Maynooth. The embankment is approximately 30m (100 feet) above the level of the river. There is a path to the side of the derelict building that leads down the embankment to the river below where you can inspect the tunnel through which the river passes. However, the path has become overgrown and you may have some difficulty negotiating your way down and up.

In 1791 workmen digging the canal discovered a spa close to Leixlip and this attraction soon became popular once passenger boats were introduced on the canal. The remains of the spa are to the right, close to the aqueduct.

This tour finishes at Louisa Bridge. For those who wish to visit Leixlip the bridge road leads down the hill to the village. Leixlip is derived from a Danish word, *lax-hlaup*, meaning salmon leap and relates to a waterfall which salmon had to negotiate when they moved up the River Liffey to spawn. In more recent times a hydro-electric generating facility was installed on the river at the point of the waterfall. In order not to disturb the breeding habits of the river's salmon an ingenious device was installed to ensure that the salmon could still progress to their breeding grounds. The world's first hydraulic fish lift was invented by two engineers attached to the Electricity Supply Board operating like a canal lock to lift the fish upstream. The design has since been used by other hydro-electric schemes around the world.

Tour 2
Leixlip to Enfield
(24.5 Kilometres)

Venturing deeper into County Kildare this tour passes the towns of Maynooth and Kilcock as it follows the canal's zigzag course into County Meath and back again to Kildare. The Kildare/Meath county boundary is crossed three times before its final crossing at the River Blackwater aqueduct 18km into your journey. For the first half of the tour the canal is hemmed in between the road and the rail track and whilst the scenery is serene the traffic noise from the nearby road is almost constant. This contrasts sharply with the second half of the journey which goes through Cappagh Bog. While the N4 remains a constant companion it is sufficiently removed to allow you to savour the peace and tranquillity of a stretch of the canal that appears rarely visited except by farm animals and wildlife.

How to get there
Leixlip is situated in the north east of County Kildare, close to the boundary with County Dublin. It is approximately 20km from Dublin city centre and can be accessed using the M4 and taking the R148 exit for Leixlip. The start of this tour is at Louisa

Tour 2 - Royal Canal
Leixlip to Enfield

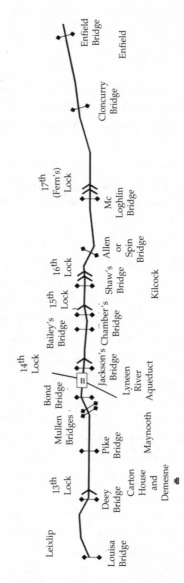

Bridge, located to the western end of the town following the directions for Maynooth.

MAPS

Ordnance Survey of Ireland Discovery Series:

Map 50 Dublin City and District (ISBN 1-901496-64-3)

Map 49 Kildare, Meath, Offaly and Westmeath (ISBN 1-901496-16-3)

Taking the right-hand towpath and leaving Louisa Bridge behind, the canal starts to curve gently to the right before passing under the newly-built bridge which links the R148 roadway to the M4 motorway. Initially the path surface is firm and as you approach Deey Bridge and the 13th Lock, 1.6km into your journey, it becomes more grassy. On occasions the use of heavy-ridged tyres on the tractors used to haul the grass-cutting mowers can result in an uncomfortable ride on some of this stretch.

Deey Bridge is named after Robert Deey who was a director of the original Royal Canal Company between 1794 and 1806. In excess of 100 directors served the company in its relatively short 24-year history yet only a small number were awarded the honour of a bridge in their memory.

The area around the 13th Lock and Deey Bridge is said to have been haunted, though the reason is no longer known, and none of the boatmen who plied their trade on the canal would ever moor their boats nearby. Perhaps it had something to do with the number 13.

Beyond Deey Bridge your journey continues on a grass path in a relatively straight line, as the canal runs parallel to the stone walls of Carton House and Demesne which lies across the R148. This was the home of the Duke of Leinster who owned the nearby town of Maynooth and was a director of the Royal Canal Company. It is said that it was at his insistence the canal was re-routed at great expense and considerable difficulty, to ensure it passed through Maynooth. Midway point along its passage, by Carton House estate, the canal passes under Pike Bridge named after William Pike, a director of the Royal Canal Company from 1794 to 1800. Just before this bridge, which lies opposite the side entrance to the estate, is a small stone harbour, discovered when the canal was being restored. This was the Duke of Leinster's private harbour.

After a further 2km, the old and new Mullen Bridges mark the entrance to the town of Maynooth, where there is a substantial harbour. A diversion off the canal to explore Maynooth is worthwhile. The town is the location for Carton House and St Patrick's College, the entrances to which are at opposite ends of the wide main street a short cycle north from the harbour. Carton House and Demesne was built by James Fitzgerald, Earl of Kildare, in the 1740s as his principal country residence. His town residence, Leinster House, which is now the seat of the Irish Parliament, was developed at the same time as Carton House. Carton House is now being redeveloped as a golf and country club and will also be the headquarters of the Golfing Union of Ireland, complete with a golfing museum.

St Patrick's College has educated many of Ireland's Roman Catholic priests and in recent years has expanded to become a flourishing third level institution. At the entrance to the college are the keep and gatehouse of a Norman Fitzgerald castle. The Norman Fitzgeralds were the Earls of Kildare.

The first college at Maynooth was established in 1518 but had a short-lived history before succumbing to the Reformation after twenty years. The present college was founded in 1795.

Curiously, since it is known as a bastion of Roman Catholicism, the former Fitzgerald Chapel which lies inside the grounds of the college is a Church of Ireland church.

Returning to the canal, resume on the right-hand towpath which follows the college's boundary wall . The next landmark is Jackson's Bridge and the 14th Lock. Henry Jackson served as a director of the Canal Company from 1793 until 1798. The bridge named in his honour is unusual in that there is a separate arch for the towpath.

On the 3.75km section to Kilcock from here you will encounter two more bridges: an accommodation bridge known as Bailey's Bridge; and Chamber's Bridge, followed immediately by the 15th Lock. It is likely that this accommodation bridge was named after the landowner or farmer whose land it connected.

For the last kilometre into Kilcock the R148 becomes clearly visible again as the canal opens out into a well restored harbour before reaching Shaw's Bridge (named after another director) and the double-chambered 16th Lock. Kilcock is well served by several establishments where refreshments are available, including two coffee shops that overlook the harbour. Unfortunately neither seems to open on Sundays.

The canal turns gently to the right as it leaves Kilcock and begins its passage underneath Allen or Spin Bridge through to a quieter and more tranquil setting. The quality of the grass towpath is well maintained, making for a pleasant cycle all the way to McLoghlin Bridge and the 17th Lock, known as Fern's Lock, which is double chambered. At this point you will have to change sides and you will note a deterioration in the quality of the towpath, which becomes wilder and softer but does not present any great discomfort as the canal makes its way towards Cappagh Bog. Compared with the extensive bogs along the Grand Canal and the Royal Canal, Cappagh Bog appears very tame with no significant bog workings or activity. However, the construction of the canal through this stretch occupied the minds of the canal engineers and the efforts of the labourers for several years. Despite extensive drainage works in preparation for the cutting of the canal, they still encountered frequent side slips and swellings in the bottom of the channel they had cut. It is notable that the canal along this stretch is wider than elsewhere and has matured in handsome fashion, with an abundance of trees on both sides to make it a very attractive and peaceful section.

Cappagh Bog was also the location of the first factory in Ireland to process turf mechanically. This was established in 1844 by Charles Wye Williams whose method of drying and compressing wet turf eventually spawned a peat-based industry which provided fuel for boats and for the generation of electricity. Unfortunately Williams' venture failed but his pioneering work had enduring benefit.

Along this stretch, just as the canal starts to take a gentle but prolonged turn left, you will encounter one of the few remaining milestones still in existence along the canal. Although the inscription has suffered the ravages of time it is still possible to make out the figure 23 on the stonework.

At Cloncurry Bridge the towpath on the south side comes to an abrupt end and you will once again have to change sides. You will first have to negotiate the gate, marking the end of this section of the towpath, which unfortunately is padlocked and inhospitably covered with rusted barbed wire. It is preferable to carry your bike over the pedestrian turnstile. There is a good tarred surface for the first 1.5km of the north towpath as it leads you towards Enfield, before the path resumes its grassy covering for the last few hundred metres to where the canal passes under the N4 marking the end of the tour.

TOUR 3
ENFIELD TO THOMASTOWN
(23.4 Kilometres)

Reaching into County Westmeath, this tour is perhaps the most appealing of the Royal Canal tours as it is full of variety in terms of scenery and items of interest. It includes the magnificent aqueduct over the River Boyne and a beautiful tree-lined stretch approaching Moyvalley. The quality of the towpaths is generally good throughout, with only a few kilometres presenting a challenging surface.

HOW TO GET THERE
Enfield, County Meath, and is 42km from Dublin. The N4/M4 west out of Dublin leads all the way to Enfield. Go straight into the town rather than taking the recently constructed bypass. Access to the canal is located at the western end of the town. An attractive amenity park, with a car park and facilities for the mooring of boats, has been built on the canal's north bank.

Tour 3 - Royal Canal
Enfield to Thomastown

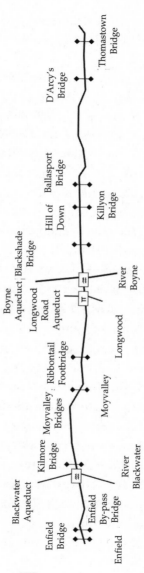

159

MAPS

Ordnance Survey of Ireland Discovery Series:

Map 49 Kildare, Meath, Offaly and Westmeath (ISBN 1-901496-16-3)

While there is a path on the north bank leading from the amenity park, it is preferable to switch to the south bank as the towpath is of superior hard-core quality. Be careful because cars also use this path to access a stretch of waterway 1.5km further on which regularly features in angling competitions. In addition, when you encounter the fishermen be sure to make them aware of your impending arrival as the rods they use tend to be of a stretched pole variety, allowing them to access the far bank. Sometimes they lie these along the ground and you may not see them until you are almost running over them.

After less than 3km, the quality of the path begins to deteriorate leading up to and beyond the Blackwater Aqueduct. This is an area that is regularly frequented by farm livestock and in some places along this stretch there is the added danger of exposed tree roots, which are sometimes hidden by the long grass.

The area around the Blackwater Aqueduct was the location for some of the earliest malicious attacks on the Royal Canal that became an unfortunate feature of the canal's life in the 1820s. These attacks consisted of embankment breaches, stone throwing to prevent closure of the stop gates and personal attacks on boatmen. The attacks were against the background of chronic unemployment and general hardship following the failure of the potato crop in the years up to 1820. The reason why some of the local populace caused breaches was that they hoped to participate in the repair work for reward. The going rate for a labourer involved in repair work was between ten and twelve shillings per week, the equivalent of between 39 and 47 cents in today's money. Similar activity, though not as prolific, took place on the Grand Canal and one of the solutions which proved successful on that waterway was to ban the use of local labour in the repair work. However, the people living near the Royal Canal appeared to have been more militant and eventually the Royal Canal Company had to resort to armed protection while the troubles persisted.

Kilmore Bridge marks the end of the rutted section referred to earlier and the beginning of a stunningly attractive stretch leading all the way to Moyvalley. Switch at the bridge to the well-maintained towpath on the north bank and savour the beauty of a tree-lined gently curving stretch of canal that has no equal among the waterways of Ireland. You will not wish to hurry through the tunnel of trees which is just as well because you will be frequently jolted by exposed roots. If there is one source of annoyance in this otherwise idyllic scene it is the necessity to dismount on at least a half dozen occasions to carry your bike over pedestrian stiles that have been erected along the route without making allowance for cyclists.

At Moyvalley the construction of the new bridge which carries the N4 over the canal did not allow for a wide towpath so you will have to brave the traffic across the busy roadway to resume your journey just past the bridge. There is an attractive pub called 'Furey's' just beside the canal at the old bridge that serves good food and is a worthwhile stop off point.

Moyvalley was the location for one of the two hotels that the Royal Canal Company built to service its passengers. The other was at Broadstone in Dublin. A third was to have been built at Mullingar but this project never came to fruition. The Moyvalley

Hotel was built in 1806 and was never a commercial success. It served as a factory, corn store, private residence and, most curiously, in 1848 as a centre for hydropathy, a treatment involving the application of water as a stimulant, sedative and a solvent to relieve disease. The building was eventually demolished in 1974 to cater for road realignment and the construction of the new bridge across the canal.

The north towpath from Furey's for the next 4km to the Boyne Aqueduct is good with the exception of a small stretch leading up to Ribbontail Footbridge. It is thought that this bridge got its name from an association known as the Ribbonmen, a militant group formed in the early part of the nineteenth century to protect the interests of the labouring classes who appear to have been active in the area. Just a short step back from the Boyne Aqueduct is a small semi-circular harbour that lies beside another aqueduct which carries the canal over the Longwood Road. The triple arched Boyne Aqueduct is an engineering marvel. It is possible to descend to the River Boyne by a path accessible at the Longwood end of the aqueduct.

Like many of Ireland's principal waterways, the name Boyne is derived from Celtic mythology. Legend has it that the Boyne is presided over by a goddess called Boand. According to legend, she was the lover of Dagda, the father of the Celtic gods.

The hard-core path continues past the Boyne Aqueduct for 1km before reverting to a grassy surface as the canal makes its way to Blackshade Bridge. Beyond this bridge the canal widens and is attractively bounded by woodland on the south side. The next bridge you meet is Killyon Bridge, located at the Hill of Down village. There is an attractive café here, The Parlour Coffee Shop, on the north bank of the canal and this is also the base of Royal Canal Ventures (Tel: 046-9546731) where small boats can be hired to explore the canal by water. A B&B is also available at this venue.

There is a good tarred surface for the next 1.3km to the slightly skewed Ballasport Bridge, one of only two skewed or oblique arched bridges on the Royal Canal system. The other is at Ballinea. Skewed or oblique arched bridges are rare and rather than deal with the engineering complexities of erecting a skewed bridge, the canal's engineers preferred to re-align the roads to cross the waterway at right angles. They were also rare on the Grand Canal but there is a good example near Allenwood on the Shannon Line, aptly called Scow Bridge, thought to be a derivation of the word skew. The only other one is the railway arch at Ringsend in Dublin.

At this point a change to the south towpath is once again required as the canal starts to make its way across another stretch of boggy terrain. The path's surface is very good but in windy conditions progress can be slow as the first part of this stretch is quite exposed. However, this allows for fine panoramic views. As the canal winds its way around Croboy Lough to the north a derelict dredger lies lopsided against the canal bank. The only signs of life in this delightfully quiet stretch are the numerous herons and moorhens you will disturb as you advance.

The boundaries of the canal start to fill with trees as you make your way towards D'Arcy's Bridge where once again a change in sides is required for the relatively short final leg of this tour to Thomastown. D'Arcy's Bridge is named after the D'Arcys of Killucan who were the builders of Hyde Park, an attractive mid-Georgian gentleman's farmhouse built in 1775, located back from the north bank a little short of the bridge.

Just before Thomastown Bridge is a fine harbour and slipway on the south side which provides the base for a canal boat hire facility run by Leisureways Holidays whose boats you will encounter frequently along the canal over the summer months. There is a feeder a short distance from the bridge to augment the canal's water supply from the nearby Riverstown River which runs a couple of hundred metres to the north. Quinn's Pub on the south of the bridge provides welcome relief for tired legs.

TOUR 4
THOMASTOWN TO MULLINGAR AND LOUGH OWEL FEEDER
(20.4 Kilometres)

A proliferation of locks dominates the early part of this tour as the canal rises by 21.6m (71 feet) to its summit level through eight locks over 3km. This is known as the Killucan Flight. Apart from the locks there is plenty of variety on this tour as the canal courses its way through bog and rock to reach one of its most important destinations, Mullingar. This tour also allows you to view the Royal Canal's principal water supply, scenic Lough Owel.

HOW TO GET THERE
Thomastown, County Westmeath, is approximately 68km from Dublin. Follow the N4/M4 west out of Dublin as far as Kinnegad. Go through Kinnegad in the direction of Mullingar and Sligo. Approximately 1km outside the village turn right and this road will lead you all the way to Thomastown Bridge, the start of the tour. There is plentiful safe parking on either side of the canal just east of the bridge.

Tour 4 - Royal Canal
Thomastown to Mullingar

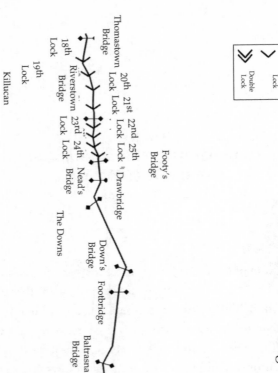

Key

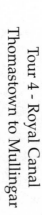

Bridge
Lock
Double Lock

Thomastown Bridge
20th Lock
21st Lock
22nd Lock
25th
"Drawbridge
Footy's Bridge
18th Lock
Riverstown Bridge
23rd Lock
24th Lock
Nead's Bridge
Down's Bridge
Footbridge
Baltrasna Bridge
19th Lock
Killucan
The Downs
Saunders Bridge
Moran's Bridge
Feeder
Towpath Bridge
Mullingar
Lough Owel Feeder

Tour 4 - Royal Canal
The Lough Owel Feeder

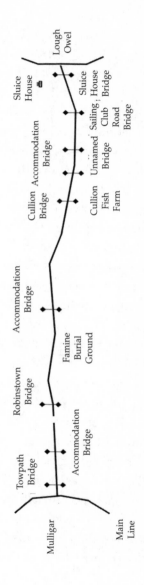

MAPS
Ordnance Survey of Ireland Discovery Series:
Map 49 Kildare, Meath, Offaly and Westmeath (ISBN 1-901496-16-3)
Map 41 Longford Meath and Westmeath (ISBN 1-901496-30-9)

Much quality restoration work has been done on the canal and the locks that dominate the early part of this tour. This is evident in the fine tarred road on the south side of the canal for the first 1.75km from Thomastown Bridge to Riverstown Bridge, passing by Locks 18-21. The lock-houses have been sympathetically extended and restored and there is a general air of care and attention to the surroundings and the canal embankments.

At Riverstown Bridge, known locally as Heatherstown Bridge, you will need to switch to the north towpath. The path is not tarred but is of good quality. The canal continues to rise sharply through Locks 22 to 25, inclusive, which come in quick succession over a distance of just over 1km before reaching Footy's Bridge where, finally, the summit level is reached. The railway track, which has been conspicuous by its absence, resumes its near parallel course just past the 23rd Lock.

The quick succession of eight locks over 3km involving a rise of 21.6m (71 feet) to reach the canal's summit level is known as the 'Killucan Flight', named after the nearby town of Killucan. The last independent canal boat trader to use the canal hailed from Killucan. James Leech ceased trading in 1951, ten years before the canal was officially closed to navigation.

After Footy's Bridge there is a comfortable tarred surface for cycling the next 2km to Nead's Bridge (or McNead's as it is sometimes referred to) which carries the wide N4 roadway over the canal. A realignment of the N4 has created a new road bridge beside the old bridge. This area is known as 'The Downs' which is an anglicised form of the Irish word *na Dúnta*, 'the forts'. Mary Lynch's Pub, located at this bridge, is a popular local hostelry widely renowned for its food.

The canal turns sharply right just after the bridge. Access to the south towpath is via a farmer's gate which, while closed, is not padlocked. From here in to Mullingar the towpath surface is good, allowing for steady progress, but you will encounter several gates all of which can be opened easily. The N4 is a regular companion for most of the way to the town. As you travel amidst open landscape, consisting of a mixture of bog, forest and farmland, you will encounter an interesting variety of bridges. Firstly, there is a drawbridge erected to accommodate a local farmer, followed by the more traditionally styled Down's Bridge which, in turn, is followed by a footbridge. A short cycle onwards leads to a more enclosed setting as the canal narrows and makes its way through a course that was expensively carved out of rock lasting for about 2km almost all the way to Mullingar. While the surface of the towpath is generally good you will need to take care as sharp rocks frequently protrude. Midway along this rocky channel is Baltrasna Bridge.

Saunder's Bridge marks the entrance of the canal into Mullingar and the start of its large horseshoe-shaped loop northwards around the town where it eventually exits in a south-westerly direction. Mullingar is sandwiched between two lakes, Lough Ennel to the south and Lough Owel to the north. The town's name is derived from the Irish, *An Muileann Cearr*, 'the left-hand mill'. This relates to the story of how a seventh-century saint, Colman, otherwise known as Colm MacLuachainn, who used miraculous powers reminiscent of the miracle of the loaves and the fishes to cause a corn-mill to turn backwards and produce enough flour to pay his parents' dues to the king of Meath. It is said that the flour sack never emptied. In terms of infrastructure the town is relatively modern, with a fire having destroyed most of it in 1747 prior to the arrival of the Royal Canal which certainly helped in promoting trade and prosperity. The canal brought coal and building materials into the town and sent corn and livestock products out. Of course, in its early years it also carried passengers in and out of the town until the arrival of the railway. The imposing Catholic Cathedral of Christ the King, with its twin towers, dominates the centre of the canal's loop around the town and indeed the skyline of the town itself. Designed by Ralph Byrne, it was built between 1932 and 1936.

As part of the intention of this tour is to visit the canal's main water source at Lough Owel you should cross over at Moran's Bridge to the right-hand or north towpath to access the feeder which is located about halfway around the loop. The feeder from Lough Owel, located just under 4km north-west of Mullingar, is a narrow and relatively shallow channel that is not suitable for navigation by boats. A small bridge spans the entrance to the feeder which facilitated the passage of horses in the era when canal boats had no engines. Initially there is a good path on the east or right-hand side of the feeder but this peters out after less than 1km when you reach a small accommodation bridge. Beyond the bridge the path is less defined but is still very passable. You will have to leave the path temporarily to cross over the busy R394 at Robinstown Bridge. There is a signpost pointing along the towpath to a famine graveyard, located on the east side of the feeder, not far from the bridge.

As the feeder meanders northwards it passes under a small accommodation bridge which has lost its walls, and then on to Cullion Fish Farm which makes good use of the nearby water supply. At Cullion Bridge beside the fish farm the path comes to an abrupt end and you will have to haul your bike over the low stone wall to access the road. To follow the line of the feeder you will have to turn right at the junction up from Cullion Bridge, having crossed the railway line. By now, you will have lost sight of the feeder but by taking the next left turn, a few hundred metres up the road where you see the signpost for the Lough Owel Sailing Club, you will regain its trail once again. The roadway leads all the way down to the lake and the Sluice House that marks the origins of the Royal Canal's main water supply and the end of this tour.

Lough Owel has a magical history. Local folklore relates its origins to a dispute between two giantesses who lived in the midlands on different sides of the River Shannon. The lake was sent on the wind by one sister to the other for a temporary loan. However, the sister to whom it was sent was so enchanted by its beauty in its new location that she refused to return it, despite many requests. In the nineteenth century the lake was the scene of an annual August festival which featured swimming races with horses on a day called 'Lough Sunday'.

TOUR 5
MULLINGAR TO BALLYNACARRIGY
(18.9 Kilometres)

Having looped around Mullingar the canal resumes its westerly path towards the River Shannon and at Ballinea finally parts company with the railway line which has been its constant companion from Dublin. A little over halfway through this tour the canal embarks on its descent from its summit level along which it has coursed for almost 25km. The tour covers a stretch that has seen much restoration in recent years yet it retains a wild and natural ambience.

HOW TO GET THERE
The starting point for this tour is the harbour at Mullingar just beside Scanlan's Bridge, where there is ample car parking. Mullingar is 75km from Dublin and can be accessed using the N4/M4 road network all the way to the Mullingar bypass. To reach Scanlan's Bridge you will need to take either the N52 exit for the town centre or, alternatively, the later R394 exit which will lead you to the bridge from a northerly direction.

Tour 5 - Royal Canal
Mullingar to Ballynacarrigy

Key

Bridge

Lock

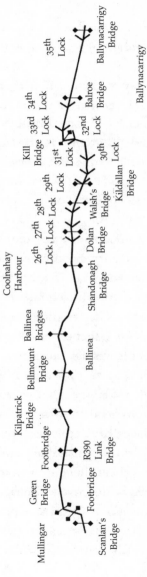

Ballynacarrigy
Bridge

35th
Lock

34th
Lock

Balroe
Bridge

33rd
Lock

32nd
Lock

Ballynacarrigy

Kill
Bridge

31st
Lock

30th
Lock

29th
Lock

Walsh's
Bridge

Kildallan
Bridge

28th
Lock

27th
Lock

26th
Lock

Dolan
Bridge

Shandonagh
Bridge

Coolnahay
Harbour

Ballinea
Bridges

Bellmount
Bridge

Ballinea

Kilpatrick
Bridge

Green
Bridge

Footbridge

R390
Link
Bridge

Footbridge

Mullingar

Scanlan's
Bridge

173

MAPS
Ordnance Survey of Ireland Discovery Series:
Map 41 Longford Meath and Westmeath (ISBN 1-901496-30-9)

The canal finally reached Mullingar in 1806. Further progress was delayed due to lengthy debate as to the best route to follow to the Shannon. One would have imagined that a route south of the town would have been the logical choice, and indeed the original plans were to follow this line. However, surveys revealed that this would have required a high embankment and as a compromise the canal's northerly loop around the town linking in with the feeder from Lough Owel was the final choice.

There is a fine harbour at Mullingar with a boat slipway and dry dock reflecting the importance of the town as a prime passenger destination and trading post along the route of the Royal Canal. The best towpath on which to start this tour is on the south side or the side opposite the car park at the harbour. To access this you can either use Scanlan's Bridge or, alternatively, the footbridge a little further upstream which leads to the street on which you will find the cathedral. You will soon pass under Green Bridge and then skirt the railway station before arriving at a fine, recently-built bridge that provides a link to the R390. Beyond the new bridge the canal continues into more open countryside along a reasonably firm and passable path before reaching Kilpatrick Bridge. At this point there is a marked deterioration in the path, which is regularly trodden on by farm stock, but fortunately the grass is kept reasonably trim, depending on how recently the Waterways Ireland maintenance crews have come this way.

The next landmark is Bellmount Bridge, also known as

Belmont Bridge, where you will need to switch to the right-hand side for a short ride to Ballinea. There are two bridges at Ballinea, as well as a small harbour and boat slipway. On one bridge is a plaque in memory of Fr Paul Walsh, or Pól Breathnach as he is described, a Celtic scholar who served in the Ballinea parish in the early to middle part of the twentieth century. One of the two bridges at Ballinea is another example of the skewed humpbacked bridge, like that at Ballasport Bridge.

In 1964 the canal was dammed at Ballinea, cutting off the main supply of water to all points west. The damming was carried out under the provisions of the 1960 Transport Act which gave Córas Iompair Éireann (CIE), the company which at that time was the owner of the Royal and Grand Canals, the power to close the canals to navigation. The Royal Canal was officially closed to navigation in 1961 and the dam at Ballinea was followed by permission being given to certain local authorities to build low-level bridges across the canal to the west of Mullingar to level the roads for the comfort of traffic. Fortunately the dam has since been removed as part of the ongoing efforts to restore the canal to full navigation all the way to the Shannon.

The journey continues on the left towpath after the second of the two bridges at Ballinea. For the next 200m the path is once again uneven due to the regular passage of farm animals. One of the few surviving milestones is to be found along this path. The inscription has long since weathered away but you will be able to make out the figure 57 on the face representing the number of miles the canal has journeyed from Dublin to this point.

As you progress you come to a section lasting for about 1km where livestock have not entered. If there was evidence needed of the remoteness of some stretches of the Royal Canal then this is it, with the almost complete absence of any person or animal having passed this route for some time. Despite the high grass the passage is easy as the base of the path is relatively smooth.

The path improves as you approach the new bridge at Shandonagh, although it is sometimes overgrown. The same applies to the stretch after the bridge all the way to the picturesque Coolnahay Harbour, the 26th Lock and Dolan Bridge. Despite the rougher surface the appeal of this section lies in the rural surroundings and the abundance of wildlife. At frequent intervals herons take flight, surprised by your disturbance of their normally placid environment. Not so the mallards and tufted ducks that frequent the harbour at Coolnahay who nonchalantly greet your arrival without so much as a shake of their feathers.

Coolnahay, which was reached in 1809, marks the end of the last stretch of the canal built by the original Royal Canal Company, and also the end of the summit level. Having completed the 96km from Dublin the company was in a bad way financially and it was also in dispute over the remaining course of the canal to the River Shannon. The result was the final dissolution of The Royal Canal Company in 1813 and, rather than leave the canal unfinished without having reached its River Shannon target, the government mandated the Commissioners of Inland Navigation to complete the canal using public funds, which they did by 1817.

Keeping to the left side you will note that a lot of work has been done in improving the towpath beyond Coolnahay. Over the next few kilometres the canal follows the contours of the land with gentle twists and turns. Not having encountered locks along the summit level you will soon be reacquainted with their structures and sounds as you pass the 27th and 28th Locks in quick succession. Having seen the magnificent restoration efforts at some lock-houses the derelict building at the 28th Lock completely overgrown with trees and bushes is a sad sight. The next landmark is Walsh's Bridge where the canal turns left and flows on towards Kildallan Bridge.

Over the next 3km the level of the canal falls by over 17.1m (56 feet) through six descending locks, the 29th to the 34th inclusive. A busy stretch for boat people but with benefits for cyclists. It is notable that where there is a quick succession of locks the towpath is improved and maintained to a higher standard.

Just after the 31st Lock the canal takes a very sharp turn left and then a couple of hundred metres later another sharp turn right just after Kill Bridge before adopting a more direct line past Balroe Bridge to the small village of Ballynacarrigy, the finishing point for this tour. The village was an important trading centre when the Royal Canal was at its commercial peak and there is a fine harbour just east of Ballynacarrigy Bridge.

Tour 6
Ballynacarrigy to Ballybrannigan Harbour
(17.7 Kilometres)

In the early stages of this route, the canal crosses into County Longford and closely tracks the River Inny which it crosses near the historic village of Abbeyshrule. High hedgerows along the route conceal the river for long stretches but the frequent twists and turns dictated by the river's course add to the mystery and variety on this tour.

How to get there
Ballynacarrigy is located approximately 18km west of Mullingar. Having reached Mullingar using the N4/M4 road network from Dublin you will have to go through the town centre to access the R393 in the direction of Longford. Ballynacarrigy is the first principal village you will encounter along this road.

Maps
Ordnance Survey of Ireland Discovery Series:
Map 41 Longford, Meath and Westmeath (ISBN 1-901496-30-9)

Tour 6 - Royal Canal
Ballynacarrigy to Ballybrannigan Harbour

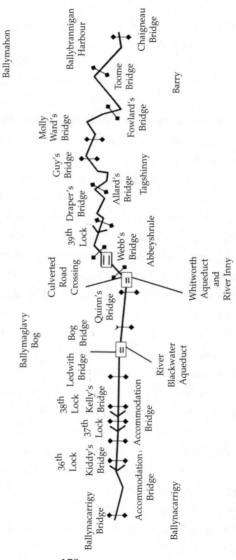

Key
Bridge
Lock

Ballymahon

Ballybrannigan Harbour

Chaigneau Bridge

Toome Bridge

Barry

Molly Ward's Bridge

Fowlard's Bridge

Guy's Bridge

Tagshinny

Draper's Bridge

Allard's Bridge

39th Lock

Culverted Road Crossing

Webb's Bridge

Abbeyshrule

Ballymaglavy Bog

Whitworth Aqueduct and River Inny

Quinn's Bridge

Ledwith Bridge

Bog Bridge

38th Lock

Kelly's Bridge

River Blackwater Aqueduct

37th Lock

36th Lock

Kiddy's Bridge

Accommodation Bridge

Accommodation Bridge

Ballynacarrigy Bridge

Ballynacarrigy

179

While it is possible to use the paths on either side of the canal for the early part of this tour, the majority of the restoration work has been carried out on the left or south towpath which is the better one to use. The surface is a mixture of tarred roadway, grass and trodden path. The initial journey away from Ballynacarrigy is relatively uninspiring. You will come across three locks, the 36th to 38th, inclusive, in quick succession as well as a series of bridges, three of which are accommodation bridges, the others being the more substantial Kiddy's Bridge and Kelly's Bridge.

After Kelly's Bridge the landscape opens out as the canal starts its course across Ballymaglavy Bog, the only extensive bog on the main line of the Royal Canal. The next few kilometres contrast sharply with the sheltered paths you will have encountered on much of your journey from Dublin and in windy conditions can be difficult. As you pass by a small aqueduct over a minor river called the Blackwater, the skyline is dominated by Bog Bridge which lies ahead, standing in splendid isolation in the midst of the bog. The access roadways to this bridge have long since being eroded. The path through the bog is very soft and it is best to keep to the edges where a firmer surface is available.

A little past Bog Bridge lies the boundary between County Westmeath and County Longford. The Longford area is noted for its rolling plains and picturesque stretches of water.

As you continue your cycle across the bog you are likely to hear aircraft engines. There is a small airfield to the north of the canal on the outskirts of Abbeyshrule. The airfield was officially established in 1977 but dates back to the 1950s. The Abbeyshrule Air Show takes place annually on the second Sunday in August.

Nearing Quinn's Bridge the path merges with the road leading up to the very fine Whitworth Aqueduct which carries the canal over the River Inny, a tributary of the River Shannon. In keeping with an age-old custom, the river is named after a mythological princess Eithne, daughter of Eochai Féileach. The River Shannon also has its own goddess, Sinann, who in Celtic mythology was daughter of Lodan, the son of Ler. Ler was one of the more prominent figures in Celtic legend, being the sea lord of the people of Dann, known in the Irish language as Tuatha Dé Danann. Legend has it that Sinann went in search of forbidden knowledge at a sacred well, only for the well to erupt on her approach and sweep her away in a flood of water to create the waterway over which she now proudly presides.

After crossing the river the canal takes a very sharp turn to the left near Scally's Bridge as it makes the short journey into Abbeyshrule.

Abbeyshrule is an historic and picturesque village which takes its name from the Irish word for stream or river. It is sited on a major ford or crossing on the River Inny. A thriving water-milling industry used to exist in the village and its surrounding areas but the last of the mills was lost in the 1960s by a river drainage scheme. The Royal Canal reached the village in 1817 and its effect was to transform the economic life of the village. With the canal's demise and the loss of its milling industry the village has retreated into rural tranquillity.

The canal harbour at Abbeyshrule has been restored and a new boat slipway was added in 1996. The village area in the immediate vicinity of the canal is very welcoming.

The ruins of an abbey are located a short distance to the south of the canal. The abbey was founded by the Cistercians in 1150 during the lifetime of their founder, St Bernard of Clairvaux. It was built on the site of an earlier Christian settlement dating back to the ninth century. Located in the village itself is an early Christian High Cross, associated with this settlement. As happened to similar establishments the monastery was sacked on two occasions and was later suppressed during the reign of Queen Elizabeth I. It was eventually confiscated by the Earl of Roscommon.

Pallas, which is approximately 5km from Abbeyshrule, is said to be the birthplace of Oliver Goldsmith, the renowned poet, novelist and playwright. He was born on 10 November 1728, the son of a clergyman, and he was a student of Trinity College Dublin from the early age of fourteen. He is best remembered for his poem, *The Deserted Village* which was published in 1770 and describes life in his native countryside. It is said that Goldsmith may not have been born in Pallas but at the home of his maternal grandmother near Elphin, County Roscommon, as he was born prematurely while his mother was visiting her. In any event there is a statue at Pallas marking the location of the Goldsmith homestead. The Oliver Goldsmith Summer School takes place every June and July in Abbeyshrule and Ballymahon.

A grassy towpath on the left-hand side of the canal takes you out of Abbeyshrule. The canal curves to the right, matching the course of the nearby Inny which is clearly visible to the left for a short while before becoming hidden by high hedgerows. As no water-borne craft has passed this way for some time the quality and depth of the water in the canal is poor, with the surface coated by a thick carpet of weeds. After the 39th Lock, adjacent to Draper's Bridge, the canal's water supply virtually disappears. From here onwards there is ongoing restoration work proceeding both on the channel of the canal itself but also on the towpaths. Rest assured that the paths are passable, though you might encounter earthmoving equipment from time to time.

Incidentally, Draper's Bridge was named after the Secretary of the Royal Canal Company who served the company from 1812.

Beyond the next bridge, Allard's Bridge, a lot of clearance work has been done to ensure that both towpaths are wide and passable. However, you should take the opportunity to change to the right towpath here or at Guy's Bridge an accommodation bridge a little further on. The first section of the path after Allard's Bridge has a tarred surface, as has a further stretch from Molly Ward's Bridge up ahead. But the main reason for changing sides is that a section of the path on the left side further along is frequently blocked to provide a corral for horses. You would have to double back at this obstacle as the barriers are not surmountable.

There are a number of twists and turns along the route as the canal continues to match the meandering course set by the River Inny. Glimpses of the river are rare. The high hedgerows provide a calm corridor of shelter from the elements and an abundant natural environment but deny the opportunity to gaze further afield.

Two further bridges, Fowland's Bridge and then Toome Bridge, are passed before reaching your destination, where the canal opens out to the fine Ballybrannigan Harbour. There is evidence of restoration work done at Ballybrannigan Harbour in preparation for the re-watering and re-opening of the canal to this point. The bridge adjacent to the harbour is officially named Chaigneau Bridge after one of the directors of the New Royal Canal Company who was appointed to the board of the company in September 1818. However, it is known locally as Brannigan Bridge perhaps because of the difficulty in pronouncing its official title.

The nearby town of Ballymahon to the south of the canal will provide you with refreshments to sustain you on the return journey.

TOUR 7
BALLYBRANNIGAN HARBOUR TO CLOONSHEERIN
(15.9 Kilometres)

The absence of water in the canal channel and the ongoing restoration work do not detract from the pleasure of this tour. Traversing deeper into County Longford, the canal parts company with the Inny Valley and despite coming within 3km of Lough Ree and the River Shannon turns northwards for an extended journey through the plains of Longford. The tour finishes at the junction with the Longford Branch.

HOW TO GET THERE
Ballybrannigan Harbour is adjacent to the town of Ballymahon, County Longford. Ballymahon is approximately 30km from Mullingar. Having reached Mullingar using the N4/M4 road network from Dublin you will have to go through the town centre to access firstly the R390 in the direction of Athlone from which you change to the R392 in the direction of Ballymahon.

Tour 7 - Royal Canal
Ballybrannigan Harbour to Cloonsheerin

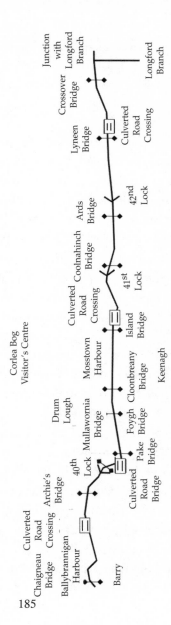

Key
Bridge
Lock

Ballymahon

Corlea Bog
Visitor's Centre

Culverted
Road
Crossing

Chaigneau
Bridge

Ballybrannigan
Harbour

Barry

Archie's
Bridge

40th
Lock

Drum
Lough

Mullawornia
Bridge

Culverted
Road
Bridge

Pake
Bridge

Foygh
Bridge

Cloonbreany
Bridge

Keenagh

Mosstown
Harbour

Island
Bridge

Culverted
Road
Crossing

41st
Lock

Coolnahinch
Bridge

Ards
Bridge

42nd
Lock

Lyneen
Bridge

Culverted
Road
Crossing

Crossover
Bridge

Junction
with
Longford
Branch

Longford
Branch

Maps

Ordnance Survey of Ireland Discovery Series:
Map 41 Longford, Meath and Westmeath (ISBN 1-901496-30-9)
Map 40 Galway, Longford, Roscommon and Westmeath (ISBN 1-901496-25-2)

On the initial part of this tour the twists and turns that have been a feature of the canal's course from Abbeyshrule as it tracked the River Inny to Ballymahon are replaced by the more familiar straight lines that one associates with canals. The Inny pursues its own journey to the Shannon from Ballymahon by a meandering southerly course towards its access point via Lough Ree.

Starting on the left-hand towpath, do not be deceived by the ease of the initial part of the journey from Ballybrannigan Harbour. A lot of quality work has been done on the banks of the canal as it courses past the outskirts of Ballymahon. The grass path and boundary hedges are extremely well maintained and the stretch to the culverted crossing for the R392 is a popular walk for locals. The culvert was the location of Longford Bridge and is one of a number that you will encounter along this tour owing to the demolition of several bridges in this area when the canal was closed to navigation. All these are being reinstated to render the waterway navigable once again.

At Archie's Bridge the path's surface becomes rougher and once again the hedgerows start to enclose the embankments. There are two large derelict buildings just beyond the bridge that were once used as storage warehouses but are now attractively coated in thick ivy. Along this stretch the canal bed is not completely dry but whatever water exists is hidden by a dense mass of sedge grass, reeds and other marshy plants, and is home to a lot of wildlife. The fact there is no regular traffic of humanity to disturb them has resulted in a prolific array of animals and birds on display and if you cycle along slowly your chances of spotting them are enhanced. There can be downsides. On one occasion about 200m from Archie's Bridge I was hit head on by a swarm of wasps and spent the next few minutes extracting wasps from my hair and clothing, as well as a number of stings from my body.

Just past Archie's Bridge the canal starts to gently curve around Mullawornia Hill located to the right. On the left-hand side the ground falls away to a forested valley and at this point the canal is only about 3km from Lough Ree. It appears strange that as soon as the canal comes within a relatively short distance of the River Shannon, its ultimate objective in terms of destination, it immediately turns north and adds another 20km to its journey. This was all part of the debate that delayed the progress of the canal when it was being built. A number of reasons were put forward for the adoption of a more northerly route. Perhaps the strongest was to service the coal trade from Arigna Collieries located near Lough Allen. It is ironic that the coal trade ultimately went in the opposite direction, with imported coal from English collieries being transported down the canal from Dublin. The difficulties of linking into a large lake, which was known to be subject to difficult boating conditions in stormy weather, was another of the justifications put forward at the time. Whatever the reason we should be thankful that the canal did extend northwards because it provides increased access to parts of Ireland and, indeed, County Longford which otherwise would have been well and truly hidden.

The 40th Lock at Mullawornia is the first lock for over 11km and is followed immediately by an accommodation bridge. The lock-house has been partially restored and enjoys delightful views across the valley towards Lough Ree. There are very fine views of Lough Ree and the surrounding areas from the top of Mullawornia Hill which has been partially eroded by a commercial quarrying operation that has destroyed one side of the hill. To access the hill cross the accommodation bridge at the 40th Lock and leave your bike at the entrance to the quarry which is about 0.5km up the road from the bridge.

Returning to the canal, there is a short scenic ride on the left-hand towpath to Pake Bridge passing a small lake called Drum Lough. At this point the towpath ends temporarily as the old bridge is no longer used and the R392 road crosses the canal for the second time by means of a culvert. Having crossed the road you can resume the path through a gateway which is not locked. However, there is a marked deterioration in the quality of the towpath. At first sight the path looks relatively clear but unfortunately this is one area where thorny briars run right across the path at frequent intervals. Punctures are an unavoidable hazard along this stretch so ensure you have a repair kit to hand. There is some improvement as you approach Foygh Bridge where the canal opens out into a harbour.

There is a marked change in scenery as you pass by Cloonbreany Bridge, an accommodation bridge that marks the start of a passage through scrubland and expansive bog. There is a striking contrast with the enclosed corridors that have been a feature of the Royal Canal's passage for much of its journey from Mullingar. The sheltered corridors will soon make a return once you reach the culverted crossing at Mosstown Harbour. Island Bridge at Mosstown is an ugly structure with rusted railings and will be replaced in due course. The harbour at Mosstown is extensive and marks the start of a 1.5km stretch, lined on both sides by densely planted trees offering considerable protection in otherwise open countryside. Taking the left or western towpath, the surface is reasonable but can be quite soggy after a spell of rain.

Keenagh village lies a short distance to the east of the canal at Mosstown Harbour. In the middle of the village is a clock tower erected in memory of Lawrence Harman King, a local notable who died in October 1875. There is also a small restaurant called Michael's on the Main Street that is worth a visit.

Another place to see is the Corlea Bog Visitor's Centre which is a short diversion from the canal and can be accessed by going west on the culverted crossing at Mosstown Harbour. The centre is signposted to the left about 1km along this road. The centre has on display various bog artefacts which were uncovered in this region over the latter part of the last century. Perhaps the most important item on view is an 18m section of an old bog road which used to track across the bog and which dates back to 148 BC. The Corlea bog road, which ran for about 2km, is the largest of its kind uncovered in Europe. It consists of trunks of oak trees laid down in sleeper fashion and held in place with hazel pegs.

After the 41st Lock and Coolnahinch Bridge the path for the next 3km has been improved with a tarred surface making for a very comfortable ride. A little over halfway along this route is an accommodation bridge called Ards Bridge followed soon afterwards by the 41st Lock. All along this way the canal continues to be a bed of weeds and marsh plants but the banks and locks are in good condition. The tarred path comes to an end at Lyneen Bridge where once again there is a culverted crossing to facilitate the passing of the R398 across the canal – yet another obstacle to be removed in the efforts to restore the Royal Canal to its former glory.

East of Lyneen Bridge are the ivy clad ruined walls of what was once a fortified house known as Ballinamore Castle. There is a line of square musket holes still visible in one of the walls. The castle was built by Sir Richard Browne in the middle of the seventeenth century.

After crossing the R398 there is a farm gate allowing access to a once-again grassy path for the final part of the journey. The bridge just short of the junction with the Longford Branch is aptly called Crossover Bridge and in the days of horse-drawn boats facilitated the passage of horses for those boats whose destination was Longford town. At the mouth of the junction the canal is extremely wide and the terrain is boggy and isolated. The rusting hull of a canal boat lies forlornly beyond salvation on the western bank of the canal to mark the end of the tour.

TOUR 8
CLOONSHEERIN TO CLOONDARA AND LONGFORD BRANCH
(16.2 Kilometres)

Raw and wild is the best description that can be applied to the canal and its environs as it advances to its rendezvous with the River Shannon. For the time being there is a pioneering quality to this tour as the ongoing restoration work has only partially impacted on the canal's route. As you witness at first hand the work being undertaken, you will appreciate not only the efforts of today's workmen but more so those of yesteryear who broke virgin soil and rock without the support of today's earthmoving equipment. Thankfully their legacy is once more receiving the attention it so richly deserves.

HOW TO GET THERE

Cloonsheerin is merely a townland name for the area where the Longford Branch of the Royal Canal parts company with the main line. The nearest village is Killashee through which the N63 national secondary road runs. The best way to get there is to travel

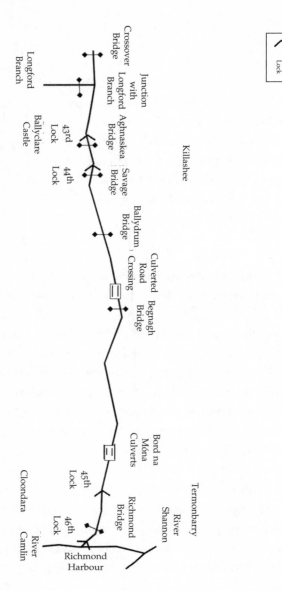

Tour 8 - Royal Canal
Cloonsheerin to Cloondara

firstly to the town of Longford (122 km from Dublin) using the N4/M4 road network out of Dublin and then take the N63 in the direction of Lanesborough. The village of Killashee is midpoint along this road. You will have crossed over the canal at Aghnaskea Bridge. At Killashee take the road south out of the village for approximately 1km where you will come to a minor road or track on the left-hand side. Watch carefully as it is easy to miss. This will lead you to the route of the canal north of the Longford Branch junction. Alternatively, you can make your way back to Aghnaskea Bridge from Killashee and cycle down the towpath to the junction before doubling back.

Maps

Ordnance Survey of Ireland Discovery Series:

Map 40 Galway, Longford, Roscommon and Westmeath (ISBN 1-901496-25-2)

Map 41 Longford, Meath and Westmeath (ISBN 1-901496-30-9)

There are two elements to this tour. Firstly, the completion of the fairly brief journey northwards to the River Shannon and, secondly, the exploration of the branch extending to Longford town. Which should be completed first is a matter for personal choice. For the purposes of this guide we will complete the journey on the main line first.

Leaving the Longford Branch junction behind via the left-hand or western towpath, there is a depressing quality to the land in the immediate vicinity of the canal. Scrubland and bog, both of which have their own quirky appeal, dominate the area and it is understandable that there was widespread emigration from this area in the nineteenth century. The canal had its own part to play in this, facilitating many emigrants in taking their first steps to a new life when they boarded the passenger boats that were a feature of the canal in its early years. Some would have embarked at the harbour at Savage Bridge a little bit further on our journey.

The first landmarks reached are the 43rd Lock and Aghnaskea Bridge. Killashee village lies a short distance to the west. The name means 'Church of the Fairy Mound', most likely due to some long-forgotten local legend. Close to this village are the ruins of Ballyclare Castle, built around 1430 by a local chieftain, O'Farrell Buí. The O'Farrell clan ruled the Longford region from the eleventh century. The county, whose Irish name is *Long phort* (long fort) takes its name from an ancient stronghold of the O'Farrell family. During the plantation of James I the O'Farrell's were dispossessed and Ballyclare Castle and surrounding lands were given to English and Scottish settlers.

Resuming the canal journey, it is noticeable that the canal bed soon becomes completely dry, with an absence of the weeds and plants that have become familiar. The canal bed requires sealing in order to stem water loss through its base. In the meantime it has become home to thousands of rabbits. Rabbits are familiar companions on towpath travels. Normally they scurry away in to the undergrowth as you approach but along this section there are so many that they appear to believe there is safety in numbers. They are slow to interrupt their feeding just because humans are passing by.

There is an interesting story relating to the lock-house at Savage Bridge which is adjacent to the 44th Lock. The building is now known as 'Frances' Cottage'. There is a plaque on the front wall which states that the building was originally erected around 1840 at a cost of £45 and it was restored in 1990 by Frances K. Kelly of Forest Hills, New York, USA. Ms Kelly has since died. It is a pity she did not live to see the canal in a fully restored state.

Through the summers of 2003 and 2004 the journey from Savage Bridge to Begnagh Bridge was quite hazardous due to the presence of a lot of machinery and equipment being used by Waterways Ireland in the ongoing restoration of this section of the canal. Once finished the cleared towpaths will be a delight for cyclists and walkers. For the time being you will be able to appreciate the extent of the clearance and restorative work being undertaken when you witness the state of the canal and paths beyond Begnagh Bridge. From this point onwards the canal is bounded on both sides by an extensive bog which is being actively worked. The canal and towpaths lose their hitherto defined course because of their neglect for over 40 years. They have become overgrown. Up to recently it would have been a futile exercise to attempt passage along what used to be the towpaths. However, some of the growth has been mowed down and it is now possible to reach the 45th Lock by changing to the eastern side of the canal at the site of the rail and road culverts installed by Bord na Móna 200m back from the lock.

The 45th Lock is the penultimate lock on the Royal Canal system and during the summer months of 2003 it was stripped down for repair and restoration. This event provided the opportunity to inspect at first hand the engineering marvels that constitute the components of a canal lock. The type of lock used on the Royal Canal is known as a 'pound lock', which has its origins in the fourteenth century. It consists of two sets of swinging gates set close to each other forming a chamber. Leonardo da Vinci is credited with the invention of the type of gate used on Irish canals. It is only when the lock chamber is empty and stripped back beneath and beyond the original stonework that you can truly appreciate the workmanship that went into building them. The restorers had carefully numbered all the stones that had been removed so they could be refitted in their correct positions.

The massive gates were lying on the bank. Originally these would have been made of oak but now the canal engineers use timber imported from West Africa with central steel cores.

Returning to the western side of the canal, it is a short cycle on a tarred surface to the village of Cloondara, passing by Richmond Bridge and onwards to Richmond Harbour. The harbour was named in honour of the then Lord Lieutenant of Ireland. Cloondara village was purpose built to cater for the canal traffic. The harbour is extensive and nowadays is lined with boats sheltering from the River Shannon. There is a fine hostelry and guesthouse on the waterfront that serves good food. There is also a restored dry dock at the far end of the harbour.

Currently the harbour gets its water supply from the nearby Camlin River which also provides the canal with its access to the Shannon. There is a small canal channel with a single lock midway which facilitates this. To view it, take the road that leads west out of Cloondara over Richmond Bridge in the direction of Termonbarry. The large four-storey rubble-built structure on the left was originally a distillery and was later used as a cornmill. It is now used by a waste recycling company. At its peak in the 1830s the distillery produced 45,460 litres (10,000 gallons) of whiskey each year. A little further on, to the right, is a church and graveyard. Just past this, the road passes over the Camlin canal and on the left side there is a small opening which leads down a tree-covered passage to the lock which allows access to the River Shannon. This is a pleasant place to sit and rest prior to the return journey.

Before setting off for the return journey it is worthwhile taking the short ride to Termonbarry where there is a fine array of establishments which mainly cater for the passing cruising trade from the River Shannon.

Tour 8 - Royal Canal
Longford Branch

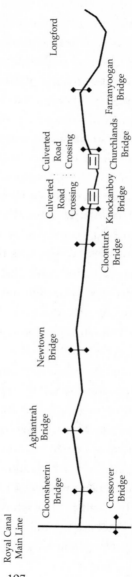

Longford

Key
Bridge

Farranyoogan
Bridge

Culverted
Road
Crossing

Churchlands
Bridge

Culverted
Road
Crossing

Knockanboy
Bridge

Cloonturk
Bridge

Newtown
Bridge

Aghantrah
Bridge

Cloonsheerin
Bridge

Crossover
Bridge

Royal Canal
Main Line

THE LONGFORD BRANCH

The main canal line finally reached the River Shannon in 1817. The Longford Branch was a later addition, taking three years to build at a cost of £12,651, before being opened in 1830. While being built it was the subject of protest mainly from the villagers of Killashee and Richmond Harbour who correctly believed the branch would divert trade from their respective locations. It was subjected to frequent malicious breaches of its banks both during and after its construction.

As it presently stands the branch presents a mixture of excellent and difficult cycling conditions. The section closest to Longford is partially rewatered, the banks have been landscaped and the towpath has been smoothed and resurfaced for a distance of almost 5km. Beyond that, conditions are considerably wilder and very little clearance work has been done to date while all efforts are concentrated on the main line. Do not let the difficult conditions deter you. It would be a pity to be thwarted from completing a tour of the full extent of the Royal Canal system by a section of rough terrain.

The starting point is the junction with the main line at Cloonsheerin. Using the Crossover Bridge, which is 750m south of the junction, you can access the southern or right-hand towpath of the branch. Having made your way back up to the junction you will see that both the canal bed and the towpath are reasonably clear for the first few hundred metres up to the accommodation bridge, Cloonsheerin Bridge. After the bridge the path deteriorates. The biggest obstacle is the proliferation of brambles that creep across the path and their prominent thorns can be the cause of frequent punctures. The stretch from Cloonsheerin

Bridge to Aghantrah Bridge is the worst.

At Aghantrah Bridge, switch to the left-hand towpath. From here to the next bridge, Newtown Bridge, the path improves. You will enter a stretch where the passage of either people or animals is rare, allowing the grass to grow to prodigious heights. The stretch is not long and ends at a pretty cottage where there is a footbridge across the marshy bed of the canal that you should use to cross over once again to the southern side. You can make swift progress on a good surface to Cloonturk Bridge.

There are two culverted crossings ahead that facilitate the passage of the N63 by the locations of the redundant Knockanboy and Churchlands Bridges. At times the curving towpath between these bridges is used to graze horses so you might find the surface becomes churned up after spells of wet weather. From Churchlands Bridge up to the railway line in the town, you will enjoy excellent cycling conditions on a tarred surface. At present the branch ends abruptly just short of the railway line. When the canal was operational it terminated in a harbour to the other side of the line which has since been filled in and is now occupied by an indoor swimming pool.

Longford Harbour was the scene a terrible accident. In 1845 a boat full of emigrants capsized at the harbour and tragically twelve people drowned.

Another tragedy took place on the Longford Branch on 6 January 1839, known as the 'night of the big wind', when about 15m (50 feet) of the canal bank was swept away in the middle of the night. A Mr Bracken and his three children perished in the flood of water when they fled their home, thinking it was about to be swamped by the torrent.

Historically and physically Longford town is relatively

unremarkable, although it has always had the reputation of being an active market town. The oldest surviving building in the town is the markethouse which is within the precint of Sean Connolly Barracks. Longford Castle, built by the then Lord Longford, Francis Aungier, in the early seventeenth century also stood on this site but did not survive.

SECTION D

THE SHANNON-ERNE WATERWAY

HISTORY OF THE SHANNON-ERNE WATERWAY

It is said that property in County Leitrim is sold not by the acre but by the gallon, such is the extent of land under water in the county particularly during the winter months. It is not surprising therefore that County Leitrim and its neighbouring counties of Cavan and Fermanagh are host to a very fine waterway that is a blend of still-water canal, lakes and canalised river. The waterway links the mighty River Shannon with the vigorous River Erne. Its existence was under threat for many years due, among other things, to its lack of commercial success but thanks to an initiative that arose out of North-South co-operation it has been restored and stands proud as one of the most modern waterways in these islands.

Once part of a navigation system that linked Belfast with Limerick for a short time, the Shannon-Erne Waterway is unusual because it was undertaken with a dual purpose. As originally conceived it was intended not only as a navigable waterway but also to play a key role in the drainage of the water retentive lands through which it passed. For the greater part of its history it is the latter role which has governed both its existence and its preservation.

The principal criterion for inclusion of a waterway in this book is that it must have a discernible towpath along its route. For a waterway that has a course through many lakes making independent propulsion essential for boats, it is understandable that there is no towpath for its entire length. However, when it was being originally built in the middle of the nineteenth century the Office of Public Works insisted on having a towpath where practicable. A towpath fenced off from adjoining lands was included in the original construction for most of the way. However, it was badly made as reported by James Butler Pratt in his description of the canal in 1860. When the waterway was being restored in the 1990s attention was given to ensuring this towpath would largely remain. However, in a number of places towpaths under bridges were removed in order to widen the navigation channel. In its present state a rough towpath exists along virtually the entire navigation with the exception of the lakeshores. In some areas this towpath has deteriorated due to lack of maintenance and is not currently passable but it is possible to track the length of the waterway by bicycle without losing sight of it for lengthy periods. As such it merits inclusion here. Furthermore its omission would deny the opportunity to bring to a wider audience the intrinsic beauty of this remarkable waterway and its surrounding hinterland. Hopefully Waterways Ireland will give more attention to maintaining the towpath so that more people will have the opportunity of savouring this amenity.

The tours in this section are slightly different in their

presentation to those for the other waterways. Because of the absence of a towpath surrounding the lake navigations and the necessity to use the roads for the intervals between towpaths, the tours are arranged in circuits which sometimes involve parting company with the environs of the waterway for extended stretches. This enhances the enjoyment of the tours while providing an overview of a captivating lake-filled countryside. In addition, the roads in this region are quiet and peaceful. Finally, it should be noted that the distances shown for each tour are for the complete circuit.

The Shannon-Erne Waterway is the modern name given to what used to be known as the Ballinamore-Ballyconnell Canal. Its origins were rooted in a period in the eighteenth century when canal building had captured the attention of governments and private enterprises. In the 1770s Richard Evans, an engineer who was closely involved in the construction of both the Grand and Royal Canals, developed a plan for an extensive navigation involving the River Erne. This would start at Ballyshannon where the river flows into the Atlantic and pass through Upper and Lower Lough Erne to reach Belturbet. Branches were proposed to Ballyconnell and Ballinamore. Work on this waterway started in 1780 but the project was never completed due to financial problems. Later, a Newcastle engineer, William Chapman, attempted to canalise the Woodford River but he also ran into financial difficulties.

Almost another half century went by before the passage of drainage legislation reawakened interest in a waterway in this region linking the Erne and the Shannon. Another spur to interest was the opening of the Ulster Canal in 1842 and a desire by the company behind this project to extend westwards to the River Shannon. The focus, however, was mainly on drainage and this work started in June 1846 with navigation works starting a year later as part of a famine relief employment programme. The original estimate to complete the canal was over £131,000 with £103,000 of this attributable to navigation works. In common with most canal ventures costs were underestimated and when the canal was completed in 1858 it had cost over £274,000 with the navigation works accounting for almost £229,000.

The canal was designed by a Dublin engineer, Thomas Mulvany (1806-1885), who specialised in arterial drainage works. He later moved to Germany where he got involved in deep coal mining in the Ruhr Valley. He went on to found a mining empire that grew into VEBA, now a major industrial group in Germany, and he even has a street named after him in Dusseldörf called Mulvanystrasse.

The first official trial of the newly built canal took place in 1858 when a boat hired from the Ulster Canal Company carried a load of tiles from Florencecourt Tilery to Ballyduff near Ballinamore. The boat also took on board gravel and coal and delivered them to Leitrim and Lough Allen. In July 1860 the canal was officially handed over to a Board of Trustees who were responsible for the Navigation Works. In a rather bizarre move a separate group of trustees was established to oversee the drainage works.

As a commercial venture the waterway was a resounding failure and remained officially open only until 1867. It is said that only eight boats ever used the canal during its official life and that the trustees made more money from selling hay from along the banks and leasing water power for mills than they ever did from boat tolls. The last boat to pass through the canal was a yacht owned by a W. Potts called the *Audax* which sailed from the Erne to the Shannon in 1873. With no boating interest the navigation trustees held their last meeting in 1878 and so from then on it was up to the drainage trustees to maintain the canal in good order to serve their own purposes as a drainage artery.

In 1906 the Royal Commission on Canals and Waterways recommended that the waterway should be maintained as a drain but also that it should be kept in good order so it could be readily converted into a navigable waterway once again should the circumstances so dictate. The navigation trustees continued to discharge this responsibility until their appointments were terminated by Leitrim County Council in 1936.

As the twentieth century moved into its second half there were some calls for restoration of the waterway as a navigable channel most notably by the Inland Waterways Association of Ireland who in 1969 called for a survey to be carried out. The first hint of restoration as part of North-South co-operation was mooted in the press in 1971 but it took almost twenty years and several surveys and feasibility studies for the restoration to get underway. In 1989 a consultancy arm of the Electricity Supply Board was given the task of executing a restoration project which was estimated to cost £30 million and take three years to complete. Funding was to come from both governments supplemented by assistance from the International Fund for Ireland and also from European Community Structural Funds. Work started in late 1990 and traffic on the newly restored waterway commenced in April 1994. The official opening took place on 23 May 1994.

SHANNON-ERNE WATERWAY ROUTE OVERVIEW

Being a combination of still-water canal, lakes and canalised river this is a waterway of great variety and ever changing profile. Commencing at Leitrim village the waterway has three distinct sections. Firstly, there is a still-water section extending from the River

Shannon at Leitrim village over 8km to the village of Kilclare. There are eight rising locks on this section bringing the waterway to its summit level of 67m as it enters Lough Scur. The middle section is the summit level which extends for 7.6km from Kilclare to Castlefore passing through Lough Scur and Lough Marrave. The remainder of its 63km length comprising the final section from Castlefore to the River Erne consists of the canalised Woodford River. There are eight descending locks along this section as it courses through the towns of Ballinamore and Ballyconnell. While the waterway resides mainly in Leitrim a significant part of its meandering course forms the boundaries between counties Cavan and Leitrim and also Fermanagh and Cavan.

The restoration programme required the removal of five of the 34 bridges that were an original part of the waterway network. Two of these were old railway bridges on the now defunct Cavan-Leitrim Railway and three were redundant accommodation bridges. Two additional accommodation bridges were constructed at locks for users of the waterway leaving the present complement of 31 bridges. The bridges are all numbered and for some reason the bridges are numbered from west to east while the locks are numbered in the reverse direction.

There are a total of twelve weirs along the waterway four of which, along the still-water section at Locks 13-16, are fairly small affairs running parallel to the navigation channel. The remaining eight are adjacent to the locks along the Woodford River section and these are far more substantial running either straight across or at an angle to the channel. The weir at Castlefore Lock has a regulating sluice but the rest are fixed.

For those who are used to the profile of the traditional locks along our waterways, those on the Shannon-Erne Waterway are surprising. The locks on this waterway are fully automated using an electro-hydraulic system that is operated by a key card. Lock-keepers have been dispensed with but there are a number of rangers with responsibility for controlling the waterway. The gates themselves are made of steel with galvanised steel footboards. Another distinctive modern feature of this waterway is the presence of traffic lights at each of the locks. Lock operation cards are available from outlets along the route displaying the waterways logo.

As part of the restoration project much attention was given to the waterway's water supply. In a water retentive region such as Leitrim and Cavan the issue of an adequate water supply should not be a priority. However, given its multi-faceted profile, being comprised of a mix of watercourses, this was a subject that received a lot of attention. The object was to provide for a minimum water depth that would allow for trouble-free summer season navigation. This was chosen at 1.55m allowing 1.2m for boat draught and the balance for squat and weed growth. The maximum draught for boats on the navigation is now fixed by bye-law at 1.25m. With this in mind the restored waterway is designed so that the water now discharges eastwards to the River Erne and not to the other side of the Lough Scur summit as used to happen prior to the reconstruction. In addition, powerful pumps were installed below each of the locks on the still-water section to cater for water to be pumped to the summit level from the Shannon.

TOUR 1
LOUGH SCUR AND LOUGH MARRAVE CIRCUIT
(30 Kilometres)

This tour starts at Leitrim village and embraces the still-water section of the waterway, its summit through Lough Scur and Lough Marrave and the first of the descending locks before returning to Leitrim village by the northern shores of the two lakes.

HOW TO GET THERE
Leitrim village provides the name for the virtually landlocked county of Leitrim. It is located in the north west of Ireland approximately 172km from Dublin. Follow the M4/N4 road network to approximately 7km south of Carrick-on-Shannon and take the signposted turn to the R299 which leads to the R280. For Leitrim village follow the R280 in the direction of Drumshanbo and Manorhamilton.

MAPS
Ordnance Survey of Ireland Discovery Series
Map 27A Cavan, Fermanagh, Leitrim and Monaghan (ISBN 1-901496-49-X)

Tour 1 - Shannon-Erne Waterway
Lough Scur and Lough Marrave Circuit

Key
Bridge
Locks

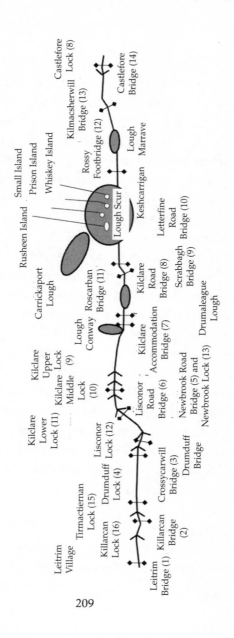

Castlefore
Kilmacsherwill Lock (8)

Castlefore
Bridge (14)

Small Island
Prison Island
Whiskey Island

Rusheen Island

Lough
Marrave

Rossy
Footbridge (12)

Kilmacsherwill
Bridge (13)

Carrickaport
Lough

Lough Scur

Keshcarrigan

Letterfine
Road
Bridge (10)

Lough
Conway

Roscarban
Bridge (11)

Kilclare
Road
Bridge (8)

Scrabbagh
Bridge (9)

Kilclare
Upper Lock (9)
Kilclare
Middle Lock (10)

Kilclare
Accommodation
Bridge (7)

Drumaleague
Lough

Kilclare
Lower
Lock (11)

Lisconor
Lock (12)

Lisconor
Road
Bridge (6)

Newbrook Road
Bridge (5) and
Newbrook Lock (13)

Tirmactiernan
Lock (15)

Drumduff
Lock (4)

Crossycarwill
Bridge (3)

Drumduff
Bridge

Leitrim
Village

Killarcan
Lock (16)

Killarcan
Bridge
(2)

Leitrim
Bridge (1)

209

Map 33 Leitrim, Longford, Roscommon and Sligo (ISBN 1-901496-05-8)

The starting point for this tour is Leitrim village whose name and that of the county are anglicised variations of the Irish *Liath Druim*, 'the grey ridge'. It is a common place name in Ireland with over 40 other Leitrims to be found as townlands, villages or streets throughout Ireland.

The county of Leitrim originally formed part of the old Gaelic kingdom of Breffni which was ruled by a powerful Irish clan, the O'Rourkes. A Norman invasion of the kingdom in the thirteenth century was resisted in the northern region which remained in the hands of the O'Rourkes until the sixteenth century. At that time large parts of the county were planted with English settlers but the plantation was largely unsuccessful, most likely because of the poor quality of the land. In 1583 the Lord Deputy, Sir John Perrott, marked out the boundaries of what now constitutes the county, with the principal town being Carrick-on-Shannon.

The county was badly affected by the Great Famine of the late 1840s and in ten years the population dropped from 155,000 to 112,000. It is interesting to compare these figures with today's population of 25,000. The poor agricultural quality of the land and the lack of other indigenous industry paved the way for sustained emigration, resulting in the massive decline in population to today's levels.

The village of Leitrim was an O'Rourke stronghold and occupied a strategic crossing point on the River Shannon. In January 1603 Brian Óg O'Rourke, who was known as Brian of the Battleaxes, provided respite at his Leitrim castle to Donal Cam

O'Sullivan Beare on his epic fighting march northwards from his fiefdom in Glengarriff in the south-west corner of Ireland. He was heading for Ulster to team up with Hugh O'Neill in order to return to the south to again lock horns with his nemesis, George Carew, the 'Lord President of Munster'. It was Carew who was responsible for taking O'Sullivan Beare's lands from him. The march took place in the depths of winter and having set off with over 1,000 men he arrived at Leitrim Castle fourteen days later with no more than 35. All the rest perished en route or had fallen by the wayside in a far from glorious episode in Irish history. Along the way O'Sullivan Beare and his followers were harassed and attacked from the rear by their own fellow Irishmen who professed loyalty to Britain. The respite provided at Leitrim is commemorated today by a memorial stone in the village that bears the coats of arms of the O'Rourkes and O'Sullivan Beare. The last remaining wall of the castle is still visible near the waterway. O'Sullivan Beare fled into exile to Spain where he became the first Irishman to be knighted by the king of Spain, a privilege not accorded to many non-nationals.

Today Leitrim still provides a welcome for those on a long journey. It is a quiet and pleasant village which has benefited from its location as the access point for the restored waterway and it comes alive when the summer boating season arrives. Several holiday home schemes have been sympathetically constructed in the immediate vicinity of the village. The Riverside coffee shop is located at the top of the hill on the Main Street as you exit the village in the direction of Manorhamilton. This delightful café is open all year round and opens at 8am, enabling you to tuck into a substantial breakfast before tackling the towpaths. Try the homemade treacle bread which is a treat.

The new public moorings in the village are a good place to start this tour. They are near the single-arched bridge (Bridge 1) carrying the road from Carrick-on Shannon to Drumshanbo which is the first official bridge on the navigation and dates back to 1850. The route along the towpath to the first lock is not in good condition so it is preferable to make the short journey to Killarcan Lock (Lock 16) by the road running eastwards out of the village from the bridge. Directions for Killarcan Lock are well signposted from this road. Originally there was a small lake called the Black Lough on the outskirts of the village which was sub-sumed into the waterway. This extended beyond Killarcan Lock. The area surrounding the waterway along this section is now one of botanical interest. The channel is bounded by a well-developed reed swamp on the southern bank and a species rich marsh on the western bank.

There used to be a lock-keeper's house on the southern bank which had been inhabited up to the 1950s. Unfortunately, despite local calls for its restoration and use as a waterway heritage centre, it was knocked down. As you set off from Killarcan Lock you will see to the right Sheemore Mountain with its distinctive cross on its summit, erected in 1950 to mark the Holy Year. The mountain is the site of a megalithic tomb with an ancient passage grave. There is a well-maintained grassy surface for 0.7km on the right-hand or southern towpath until you come to Killarcan Accommodation Bridge (Bridge 2) where the path ends. A stile allows access to the road for a short 100m cycle to Tirmactiernan Lock (Lock 15). From here the path is challenging due to lack of regular maintenance and it is frequently preferable to return to the small road which runs parallel to the waterway and links up with the R209. Using this road you will get a good view of a small single-arched accommodation bridge called Crossycarwill Bridge (Bridge 3), also sometimes called Ballinwing Bridge after the townland in which it is situated.

Keeping to the road the next bridge encountered is another accommodation bridge, Drumduff Bridge (Bridge 4), which is adjacent to Drumduff Lock (Lock 14) after which the waterway passes under the R209 by way of the skew arched Newbrook Bridge (Bridge 5). Just after this bridge you can resume the towpath on the northern bank beside Newbrook Lock (Lock 13). This section of towpath is wide and well maintained and will lead to Lisconor Bridge (Bridge 6) quickly followed by Lisconor Lock (Lock 12). Here you will have to change sides to the south bank. Once again the towpath is wide and well maintained although the surface in the early stages is quite rocky immediately below the surface, and the ride is bumpy.

Locks 11, 10 and 9 come in quick succession in an area that is beautifully maintained. The locks – Kilclare Lower, Kilclare Middle and Kilclare Upper – span the stretch of canal that adjoins Kilclare village. Just after the 11th Lock is The Sheemore Inn. There is an old handball court beside the pub and the remains of an old waterwheel on the canal bank is all that is left of a mill that used to be at this location. Between the lower and middle locks is Kilclare Accommodation Bridge (Bridge 7).

Past the 9th Lock there is no towpath but the R209 runs directly along the canal to Kilclare Road Bridge (Bridge 8). The canal merges seamlessly with Lough Conway here, with the skeleton of a tree eerily lying in the channel between the canal and the lake. A coniferous forest runs off to the north and on the distant hills can be seen the turbines of the wind farms which increasingly populate this region.

Remain on the R209 as the towpath is badly overgrown and not passable. However, the road runs close to the waterway and its elevated position allows uninterrupted views of the canal. Scrabbagh Bridge (Bridge 9) is a small and narrow single-arched bridge off the R209 after which the canal gives the appearance of seeping into the adjoining fields. This is where it merges with Drumaleague Lough, a small lake in summer time but during the rainy winter months it absorbs the adjacent fields into its mass.

As the R209 turns sharply to the right, follow in the direction of Keshcarrigan across Letterfine Road Bridge (Bridge 10). At this bridge you can resume the towpath briefly on the north or left side by crossing the padlocked gate. The path is well trodden by the horse that grazes in the nearby field. Along this stretch the canal was deeply cut out of heavy rock and the cut channel is well defined all the way to Lough Scur, the waterway's summit level. Originally the cut only extended 8m across but during the restoration this was extended to 15m to allow boats to pass each other with ease. Before the canal enters Lough Scur the path leads to a small bridge called Roscarban Bridge (Bridge 11) where you will have to leave the towpath and resume your journey on the R209 road as it rises above Lough Scur.

Roscarban Bridge is on the route of the O'Carolan Walkway commemorating the blind musician Turlough O'Carolan (1670-1738) who at one time was a resident of nearby Letterfine House. Sheebeg Mountain, which slopes away to the south of the waterway, is crowned by a passage mound that is the reputed burial site of Finn McCool. The mountain's name is derived from the Gaelic words *na sidhe,* 'the little people' or 'the fairies'. Close to the shore of Lough Scur on your left as you make for the R209 is a collapsed dolmen known as Diarmuid and Grainne's bed.

As you climb away from Lough Scur there is a great view across the lake towards the often mist-shrouded Sliabh an Iarainn. The lake has a number of islands which, going eastwards are identified as Rusheen Island, Small Island, Prison Island and Whiskey Island. Prison Island takes its name from a prison that was erected there some time around 1570 by the county's High Sheriff, John Reynolds, to hold rebellious locals. Reynolds was by repute an unsavoury and cruel individual who had a penchant for decapitation. He also built Castle John, the ruined fortified house on the lakeshore. It was there that he was reputed to have slain some local chieftains after inviting them to a banquet and having asked them to hand up their swords. A turn off to the left a short way up the R209 leads to a track which skirts the banks of the lake around Gowly Hill to link up with another small road leading into the village of Keshcarrigan.

In the 1850s a fine golden-spun bronze bowl dating back to the first century was found to the north of the village. Known locally as the Keshcarrigan Bowl the relatively small vessel is on display in the National Museum in Dublin. There is a plaque commemorating the find in the centre of the village. There are several pubs and coffee shops in the village. Keshcarrigan Moorings located at the north-eastern end of the village has car parking and picnic facilities and a small marina.

Keshcarrigan is one of the villages visited in a cycle tour known as the 'Tour de Humbert'. This tour follows the route of the march taken by General Humbert at the head of a revolutionary expedition to Ireland during the 1798 rebellion. It extends 225km (140 miles) from Mayo and Sligo through Leitrim and on to Ballinamuck in County Longford where the rebels were eventually defeated.

The road tracks the canal out of Keshcarrigan past an arched steel pedestrian bridge called Rossy Footbridge (Bridge 12) in the direction of Lough Marrave. From here you will lose sight of the waterway for a short time as the road rises around Kilmacsherwill Hill passing Castlefore Lake which has an extensive forest on its shores. At the next junction there is a signpost indicating Kilamacsherwill Bridge (Bridge 13) 1km to the left. This road leads down to Castlefore Lock (Lock 8) which is the first of the descending locks on the canalised river section of the waterway. Cross over the footbridge that spans the weir alongside Castlefore Lock to access the northern towpath for the short ride back to Kimacsherwill Bridge where you part company with the waterway for the journey back to Leitrim village.

The small tree-lined road that leads from the bridge rises steeply passing a derelict school building and leading to a secluded area surrounded by deciduous forest, mostly of silver birch, and blanket bog. This road rises above the northern shore of Lough Scur and links up with the R208, the main road between Carrick-on-Shannon and Ballinamore. Turning westward along the R208 provides a fine view across Lough Scur towards Keshcarrigan in the distance. The road carries you along the lakeshore to the village of Drumcong, with its two prominent churches. As you leave Drumcong the road is sandwiched between Lough Scur and another delightful lake, Carrickaport Lough. At one stage it was proposed that this lake would be used to supplement the water supply of the Shannon-Erne Waterway but nothing came of this proposal.

The R208 links up with the R209 at the junction where earlier you took a sharp right turn towards Letterfine Road Bridge and Keshcarrigan. From here you retrace your path via the R209 all the way back to Leitrim village where another visit to a café would be well deserved.

Tour 2
Castlefore to Garadice Lough
(50 Kilometres)

Leaving its summit level the waterway makes a short journey through three lakes before heading for Ballinamore, the town that gave its name to its original title. From here this tour embarks on a circuit that maintains close contact with the waterway criss-crossing its course several times before circling Garadice Lough, one of the largest lakes in Leitrim, through which the waterway flows.

How to get there

Castlefore is approximately 10km east of Ballinamore, County Leitrim. There are several alternative routes from Dublin to Ballinamore. You can follow the M4/N4 road network from Dublin as far as Dromod and proceed to Ballinamore via Mohill using the R202. Alternatively, you can travel via Cavan and Ballyconnell using the N3 and N87. My preference is for the latter route, perhaps due to the historic waterway connection between the towns of Ballinamore and Ballyconnell, and the latter part of the journey allows you to track the waterway by road. Follow the M3/N3 from Dublin to Cavan and then to Belturbet

Tour 2 - Shannon-Erne Waterway
Castlefore to Garadice Lough

Key

Bridge

Lock

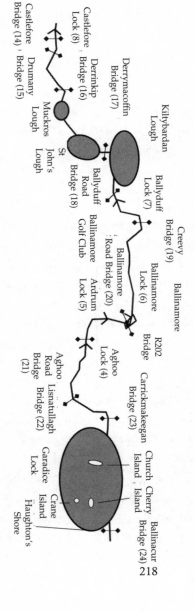

Castlefore Lock (8)

Castlefore Bridge (14)

Drumany Bridge (15)

Derrinkip Bridge (16)

Derrymacoffin Bridge (17)

Muckros Lough

St John's Lough

Ballyduff Road Bridge (18)

Kiltybardan Lough

Ballyduff Lock (7)

Creevy Bridge (19)

Ballinamore

Ballinamore Golf Club

Ballinamore Road Bridge (20)

Ballinamore Lock (6)

Ardrum Lock (5)

R202 Bridge

Aghoo Lock (4)

Carrickmakeegan Bridge (23)

Aghoo Road Bridge (21)

Lisnatullagh Bridge (22)

Garadice Lock

Church Island

Cherry Island

Crane Island

Ballinacur Bridge (24)

Haughton's Shore

218

where you take the N87 to Ballyconnell. From there the road to Ballinamore is well signposted using the R205 and R199. The total journey from Dublin to Castlefore is approximately 175km.

MAPS

Ordnance Survey of Ireland Discovery Series:

Map 27A Cavan, Fermanagh, Leitrim and Monaghan (ISBN 1-901496-49-X)

Map 33 Leitrim, Longford, Roscommon and Sligo (ISBN 1-901496-05-8)

Car-parking facilities are available beside Castlefore Lock (Lock 8). The towpath on the southern bank can at times be overgrown and difficult but it is only a short journey to Drumany Bridge (Bridge 15), a small accommodation bridge. You should switch here to the northern bank where again the towpath can at times be challenging as the canal gently bends around Drumany Hill before reaching Derrinkip Bridge (Bridge 16) about 1.3km further on. At this point it is necessary to leave the towpath which terminates its wood-bounded path about 0.5km further on as the canal enters Muckros Lough. The small road north from Derrinkip Bridge links up with the R208, the main road from Drumshanbo to Ballinamore, and allows you to maintain contact with the waterway to the east as it flows from the narrow Muckros Lough into St John's Lough.

According to the maps there are two parts to St John's Lough connected by narrows spanned by Derrymacoffin Bridge (Bridge 17). However, locally the northern part of the lake is better known as Kiltybardan Lough and the road tracks the lakeshore all the way to the point where the waterway exits the lake at Ballyduff

Bridge (Bridge 18). The bridge between the two parts collapsed in 1948 when it was being crossed by two men with a horse and cart. A modern, high, single-span bridge was erected here during the restoration. It is not possible to reach this bridge from this side of Kiltybardan Lough but it can be inspected later by turning south off the R208 beyond the point where the canal exits the lake near Ballyduff Bridge.

At Ballyduff Bridge leave the R208 to avail of a delightful narrow road, part of the Kingfisher Cycle Trail, which tracks directly alongside the waterway for 4km to Ballinamore. This roadway used to be the route of a branch line of the Cavan and Leitrim Railway built to serve the coalfields of Arigna. The line was closed in 1959 when the Electricity Supply Board built a coal-fired power station at Arigna capable of absorbing all the coal output of the mines. Just under a kilometre of the old narrow guage railway has been restored at Dromod where railway enthusiasts can enjoy nostalgic steam train journeys during the summer months. About halfway along this road is Ballinamore Golf Club, whose members access their course over the waterway via Creevy Bridge (Bridge 19).

The narrow roadway finishes at Ballinamore Quay where the waterway expands, and as it enters the town it is divided by an artificial island. On the town side of this island one section of the waterway pursues the old course of the Yellow River which has been integrated into the waterway flowing under a walkway, through a weir and on to a three-arch stone bridge which carries the R202 into Ballinamore. This bridge is not one of those numbered as part of the navigation. There is a small basin on the other side of this bridge where the small Fohera River flows into the waterway. A limestone memorial marks the visit of An Taoiseach,

C.J. Haughey to inaugurate the restoration project on 26 November 1990.

On the other side of the island the navigation element of the waterway courses through Ballinamore Lock (Lock 6) by a steep cutting, passing under a separate bridge, Ballinamore Road Bridge (Bridge 20).

The name of Ballinamore is derived from the Irish *Béal an Átha Móir*, the 'mouth of the big ford'. The town was the main crossing point on the Yellow River which has been integrated into Shannon-Erne Waterway. It is situated in the Valley of the Black Pig, the name given in historic times to the frontier between the province of Ulster and the rest of Ireland. Smyth's coffee shop on the Main Street beside the same proprietor's *Siopa Ól* is worth a visit. *An Siopa Brontanas*, which you will find towards the top of Main Street, has a wide range of maps and guide books covering the area and the Irish inland waterways in general.

The waterway takes a distinct southerly course out of Ballinamore that can be followed by road on the R202 in the direction of Fenagh. The boat-hire company, Locaboat, has a depot on the outskirts of the town and during the winter months there is an impressive array of cruisers on display. The access to Ardrum Lock (Lock 5) is a little further on. From this lock you can resume your journey on the right-hand towpath for about 1km before the path is intersected by a small but deep stream over which there is no passage. However, there is a track adjacent to the canal that leads away for about 300m to a roadway. This small but well surfaced road runs parallel to the canal and eventually leads around Drumraine Glebe to link up with the waterway again at Aghoo Road Bridge (Bridge 21).

At Aghoo Road Bridge the canal resumes its westerly course.

As with most of the bridges along this waterway there is no towpath facility underneath Aghoo Road Bridge and access to the towpath leading away from the bridge is impossible. However, the R204 in the direction of Carrigallen provides a decent substitute and it is a short journey to Aghoo Lock (Lock 4). From this lock the towpath proceeds on the northern bank and can be accessed across the waterway over the weir. The towpath is quite challenging and requires frequent dismounting. An alternative route is to use the R204 which maintains a reasonably close distance to the canal until the canal embarks on a north-easterly course through open country dominated by scrubland about 1km before Drumcoura Lough.

The R204 allows you to skirt around the lake until you come to a crossroads where it takes a sharp deviation to the right in the direction of Carrigallen. In order to link up with the canal again turn left at this crossroads where you pass directly in front of the impressive Drumcoura City Lake Resort which specialises in western style horse riding. There is a bar designed in the style of a western saloon where during the summer months you can obtain refreshments.

Continuing on a sharp incline you are soon reunited with the canal at Lisnatullagh Bridge (Bridge 22). This bridge is also known as the Derrygoan Road Bridge so as not to confuse it with an earlier accommodation bridge sited 0.5km east that no longer exists and which was also known as Lisnatullagh Bridge. Here you have a choice. The towpath on the left-hand side is passable but once again is quite challenging and you will find yourself hurdling some fences and small streams on your way. The alternative is to continue north on the Derrygoan Road to link up with the R199 (Ballinamore-Ballyconnell Road). The 2km journey from the canal to the R199 is a hilly route with a couple of steep climbs.

At the R199 junction turn right and after approximately 1km turn right again off this road where it is signposted for Carrickmakeegan Bridge (Bridge 23). This bridge is about 500m shy of the canal's westerly entrance to Garadice Lake. The continuation of this road southwards runs parallel to the Derrygoan Road which took you away from Drumcoura Lake. Turning left at the end of this road will put you on course for the southerly shores of Garadice Lough. As you descend towards the lake there is a good view of Church Island, the largest island on this imposing lake, on which are found the ruins of a seventeenth-century church. There are two other islands near the southern shores of this lake: the larger is Cherry Island, on which are sited the ruins of a castle; and the smaller island is called Crane Island.

Situated beside the lake, with convenient moorings for boa-towners, is Swan Island Visitors Farm and Davy's Cottage which is worthy of a visit. There is an animal farm with a fine array of unusual species, and a restaurant enjoying delightful views across the lake. Part of the restaurant is housed in the cottage which originally stood on these grounds and which the friendly proprietors have painstakingly restored. A local story tells of an old woman who used to live in the cottage. A local farmer noticed that his cow, which grazed in the field beside the cottage, was not yielding her usual amount of milk but he could not fathom why. He suspected somebody had been furtively milking the cow before he had the opportunity. Early one morning, armed with a shotgun, he laid in wait and after some time he noticed a hare approach the cow, take hold of one of its udders and started to suckle the cow. When the farmer yelled out the hare ran away in direction of the cottage. The farmer managed to let off a round from his shotgun and wounded the hare which continued on its way before the farmer lost sight of it. A short time later the farmer strolled past the cottage and on looking through the small windows he noticed the old woman beside the fire with blood streaming down her arm!

Leaving Swan Island Farm behind the road leads to the village of Newtowngore and the R199 for the return journey to Ballinamore via the northern shore of Garadice Lough. After 2km you come upon Ballinacur Bridge (Bridge 24) which crosses the waterway as it makes a short journey from Garadice Lough to enter a small lake called Woodford Lough. Just beside Ballinacur Bridge is Haughton's Shore Mooring where there are extensive quays and good car-parking facilities, making it a popular location for boatowners and anglers.

The return journey to Ballinamore passes swiftly on a well-surfaced open road with a hard shoulder making it a very comfortable and safe cycle. From Ballinamore you make your way back to Castlefore Lock by reversing the route on which you travelled earlier.

TOUR 3
HAUGHTON'S SHORE TO BALLYCONNELL
(29 Kilometres)

A mixture of canalised river and successive small lakes dominate the profile of the waterway for the early part of this tour as it moves from County Leitrim into County Cavan. It then adopts a more northerly course, meandering its way through a remote wilderness where you can begin to understand the sound of silence. For the latter part of the tour the looming presence of the Slieve Russell Mountains, which have Ballyconnell at their feet, accompanies the cyclist.

HOW TO GET THERE

Haughton's Shore is located 11km west of Ballyconnell, County Cavan, on the fringes of Garadice Lough and adjacent to Ballinacur Bridge on the Shannon-Erne Waterway. It is almost at the mid-point between Ballyconnell and Ballinamore. There are several alternative routes from Dublin to Ballinamore. You can follow the M4/N4 road network from Dublin as far as Dromod and proceed to Ballinamore via Mohill using the R202. Alternatively, you can travel via Cavan and Ballyconnell using the

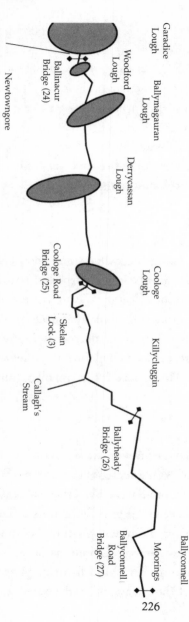

Tour 3 - Shannon-Erne Waterway
Haughton's Shore to Ballyconnell

Key

Bridge

Lock

Garadice Lough

Haughton's Shore

Woodford Lough

Ballinacur Bridge (24)

Ballymagauran Lough

Newtowngore

Derrycassan Lough

Coologe Road Bridge (25)

Coologe Lough

Skelan Lock (3)

Killycluggin

Callagh's Stream

Ballyheady Bridge (26)

Ballyconnell Road Bridge (27)

Moorings

Ballyconnell

N3 and N87. My preference is for the latter route, perhaps due to the historic waterway connection between the towns of Ballinamore and Ballyconnell, and the latter part of the journey allows you to track the waterway by road. Follow the M3/N3 from Dublin to Cavan and then to Belturbet where you take the N87 to Ballyconnell. From there the road to Ballinamore is well sign-posted using the R205. Haughton's Shore is located to the left of the junction between the R205 and the R 209. There are excellent car parking facilities beside the moorings.

MAPS

Ordnance Survey of Ireland Discovery Series:
Map 27A Cavan, Fermanagh, Leitrim and Monaghan (ISBN 1-901496-49-X)

Recourse to the road is necessary for a significant amount of this tour. There are a number of reasons for this: firstly, the waterway courses through a chain of four lakes for the early part of the tour where no towpath exists; secondly, the quality of the towpath beyond these lakes is poor. In some places poaching of the canal banks by local farmers is evident providing fencing obstacles to be hurdled; thirdly, there are also some locations where the outfall of a small stream presents an obstruction that in the wetter winter months becomes impassable; fourthly, in some locations there is evidence of erosion leaving the path in a poor state. On the positive side the roads are well surfaced and very quiet even in the height of the summer tourist season. In the winter months you can find yourself travelling for several kilometres on the smaller roads without encountering traffic.

Leaving Haughton's Shore turn right on to the R199 in the direction of Newtowngore. On your left the waterway flows under

Ballinacur Bridge (Bridge 24) into a very small lake called Woodford Lough which is more like a widening of the Woodford River. You will be able to see the waterway leaving Woodford Lough on its short journey into the larger Ballymagauran Lough but your sight of it coursing through the lower reaches of that lake is obscured by Woodford Demesne.

On reaching Newtowngore continue through the village and as you proceed to a junction 2km east of the village there will be glimpses of the third of the four lakes the waterway passes through, Derrycassan Lough, which is just over 0.5km from the road. At the junction turn left, heading towards Coologe Lough, where you will be reunited with the waterway at Coologe Bridge (Bridge 25). Depending on conditions you can resume your towpath journey using the left-hand side where there are trees between the path and the canal. After Coologe Bridge the canal embarks on a U-shaped course before reaching Skelan Lock (Lock 3), the first lock encountered on the navigation for almost 14km. This is a very isolated but scenic part of the waterway. The quality of the towpath beyond this lock is variable and is interrupted on the right by the outfall of Callagh's Stream which you can pass by accessing a small track about 200m from the canal. Because of the variable quality and lack of definition of the path in this area it is recommended returning to Coologe Bridge and resuming a tracking of the waterway by road.

Going north from Coologe Bridge the road links up with the R205 after 3km. The waterway, after its U-shaped course to Skelan Lock, follows a similar route at a distance of 1km from the road. You emerge on to the R205 near the townland of Killycluggin famous for a carved stone dating back to the first century BC. There is a sandstone replica of the decorated Killycluggin Stone on the roadside unveiled in 1992 and the original was removed to the National Museum. It was an Iron Age ritual stone and in pagan times the stone is said to have been used in the inauguration of the kings of this territory. The immediate area around Killycluggin is steeped in ancient Celtic folklore and spirituality and the location of important archaeological finds such as a golden collar discovered at nearby Lissanover. There are quite a number of standing stones as well as a stone circle, a holy well and a megalithic tomb in the locality. These are part of the Tullyhaw Heritage Trail and it is worth a temporary diversion to explore further an area which incorporates Magh Sleacht, the Plain of Slaughter, a major pagan ritual centre linked by royal road to the Hill of Tara. It is said that St Patrick journeyed to this area in 432 AD to confront an idol called Crom Cruach, or *Crom Dubh* the dark god, and eleven satellite idols representing his court. In defiance of the druids Patrick knocked the idols to the ground and established a church of his own at nearby Kilnavert. A church of more recent vintage called St Patrick's now stands prominently on a hill at Kilnavert which you will pass on your return journey.

Returning to the R205, a little over 1km further on in the direction of Ballyconnell you will see the signpost for Ballyheady Bridge (Bridge 26). There is no apparent sign of a towpath on either side of this bridge and there is evidence of the erosion of the canal bank south of the bridge. Officially the towpath continues on the right-hand side but the section nearest the bridge has been appropriated as a private mooring. The poaching of the towpath by the extension of fields down to the water's edge is a regular hindrance in this area and it is preferable to track the waterway from Ballyheady Bridge to Ballyconnell by the nearby R205.

As you approach Ballyconnell there are substantial moorings located just south of Ballyconnell Road Bridge (Bridge 27). The double-arched bridge also has a smaller arch over the towpath which is the only bridge on the waterway to do so. Ballyconnell is an attractive and well-kept town whose name is derived from the Irish *Béal Átha Conaill*, 'the mouth of the ford of Conaill'. The name commemorates the legendary warrior Conaill Cearnach (Conaill the Victorious) who was slain here and whose grave is marked by a cairn at an old church on the outskirts of the town. There are plenty of places for refreshment and the Bayleaf Coffee Shop and Restaurant on the Main Street is to be recommended. Its garden runs down to the edge of the canal as it begins to make its exit from the town.

The guide books recommend a visit to the Church of Ireland Tomregon Church, built in the seventeenth century, which is famous for the Tomregon Stone, a pagan stone depicting a human head. The stone is adjacent to the main door of the church and is a little disappointing. It has the dimensions of an upturned road cone and the inscriptions on it are barely visible. It seems unusual that a religious establishment should have such a close association with a pagan artefact but it is noteworthy that it lies outside the walls of the church building.

The ruins of Ballyconnell House are to be seen on the left of the waterway just past Ballyconnell Road Bridge. The former gateway to the house has been preserved as the entrance for the nearby Boxmore Plastics factory. The house and demesne were last occupied by Bernie Edgeworth who sold them and moved to England some time ago. He was a descendant of Maria Edgeworth, author of the novel, *Castle Rackrent,* and other works. When he died in recent years his remains were brought back to Ballyconnell and he was buried in the graveyard beside Tomregon Church.

The return journey to Haughton's Shore follows the R205 all the way to its junction with the R199.

Tour 4
Ballyconnell to Upper Lough Erne
(42 Kilometres)

For almost all this tour the waterway forms the border between Fermanagh and Cavan and also between the Republic of Ireland and Northern Ireland. At this stage the waterway is the only visible barrier between the two jurisdictions and the tour embraces a number of switches across the watery frontier. Low drumlin hills on both sides of the border provide a gentle and pleasing backdrop as the waterway meanders on a winding course to Upper Lough Erne.

How to get there
Ballyconnell is in the northern reaches of County Cavan and is 140km from Dublin. Follow the M3/N3 from Dublin to Cavan and then to Belturbet where you take the N87 to Ballyconnell. There are good car-parking facilities at Ballyconnell Moorings.

Maps
Ordnance Survey of Ireland Discovery Series:
Map *27A* Cavan, Fermanagh, Leitrim and Monaghan (ISBN 1-901496-49-X)

Key

Bridge

Lock

Tour 4 - Shannon-Erne Waterway
Ballyconnell to Upper Lough Erne

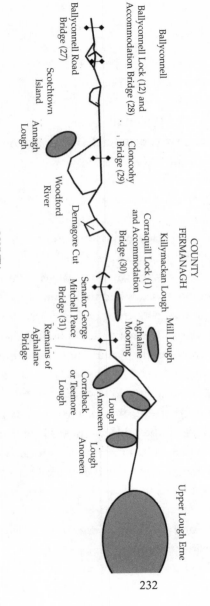

Ballyconnell

Ballyconnell Lock (12) and
Accommodation Bridge (28)

Ballyconnell Road
Bridge (27)

Scotchtown
Island

Annagh
Lough

Cloncoohy
Bridge (29)

Woodford
River

Dernagore Cut

COUNTY
CAVAN

COUNTY
FERMANAGH

Killymackan Lough

Corraquill Lock (1)
and Accommodation
Bridge (30)

Mill Lough

Aghalane
Mooring

Senator George
Mitchell Peace
Bridge (31)

Remains of
Aghalane
Bridge

Corraback
or Teemore
Lough

Lough
Amoneen

Lough
Anoneen

Upper Lough Erne

232

There is a fine path running from Ballyconnell on the southern banks of the canal which can be accessed beside Ballyconnell Road Bridge (Bridge 27) through a small park where there is a memorial to Kieran Dwyer, one of the nationalist prisoners who died while on hunger strike in Northern Ireland. The ruins of Ballyconnell House lie close by. The waterway at this point is fast flowing, particularly in the winter months. The surface of the path is reasonable but in some places can get very wet due to its proximity to the water.

On the outskirts of the town the waterway splits with the navigation channel heading left towards Ballyconnell Lock (Lock 2) and the river channel passing over a weir. After the lock there is a small accommodation bridge (Bridge 28) allowing access to the little island between the two watercourses. There is no bridge link across the river channel.

The skyline to the north of the waterway is dominated by an extensive cement production plant and behind that a series of wind turbines. As you move along the path you will also see a vast warehouse building across the river which is part of a glassmaking business. After 2.5km the path leads away from the river into dense woodland. There are several paths through the wood and it is worthwhile taking a detour to experience an exhilarating cycle leading to the shores of Annagh Lough. The forest path will lead you back towards Ballyconnell and it is possible to link up with the canal path again either by returning to the town or by making a short cross-country cycle in the direction of the river, meeting up with it just below Ballyconnell Lock. Once you emerge from the forest you will be able to get your bearings from the cement plant on the other side of the waterway. This detour will add approximately 5km to your journey.

Although it is not immediately evident it is possible to

continue along the side of the waterway from where the path diverts towards the forest. Keeping to the fringes of the forest you will have to negotiate fallen trees, a number of fences, boggy conditions underfoot and a small stream which you will be able to cross a little inland from the waterway. It is quite challenging but you emerge 200m short of Cloncoohy Bridge (Bridge 29). Here you will have to part company with the waterway for a short while as the path on the southern side is interrupted by a number of channels over which there is no easy passage.

At Cloncoohy Bridge head by road in the direction of the cement plant towards the B129, which is the Northern Ireland continuation of the R205 from Ballyconnell. Remain on the B129 for 1.5km before taking the first turn right. This road leads up a fairly steep hill where you get a fine view of the undulating landscape. Bear right at the junction located just under 1km along this road leading you back in the direction of the waterway. This road runs parallel to the waterway until you come to the A509 where you turn right. Remain on the A509 for approximately 0.5km until you see the signpost for Corraquill Lock (Lock 1). There is a commemorative stone at this lock noting that the waterway was opened on 23 May 1994 jointly by the then Tánaiste, Dick Spring, and Sir Patrick Mayhew, Secretary of State for Northern Ireland. Corraquill Bridge (Bridge 30) is an accommodation bridge linking the northern bank to the island between the navigation channel and the river channel.

Backtracking towards the main road is a small road to the right which tracks the waterway almost to the Senator George Mitchell Peace Bridge (Bridge 31) which carries the A509 across the canal near Aghalane. The bridge was constructed in 1998 and named in honour of US Senator George Mitchell in recognition of his contribution to the Good Friday Agreement of that year. The northern towpath between Corraquill and this bridge is passable but challenging. Access is difficult as there is no bridge spanning the full waterway at Corraquill.

Aghalane Mooring, on the northern bank of the waterway just over 0.5km from the Senator George Mitchell Peace Bridge, can be accessed by taking the side road to the left that you passed just after resuming the A509. On the route to the moorings you will come across the old Aghalane Road Bridge which was demolished by an explosion in the 1970s. All that is now left of the old bridge are the abutments.

While the northern towpath is marked on maps from Aghalane to the junction with Upper Lough Erne it has a number of obstacles, not least being several narrow channels leading from two small lakes, Lough Amoneen and Lough Anoneen. Accordingly, the only feasible route for tracking the waterway on its final passage towards its destination is via a small road that runs parallel to the winding course of the waterway virtually all the way. This road is to be found 1km to the north of Senator George Mitchell Peace Bridge off the A509. The road is sandwiched between several lakes on both sides and the waterway is never far away. It ends at a quaint, recently derelict cottage after which is a track behind a gate that leads down to the shore of Upper Lough Erne just north of the junction with the waterway.

During the winter months you are likely to see quite a few whooper swans here who come to escape the harsh Icelandic winter. The edge of Lough Erne is a favourite destination for some of the migrants. It is estimated that as many as five per cent of the world's population of whooper swans winter here. The swans are the beneficiaries of a government scheme in Northern Ireland that

235

encourages farmers in the area to allow them graze on their land undisturbed. Farmers are paid to take cattle off the fields early in order to accommodate the arrival of the swans who would otherwise compete with farm animals for grass. The land must be set aside for swans until 1 April by which time the swans have returned to Iceland.

The return route to Ballyconnell is via the small link road between the N3 and the N87 which is accessed just south of the Peace Bridge. This road sees very little traffic and is a delightful, undulating cycle, passing close to the southern shores of Annagh Lough where you get a good view of the woodland area through which you may have opted to cycle earlier on this tour.

SECTION E

The Newry Canal

History of the Newry Canal

Northern Ireland's Newry Canal holds an important position in the history of inland waterways in the British Isles as it was the first commercially operated summit level canal in these islands. The canal occupies a natural trough in the landscape between the towns of Newry and Portadown where it joins up with the River Bann and is part of the waterways link between Lough Neagh and the sea at Carlingford Lough. The waterway comprises two distinct elements, an inland canal stretching from Newry to Portadown and a ship canal extending 5km from Newry to Warrenpoint. The inland canal was open for navigation for over 200 years. It thrived throughout the nineteenth century and was responsible for the emergence and growth of a number of towns along its route such as Poyntzpass. The entire waterway was also responsible for much of Newry's prosperity in the eighteenth and nineteenth centuries.

The inland portion of the canal has been closed to navigation since 1947 and the water channel has deteriorated badly in places. Thanks to the work of Sustrans (a UK charity whose work involves building and designing routes for cyclists and walkers) and the local Councils, the towpath on the western bank of the canal has been cleared and a black-top surface has been installed on almost the entire route.

As a towpath cycling experience the Newry Canal is diminished by the black-top surface now in place. The route has been excessively sanitised and has ended up more like a cycling race-track than a pleasant off-road cycling adventure.

It is interesting to draw comparisons between the Newry Canal towpath and the rugged towpaths of the westerly reaches of the Royal Canal or the carpet-like, grass-covered tracks of the Barrow Navigation. The towpaths of a number of canals in England have been similarly sanitised under the banner of 'progress'. If the work carried out on the Newry Canal is an example of what the future holds for canal towpaths in the Republic of Ireland, we should actively seek to retain and maintain our towpaths in a condition that resembles their original state. This will afford cyclists, and indeed walkers, a more rewarding experience.

While the towpath is clear the same cannot be said of the canal's water channel. A significant portion of the canal has been in generally poor condition for some time, overgrown with weeds, with water hardly discernible at some points. Some work has been done on the more northerly reaches of the canal from Terryhoogan Lock and this stretch retains a semblance of how the canal must have looked in its glory days. Elsewhere most of the locks are in disrepair, with missing gates and badly deteriorated stonework. It is almost impossible to identify the location of one or two of the locks such is their state of dilapidation. This takes from some of the pleasure of cycling along this waterway.

Notwithstanding reservations regarding the surface of the towpath and the poor state of the navigation, the Newry Canal is a worthwhile and rewarding route to follow. The canal courses through the heart of the Ulster countryside and exposes an area that is full of interesting heritage and attractions.

The canal's origins date back to the Cromwellian times of the mid-seventeenth century when one of Cromwell's officers, Colonel George Monck, proposed the digging of a canal in this area. His proposals were not immediately followed up and it was not until 60 years later in 1703 that the first survey was carried out by Francis Neill. The discovery of coal deposits in east Tyrone was the spur that eventually saw the canal come into being. An Act of Parliament in 1729 provided for the funding and construction commenced in 1731.

The canal took ten years to complete and over this time three engineers were responsible for its construction for different periods. The first was Edward Lovett Pearce who died prematurely to be succeeded by his assistant, Richard Castle. Castle was dismissed after three years and was replaced in 1736 by Thomas Stears who completed the project by the summer of 1741. The canal was officially opened in early 1742. The first vessel to pass through the waterway was called *The Cope of Lough Neagh* with a cargo of coal from Lough Neagh to be brought to Newry and onwards to Dublin.

In the 1760s work started on a ship canal extending under 3km from the head of Carlingford Lough to Newry. The work was supervised by Thomas Omer, the engineer who also supervised the early stages of the Grand Canal and the Barrow Navigation. The ship canal was opened in 1769 and could accommodate ships of up to 120 tons making Newry the most important port in Northern Ireland.

In 1800 control of the canal passed to the Directors General of Inland Navigation who immediately commenced a programme of refurbishment and improvement under the supervision of the eminent engineer, John Brownrigg. In the following ten years the bridges at Jerretspass and Knock were rebuilt, as were four of the canal's fourteen locks which had fallen into disrepair. The programme also included the construction of a new landing quay and basin at Scarva and the construction of the stone and brick River Cusher aqueduct, just north of Scarva.

In 1813 William Dawson introduced a passenger service on the waterway, the only such service to have existed on the waterways of Northern Ireland. The journey time was four hours and the service endured for 30 years before falling victim to the faster transport times of the railway network introduced in the middle of the nineteenth century.

Ownership of both the inland and ship canals was transferred by the government into private hands in 1829. The new owners, the Newry Navigation Company, committed to undertake further improvements to the waterways network and in the mid-nineteenth century they extended the existing ship canal by a further 2km towards Warrenpoint to give larger ships access to four quays which were built at Newry. Albert Basin was also completed in 1850, improving Newry's port facilities by accommodating ships of over 500 tons.

In the early years of the twentieth century control of the canal changed hands yet again, on this occasion to the Newry Port and Harbour Trust who probably rued the day they assumed responsibility for the waterway. Heavy maintenance expenses, combined with declining revenues, proved an onerous liability. The rapid growth of cheaper and quicker rail transport proved its principal undoing and with trade diminishing to negligible levels it was eventually closed in 1947. As an indication of its commercial decline the last vessel to be carried along its waters was a pleasure craft to Portadown in 1937, returning south two years later. While it was closed it was not forgotten and became a designated water-course in 1954. In the late 1950s the swing bridge on the Dublin Road was replaced by a fixed bridge which thereafter prevented movement between the inland canal and the ship canal. Commercial operation of the ship canal survived until March 1974 but ceased when a decision was made to develop Warrenpoint as the main port for the area and the Newry Port and Harbour Trust went into liquidation.

Over following years various sections of the canal were pur-chased by the local Councils of the districts through which it passed. Accordingly, ownership of the waterway is now shared by the following public agencies: Newry and Mourne District Council; Banbridge District Council; Armagh City & District Council; and Craigavon Borough Council.

All these agencies are committed to restoring the canal to its former glory and are participants in a programme entitled The Newry Canal Restoration Project. Already work has been under-taken in restoring a number of locks and in constructing several visitors' centres along the route of the waterway. Installation of a black-top surface on the towpath on the western bank of the canal has also been completed, opening up the canal to the shared use of cyclists and walkers. The towpath forms part of Route 9 of the United Kingdom's National Cycle Network and is also an integral part of the Ulster Way.

NEWRY CANAL ROUTE OVERVIEW

The ship canal starts at Victoria Lock and extends for 5km to Albert Basin where it links up with the inland section just south of Buttercrane Quay. Movement between the two sections of the canal is no longer possible due to the fixed bridge that runs between Bridge Street and William Street. There are four quays along the early part of the inland section, heading north: Buttercrane Quay, Merchant's Quay, Sugar Island Quay and Canal Quay. The inland canal then navigates its way for a distance of 32km from Newry to link up with the River Bann just short of Portadown. It has a total of thirteen locks, ten of which are south of the summit level which commences at Poyntzpass. These are numbered from 2 to 14 taking into account Victoria Lock on the ship canal which is recognised as the first lock on the overall navigation. The summit level is 23.8m above sea level. Acton Lake, which is located a little over halfway along the route, plays an important part in being the main feeder for topping up the canal's water supply. The towpath is in excellent condition for cycling with a black-top surface for much of the route. The final section of the path forms the Bann Boulevard, a riverside park that runs through Portadown.

NEWRY CANAL
NEWRY TO PORTADOWN
(33 Kilometres)

Starting at Newry and going north, this tour follows the route of the inland canal and does not include the ship canal which extends south east of Newry towards Warrenpoint. The black-top surface of the towpath extends for most of the route making for a fairly easy ride that can be undertaken even in the depths of winter.

HOW TO GET THERE
Newry, County Down, is located in the south-eastern corner of Northern Ireland on the main Dublin-Belfast road and is part of the border area between the six counties of Northern Ireland and the 26 counties of the Republic of Ireland. It is 106km from Dublin and can be accessed by following the M1/A1 road network northwards from Dublin bypassing Drogheda and Dundalk. There is ample car parking throughout the town.

Newry can also be accessed by train. The Dublin-Belfast train, known as the *Enterprise*, stops at Newry and bicycles can be accommodated on this service at a charge. When booking be sure to advise the ticket office that you will be bringing a bicycle.

Tour - Newry Canal
Newry to Portadown

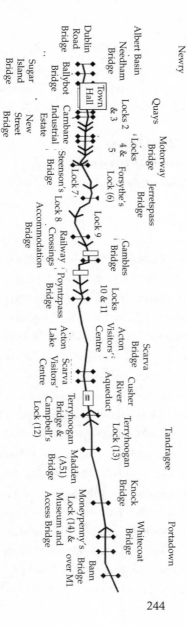

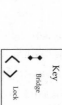

Key

Bridge

Lock

244

MAPS

Ordnance Survey of Northern Ireland Discovery Series:

Sheets 20 and 29. An Illustrated guide to the canal is published as part of Northern Ireland's Waymarked Way series and is available from the Tourist Office located in the Newry Town Hall. Tel. (04828) 30268877

While Newry is recognised as an important shopping and commercial centre for its hinterland, it is steeped in history and is worthy of a separate tour either before or after your journey alongside the canal. The area has a history of continuous settlement dating back to early records and has a fine heritage graced with interesting buildings such as Bagenal's Castle and an imposing town hall which straddles the Clanrye River. Guides to Newry's Heritage Trail are available at the Town Hall Tourist Office.

The town derives its name from the Irish *Lubhair Cinn Tragh,* 'a yew tree at the head of the strand' referring to a tree reputed to have been planted by St Patrick. This was shortened later to *Na Lubhair* and then to Newry. In 1144 thirteen Cistercian monks arrived in Newry from the mother-house at Mellifont, Collon, County Louth, and proceeded to reorganise an existing monastery they founded there which had been established by Patrician and Benedictine monks in earlier times. The abbey they established grew in prominence over following centuries before being dissolved during the reign of Henry VIII. In 1550 the Abbot's house was occupied by Nicholas Bagenal, Marshal of the English Army in Ireland, establishing a dynasty that endured for over 160 years. He is credited with developing Newry as a town. He either built a new castle on the site of the abbey or fortified the Abbot's house. The standing remains of this building were rediscovered in 1996 enveloped inside a more modern building that had been used as a bakery. This renovated premises will house the Newry and Mourne Museum and the Tourist Information Office.

Among other attractions in Newry are its Catholic Cathedral and its Anglican Church, both of which are unique. The Cathedral of St Patrick and St Colman located on Hill Street was built in 1829 and was the first Catholic Cathedral opened after the granting of Catholic Emancipation. The Church of Ireland church, also called St Patrick's, is located on High Street, enjoying a prominent position overlooking the town. It was the first Protestant church to be built in Ireland following the Reformation.

One of the more famous people to emerge from Newry was John Mitchel (1815-1875), writer and nationalist politician. For his political activities he was sentenced to fourteen years penal transportation to Australia. His book, *Jail Journal,* is regarded as a classic of prison literature.

The southern end of Buttercrane Quay on the western bank of the canal is the starting point for this tour. Looking back is Albert Basin which was completed in 1850, allowing the port of Newry to accommodate ships of over 500 tons. The Buttercrane Shopping Centre to the west of the canal takes its name from a butter crane erected at the side of the canal by Lord Kilmorey in 1808. Casks of butter were regularly transported on the inland canal in the middle of the nineteenth century. Another point to note is the proximity of the Clanrye River which runs directly parallel to the canal through Newry.

Moving onwards to Merchants' Quay, this is the second of four quays which dominated the canalside as testimony to the strong mercantile history enjoyed by Newry through the nineteenth and early twentieth centuries. The quayside has some surviving nineteenth-century warehouses and stretches to Godfrey Bridge, a modern structure that now prevents passage by boat up the canal. The bridge replaced a swing bridge whose foundations are still in the water. After Godfrey Bridge is Sugar Island Quay, an area which takes its name from the trade of importing sugar from the West Indies. Looking eastwards you can see the Town Hall which is interesting from both an architectural and engineering perspective as it is built directly over the Clanrye River. The story behind this is interesting. Newry is situated on the border of Counties Down and Armagh, and the Clanrye River forms the boundary line between the two counties. In the late eighteenth century rivalry between the two counties over the location of a new town hall resulted in the compromise of it being built on a three-arched bridge astride the river. The building was designed by William Batt and was built in 1893.

The canal narrows as it leaves Sugar Island Quay and moves under the extensive Sugar Island Bridge on to Canal Quay which is dominated by a large Venetian style red-bricked building known as Clanrye Mills. As you pass this building you will notice the strong sickly sweet aroma from the animal feed processed in these mills. The building dates from 1873 and the adjacent grey building to its north side bears a worn sign stating 'Sinclair & Sons, Steam Mills', dated 1867.

Continuing along Canal Quay you will reach the Linen Hall Arch which formed the entrance to White Linen Hall built in 1783. Irish Linen was in great demand in the second half of the eighteenth century and developed into a major manufacturing and export industry. Unfortunately the Linen Hall did not prosper and it was later used as a military barracks.

Just past a business park the canal parts company from the road and the towpath begins in earnest. It had been reported that the stretch of the canal up to and including Locks 2 and 3 on the outskirts of the town had undergone much restoration in recent years. The results of the restoration are not immediately evident and in fact the first impressions of the canal after it leaves the centre of the town are disappointing. Lock 2, the first lock of the inland canal, is in very poor condition and overgrown with weeds. There is a small culverted crossing just after the lock that is also laden with weeds right down to the water's edge. This does not augur well for the rest of the waterway. While the third lock is in a better state, ruined locks become a familiar sight as the smooth towpath facilitates speedy passage towards more open countryside. For almost the entire route to Steenson's Bridge, which is just after Forsythe's Lock (Lock 6), the canal's channel is narrowed by a blanket of duckweed, with the result that only a small amount of water is visible.

The area around the triple-arched Steenson's Bridge is called Goragh Wood, although the scarcity of trees in the immediate vicinity suggests the name has its origins back in history. Goragh Wood was important as the principal railway station for Newry and it also served as the main Customs point up until the 1960s, as it was the last stop before crossing the border between Northern Ireland and the Republic.

Lock 7 is located just past Steenson's Bridge, after which the path continues through what appears to be a trough in the terrain as the ground to the east and west slopes gently upwards. The path skirts past the small village of Jerretspass where the bridge was one of two reconstructed as part of improvement works carried out between 1801 and 1811 by the Directors General of

Inland Navigation. The bridge has an unusual and attractive design,with the parapets rising to a peak instead of the more usual rounded design.

After Lock 8 at Jerretspass the canal takes a prolonged and gentle turn to the right, following the contours of the western slopes before straightening up to pass through Lock 9 and under the first of two railway crossings that are 1km apart. Between these two crossings the canal twists like a corkscrew, firstly, to the right and then to the left while passing under Gambles Bridge. This bridge is sometimes referred to locally as Crack Bridge, although there is no obvious reason for this.

The path from Jerretspass to Poyntzpass is shared with motorised vehicles so care is needed along this stretch. Locks 10 and 11 are on the fringes of Poyntzpass. Unless you pay close attention it is easy to miss what is left of the tenth lock while the eleventh is in a particularly distressed state. The ruined remnants of one of the gates are all that remain and the lock looks every year of its 250 since it was first constructed. The first ever recipient of the Victoria Cross, Admiral Charles Lucas hailed from Poyntzpass. During the Crimean War, he risked his life by throwing a Russian shell off the deck of his ship.

After a short ride on from Poyntzpass you will emerge from the cover of the trees which line the towpath to arrive at Acton Lake, also known as Lough Shark, and it is an important source of water supply for the canal. There is now a visitors' centre adjacent to the towpath in the restored sluice keeper's cottage which is open during the summer months. When the canal was being built Acton Lake was expanded and became the main feeder for topping up the canal's water supply during periods of prolonged dry weather via a sluice close to the cottage. This is a scenic part of the route and the lake is home to hundreds of swans and other birdlife.

Just south of the visitors' centre is the first of a number of mileposts that have been erected along the towpath by Sustrans to mark the millennium and the launch of the National Cycle Network. The mileposts resemble totem poles and were designed by David Dudgeon and cast by Taylor's Foundry in Suffolk, England. On each is a short poem by the designer dated 1999 that reads as follows:

Down a wandering path I have travelled,
Where the setting sun lies upon the ground
The tracks are hard and dry smoothened with the weather's
    wear.
My mind did move with them that had before me been
Trodding down the ground a track
For me to follow leaving marks for others
A sign for them to follow.

The village of Scarva lies about 2km north of Acton Lake. The village owes its existence to the canal and the bridge built across it which was erected in 1744, using many parts of a bridge that existed in earlier times. The sharply pointed steeple of Scarva Church stands out as you approach the village. A distinctive Parish Hall lies just across the canal bridge directly under the church and steeple. North of the bridge is a newly-erected Visitors' Centre and Community Centre located at the basin and landing quay which was constructed in the early years of the nineteenth century when the Directors General of Inland Navigation assumed control of the waterway. In bygone times vast quantities of coal were unloaded at this dock for use in the local linen industry. It is now tastefully presented as a garden to the community centre and is accessible from the towpath by means of a footbridge over the canal.

Not far from Scarva are the remains of a stone and brick aqueduct dating from the nineteenth century used in the supply of water to the canal from the Cusher River. This river accompanies the canal from this point all the way to its junction with the River Bann further north. The stone aqueduct, which is now missing the section over the canal, replaced a wooden trough leading a feeder from the river into the canal. A short distance further on is Campbell's Lock (Lock 12) followed by Terryhoogan Bridge. After this bridge the towpath disappears for a short distance passing by the waterway's penultimate lock (number 13), Terryhoogan Lock. Nearby is Terryhoogan House where John Wesley, founder of the Methodist Church, is reputed to have stayed.

The towpath resumes alongside a dismantler's yard which runs for about 200m along the western bank of the canal before reaching a gateway that has an excellent side access for pedestrians and cyclists. The side gate, made of wood, has a spring lever mechanism and is easily negotiated. Perhaps Waterways Ireland could look at this type of gate for use along the Royal Canal where gates are frequently encountered and where access for cyclists is awkward.

Leaving Terryhoogan behind, the surrounding landscape takes on a boggy profile and the exposed towpath can be susceptible to strong winds. Care should be taken crossing the A51 at Madden Bridge from which Tandragee is a short cycle to the west. Though not on the canal, Tandragee has connections with the linen industry and is worth a visit. The area after Madden Bridge presented the canal builders with a lot of difficulty because of its boggy terrain, complicated by a forest of fallen oak, ash and alder trees. Today it is a haven for those interested in flora and fauna and is host to a wide variety of birdlife.

Knock Bridge is the next feature encountered, spanning the canal just before the final lock on the system, Moneypenny's Lock (Lock 14). The bridge was designed by John Brownrigg and dates back to 1861 when it replaced the original wooden bridge erected at the beginning of the nineteenth century. The cast iron section of the central span was made in England at the Lucas Soho factory.

A tree-lined path leads from Knock Bridge to Moneypenny's Lock and lock-house. The lock is in good condition in contrast to nearly all others on the waterway, and takes its name from the family who were lock-keepers here for many years. The lock-house dates back to the beginning of the nineteenth century and has been restored along with the stables and bothy, providing a canal museum that is open in the afternoon at weekends and bank holidays from 1 April to 30 September.

A short distance from Moneypenny's Lock is a fine modern bridge called Whitecoat Bridge, opened in March 1990. This was erected at a place called the Point of Whitecoat (sometimes written as Whitecote) where there is the convergence of the Newry Canal, the River Cusher and the River Bann. According to local legend the area takes its name from a local resident who was renowned for wearing a white coat and who was said to have drowned nearby. The bridge has an A-frame tubular design that was intended to compliment its relatively flat surroundings.

The wide expanse of the River Bann makes a stark contrast to the narrow canal as Portadown is approached on an excellent path which leads into what is now part of the Bann Boulevard, a riverside amenity running through Portadown. Portadown has been an important crossing point on this sizeable river going back to early history. Its name is derived from an anglicised version of an Irish phrase meaning 'landing place of the fort'. This refers to a *rath* or circular stronghold that overlooked the River Bann at this location. The canal's opening in 1742 and its proximity to Lough Neagh projected Portadown into a pivotal trading position and it soon became an important inland canal port, trading goods via not only the Newry Canal but also the other man-made inland waterways such as the Lagan, Ulster and Coalisland canals. The town has many fine establishments where refreshments can be enjoyed before going back to the towpath for the return journey.

SECTION F

THE LAGAN NAVIGATION

HISTORY OF THE LAGAN NAVIGATION

The vast expanse of Lough Neagh and its close proximity to the Irish Sea made it a frequent target for linkages by canal, especially during the canalmania era of the eighteenth and nineteenth centuries. While five canals eventually saw the light of day there were also several which were proposed but never built, such as a link with Larne on the coast north of Belfast Lough and another with the inland town of Armagh via the River Blackwater. The completed waterways were: the Newry Canal; the Tyrone Navigation, otherwise known as the Coalisland Canal, built in the middle of the eighteenth century, which secured its link to Lough Neagh via the River Blackwater; the Lower Bann Navigation, the most northerly of the waterways which was again the product of the mid-eighteenth century; the Ulster Canal completed in 1841; and, finally, the Lagan Navigation.

Unfortunately the Lagan Navigation has not survived intact. Over one-third of its length has succumbed to a less sedate transport route, having been used as part of a motorway constructed in the 1960s. However, it rightly merits inclusion, as a substantial part of the towpath still exists and even the converted section can be tracked using small country roads that are not too busy. An element of the active parts of the towpath has received similar treatment to that of the towpath of the Newry Canal. The sections from Belfast to Lisburn and from Moira to Aghalee form part of National Cycle Network Route 9 and it is proposed that the final section of the towpath from Aghalee to Lough Neagh will also become a shared use path in the near future.

Because the towpath is a popular shared use amenity you will not experience the same sense of getting away from it all that you will encounter on the Southern waterways until perhaps you close in on the shores of Lough Neagh. Its missing middle section provides a timely reminder of the threat that our waterways face. I doubt that in this more enlightened and heritage-conscious age such a development for the purposes of 'progress' would now be permitted.

One of the best reasons for visiting this waterway is that it provides access to the Lagan Valley, a part of Northern Ireland that has an important place in industrial history, where it was the centre of an extensive linen industry now celebrated at the Irish Linen Centre at Lisburn. Furthermore, the section which runs through the Lagan Valley Regional Park is a good example of what can be achieved through opening up the waterways as shared use amenities instead of focusing on the needs of one group of users alone.

The recommended tours for the Lagan Navigation both commence at Sprucefield where there are good car-parking and refreshment facilities. The first tour allows you to cycle into Belfast city by a delightful route rather than drive on the motorway and dispensing with the need for hunting for a car park.

As with nearly all the waterways covered here proposals to render the River Lagan navigable were put forward long before any work started. As early as 1637, almost a century before canalmania took a firm foothold in the British Isles, a link between Belfast and Lough Neagh was proposed. However, it was not until the Newry Canal, completed in 1741, was producing commercial benefit that the authorities considered that the desired link was justifiable. The required survey was carried out followed by the passing of the Act for the Lagan Navigation in 1753. Work on the canal started in 1756 under the direction of Thomas Omer, the same engineer who was supervising the construction of the Grand Canal which also started in that year and who had also worked on the Newry Canal.

The original plan was to canalise the river as much as possible and to use independent collateral cuts where awkward bends were encountered. Initially work on the canal progressed well and in 1763 a boat called the *Lord Hertford* negotiated its way as far as Lisburn. By 1765 Thomas Omer had reached Sprucefield but two growing problems put a halt to construction. Firstly, the project had run short of funds and, secondly, the river sections were susceptible to severe flooding preventing the safe use by boats.

In 1768 Omer's work was inspected by Robert Whitworth, an engineer, who was an assistant to James Brindley, one of the leading canal engineers of his time. Whitworth was critical of the works already completed, in particular, the proneness to flooding. He suggested that an independent canal separated from the River

Lagan would be a superior option. Due to the parlous state of the project's finances nothing was done immediately and it was not until 1779 that the project was revived, mainly due to the financial backing of the Marquess of Donegall. The Company of Undertakers of the Lagan Navigation was established and by 1782 a new engineer, Richard Owen, was appointed to supervise the construction of the remainder of the canal from Sprucefield to Lough Neagh, leaving Omer's works largely untouched despite Whitworth's earlier critical comments.

It took a further twelve years to complete the canal to its junction with Lough Neagh. The total cost was £108,231 with almost 60 per cent of this being covered by the Marquess of Donegall. The Marquess formally opened the canal by making a boat trip from Moira to Lough Neagh.

Maintenance of the canal was poor in its early years and navigation problems persisted due to flooding and silting in the canalised section of the river during winter months. In the early 1800s a number of local businessmen bought a controlling interest in the canal company and set about improving the navigation, particularly on the canalised river stretch. They also installed a suitable towpath.

With the improved navigation a greater flow of trade followed. When proposals for the canal were first mooted it was expected it would provide a means of transporting coal from the Tyrone Collieries to Belfast and onwards to other destinations. It is ironic that the traffic of coal flowed in the other direction with imported English coal being hauled to Lisburn and other centres of the burgeoning linen trade. Other cargoes to be carried on the canal at the time included agricultural produce, sand and tiles.

As happened with canals in other areas of the British Isles the

Lagan Navigation faced increasing competition from the railway networks emerging from the 1830s onwards. It had been thought that completion of the Ulster Canal in 1841 would provide a welcome boost to traffic but this failed to emerge due to significant defects in that canal, not least its inability to cope with the size of boats in use on the Lagan as the locks on the Ulster Canal were smaller than those on the Lagan. Between 1843 and 1848 a number of acts were passed in relation to the canal and these facilitated the incorporation of a new company to take over the canal. At its height the Lagan Navigation carried 174,000 tons of cargo annually and the new company traded profitably for some time. However, in 1888, it accepted responsibility for the Ulster Canal and the Tyrone Navigation (Coalisland Canal) and these proved burdensome.

In the first half of the twentieth century the Lagan Navigation remained active, albeit with declining trade. Faced with unbeatable competition from road haulage its trade dwindled and in 1954 the Lagan Navigation Company was dissolved and the canal was transferred to the Ministry of Commerce. In the same year the western end of the canal from Lisburn to Lough Neagh was officially abandoned. The same fate befell the remainder of the canal in 1958. In the 1960s the chances of a restoration of the canal took a severe blow when a motorway was built over the section from Lisburn to Moira. Any future restoration will require cutting a new replacement section along a different route.

The Lagan Navigation Route Overview

The River Lagan rises near the summit of Slieve Croob (541m) in County Down and initially flows north westwards as if it were making for Lough Neagh, the largest fresh water lake in the

British Isles. However, near Magheralin it makes a right angle turn to cross a broad plain towards Belfast Lough. The Lagan Navigation originally extended for 43.5km from Stranmillis in Belfast to Ellis' Gut at Lough Neagh. It officially started at Molly Ward's Lock which no longer exists but which was located where the Belfast Boat Club now stands. In total there were 27 locks along the navigation. There were seventeen rising locks bringing the water level to the head or summit level of 34m (112 feet) reached at Sprucefield. The summit level extended for 17.5km between Sprucefield and Aghalee before falling 21.3m (70 feet) through ten large locks to Lough Neagh. A significant portion of the summit level has disappeared having been used as the route for the motorway from Lisburn to Moira.

Most of the canal cuts originally built by Thomas Omer along what is now the Lagan Valley Regional Park have been abandoned and are now either dry or turned to marshland. There are some restricted water-filled lengths that in summer are covered with duckweed.

At least 27 bridges existed when the navigation was completed. Several of these were removed when the motorway was being built and a number of new bridges have been erected along the route to facilitate new local roads. Two railway bridges were built in the mid-nineteenth century. The one near Moira still survives but the other at Newport is gone.

Originally a towpath extended along the entire route of the navigation but this deteriorated rapidly after the canal closed. From Belfast to Sprucefield the path was restored in the 1970s as part of the Lagan Valley Regional Park and is a shared use amenity that is excellent for cycling or walking. The path is susceptible to erosion or coating with silt following heavy rains. No path exists where the motorway has been built so it is necessary to track the removed section by means of local country roads. The towpath from Lady's Bridge near Moira to Aghalee has been reclaimed and the surface is good for cycling or walking. From Aghalee to the waterway's junction with Lough Neagh portions of the towpath have been cleared and a black-top surface installed. However, some sections of the towpath appear to be in private hands and this has so far prevented completion of a similar surface for the rest of this section, requiring a number of detours while tracking the waterway to its destination.

Tour 1
Sprucefield to Clarendon Dock, Belfast
(25 Kilometres)

This tour takes you on a delightful meander through the Lagan Valley Regional Park, with its countryside settings and rich heritage. Encountering a diversity of habitats, it is hard to imagine that these exist in such close proximity to a major city. The towpath of the navigation links up with a network of cycle lanes that carry you alongside the River Lagan to Belfast's waterfront area which is being extensively rejuvenated.

How to get there
Sprucefield is on the outskirts of the city of Lisburn and is approximately 145km from Dublin and 16km from Belfast. It can be reached from Dublin via the M1/N1 road network to Newry and A1 to the Sprucefield roundabout. Then take the turn in the direction of Lisburn. From Belfast use the M1 to the Sprucefield roundabout and once again take the turn in the direction of Lisburn.

Tour 1 - Lagan Navigation
Sprucefield to Clarendon Dock, Belfast

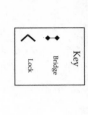

Key

Bridge

Lock

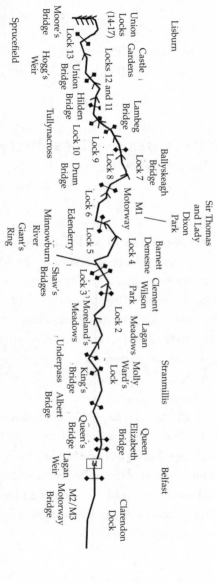

Lisburn

Castle
Gardens

Union
Locks
(14-17)

Lambeg
Bridge

Locks 12 and 11

Lock 13   Union
           Bridge

Hilden   Lock 10
Bridge

Lock 9

Drum
Bridge

Lock 8

Ballyskeagh
Bridge

Lock 7

M1
Motorway

Lock 6

Sir Thomas
and Lady
Dixon
Park

Barnett
Demesne

Lock 5

Edenderry

Clement
Wilson
Park

Lock 4

Lagan
Meadows

Lock 3

Moreland's
Meadows

Molly
Ward's
Lock

Lock 2

Shaw's
Bridge

Underpass

Minnowburn
River
Bridges

Giant's
Ring

King's
Bridge

Stranmillis

Albert
Bridge

Queen's
Bridge

Queen
Elizabeth
Bridge

Belfast

Lagan
Weir

Clarendon
Dock

M2/M3
Motorway
Bridge

Moore's
Bridge

Hogg's
Weir

Tullynacross

Sprucefield

262

MAPS

National Cycle Network Route Map Range:

Map NN9B Belfast to Ballyshannon – Panels 1 & 2

(ISBN 1-901389-21-9) available from the National Cycle Network Information Service of Sustrans.

The starting point for this tour is the Union Locks, a flight of four locks which raised the water of the Lagan Navigation the final 7.9m (26 feet) in a horizontal distance of less than 100m to its summit level of 34m (112 feet). To access the towpath alongside these locks from Sprucefield roundabout turn down the Hillsborough Road in the direction of Lisburn. At the first set of traffic lights immediately past the underpass turn left on to Blaris Road and take the first turn right which will lead you to the towpath entrance.

This was an important point along the navigation. It was just below the Union Locks that the first section of the canal, designed by Thomas Omer came to a halt. Omer had largely kept to the course of the river all the way from Stranmillis to Sprucefield, cutting channels and installing weirs and locks where there were significant bends in the river's course. From Sprucefield on, the canal was subject to the design of Richard Owen who determined that the channel for the canal should be independent from the river, having regard to the problems Omer's section had encountered with flooding in winter months. You will be able to observe where the canal continued beyond the Union Locks across what is now the Blaris Road and westwards following the route now taken by the motorway. You will also be able to see the river branching off to the north west. The bridge carrying the Blaris Road, which was known as the Warren Gate

Bridge, was removed when the motorway was being built.

The well-surfaced towpath initially runs over the course of the disused canal to reach the left-hand side of the navigation. The Union Locks were completed in 1796 three years after the navigation had reached Lough Neagh. They are presently in a dilapidated state. There used to be a basin between two of the locks in order to provide temporary stops for boats passing through the flight. The first of several millennium mileposts that are dotted along the route of this tour can be seen beside the disused locks. This indicates a distance of 13.7km (8.5 miles) to Moira and 29.4km (18.25 miles) to Oxford Island, adjacent to Lough Neagh. These attractively designed mileposts were erected by Sustrans to mark the millennium and the launch of the National Cycle Network. The towpath alongside the Lagan Navigation is part of Route 9 of that network.

A sharp bend in the canal leads to Moore's Bridge, a three-arched bridge of dressed sandstone with blackstone parapets. It was built between 1824 and 1825 and carries the Hillsborough Road from Lisburn. Just past the bridge the River Ravernet joins the navigation at the opposite bank. A little further downstream the sound of gently cascading water indicates your arrival at Hogg's Weir which is followed by Becky Hogg's Lock, the 13th Lock along the navigation from Stranmillis. Unlike the 13th locks on the Grand and Royal Canals there are no ghostly associations with this lock, despite its unlucky number.

An unsightly pipe fairly low across both the waterway and the towpath heralds your arrival in the city of Lisburn. This is quickly followed by Union Bridge, built in 1880, replacing an earlier one which would have been on the main road to Dublin before Moore's Bridge was opened. The bridge was widened in 1987 and it does not accommodate the towpath. The cycle track takes you through the busy junction over the entrance to the bridge towards Queen's Bridge at the Island Civic Centre under which you can pass. The left bank of the canal passes through the Diana, Princess of Wales Memorial Garden which finishes at a footbridge called the Millennium Bridge. You will need to cross this bridge as the towpath continues from the other side of the island.

Lisburn is a vibrant city with lots to see and explore. Its strategic location alongside the River Lagan made it an important focal point for trade and it occupies a notable position in the history of the Lagan Navigation. It was the destination for the *Lord Hertford* which was the first boat to use the navigation in 1763 and to complete the historical circle, it was also the destination for the last barge to have used it drawing a load of coal to the Island Spinning Mill in 1954. In its heyday as a port the city had as many as nine quays. One of these belonged to the Lagan Navigation Company while the others were privately operated. Shipments of coal were landed on these quays for use in the flourishing linen industry and several of the linen merchants operated their own boats.

To the left, past Union Bridge, is Castle Gardens, the site of what was Lisburn Castle once owned by Lord Conway. This was a seventeenth-century fortified manor house which dated back to the 1620s, with extensive renovations dating from the 1660s and 1670s repairing damage suffered by the castle during the 1641 rising. Unfortunately the house was burned down in a great fire which engulfed Lisburn in 1707 and was not rebuilt. The castle had extensive gardens which contained several historic monuments including a red sandstone gateway with a 1677 datestone and a drinking fountain and memorial both commemorating Lisburn's landlord, Sir Richard Wallace (1818-1890). The

Gardens are currently being restored and will become a feature of Lisburn's planned Riverfront.

Lisburn celebrates its association with the Navigation and the linen industry in various ways. Located in the Market Square is the Irish Linen Centre Museum which has free admission and provides an absorbing exhibition relating to the history of Ireland's world-famous linen industry from the past to the present day. While the nearby townland of Lambeg lays claim to origins of the linen industry in Ulster it was a Huguenot refugee, Louis Cromellin, who is credited with putting it on a true commercial footing in Lisburn in the 1780s. Manufacture of fine linen developed all along the banks of the Lagan and the area became the most important linen bleaching centre in Ireland. The river played an important part in this development, providing water power before steam power took over. Even then the river still played an important role in providing the means by which coal for the mill steam engines could be transported to the factories. By 1800 80 per cent of Irish linen was made in Ulster and to this day the province still has a vibrant linen industry whose story is told in an entertaining way at the museum. There is also a pleasant coffee shop on the premises.

The Lagan Valley Arts and Civic Centre is located right on the waterway, occupying an island formed between the canal and the river which was previously known as Vitriol Island. This relates back to the manufacture of the chemical vitriol in a factory built on the island shortly after the construction of the navigation. In 1840 the factory changed to the manufacture of linen and thread, becoming the Island Mill Spinning Company which operated until 1983. In more recent years the island has been rejuvenated with the building of a modern arts and civic centre, a multipurpose venue for business and the arts which includes a theatre and a café/restaurant. Dotted around the island are a series of art works that were commissioned as part of Lisburn City Council's public art programmes and it is well worth taking the time to explore these.

On the far side of the island the 12th lock has been restored and the quayside leads to the towpath which will take you away from Lisburn. The entrance to the path has been marked by a sculpture entitled 'Concentric Twist' by d3 Art and Design (Ngaire Jackson, Claire Lawson and Gerry Woodcock). The sculpture represents the sport of cycling and was funded by Sustrans.

As you progress through the suburbs of Lisburn there is an abiding sense of its industrial past as the river and the canal pursue different courses. The path continues under a footbridge past a weir that marks the start of the cut leading past the extensive premises of Campbell Barbour Threads. The founder of this factory was John Barbour, a native of Paisley in Scotland, who was the pioneer of the linen thread industry in Northern Ireland. Unfortunately, the buildings closest to the canal section now appear disused and in a generally rundown state. The remnants of the 11th Lock, which was known as Scott's Lock, lie beside the factory. Hilden Bridge near the factory carries the road that leads to Hilden village located to the left of the canal. This bridge is followed by the 10th Lock, known as Hilden Lock, just below where there is a distinct improvement in the surrounding scenery. The canal embarks on a sustained curve here known as 'Hunter's Corner', after the eighteenth-century owner of a nearby bleachworks.

Lambeg Bridge and Lambeg Lock (9th) follow in quick succession with Lambeg Church and graveyard prominently sited on a hill to the left. The church dates back to the middle of the nineteenth century but a medieval church and Franciscan Friary were established here earlier, around 1500. It is said that this parish gave birth to the linen industry and in the graveyard can be seen the graves of some of the prominent linen families, such as the Barbours and the Wolfendens.

Not far from Lambeg Bridge is Ballyskeagh Bridge, a striking red sandstone, double-arched bridge, otherwise known as 'High Bridge'. It was built by Thomas Omer in 1760, and the last man to be executed for stealing sheep in Northern Ireland was hanged from its parapets. A footbridge running parallel to the road bridge was added in later years. Just beyond the bridge is the 8th lock and what looks like a turning basin or a lay-by where the canal widens out.

Continuing along a lengthy stretch of independent channel there are the remnants of a number of accommodation bridges and the ruins of canalside buildings before the towpath passes under the motorway by a subway. The canal bed has dried out at this point. Just beyond the subway are the ruins of McQuiston's Lock (7th) after which the canal channel rejoins the river and the waterway embarks on a sustained curve to the right which finishes at a red footbridge where there is another millennium milepost to remind you of your progress. This was the start of another short cut away from the river. Crossing the footbridge leads to Drum Bridge that carries the Upper Malone Road. The cycle path crosses to the opposite bank under the canal arch of the bridge where the canal cut would have once flowed. In the days of the Navigation this was a point where the towpath changed sides. The horses would have to be unhitched and led across the bridge before being rehitched to continue their journey. Just past Drum Bridge is the 6th lock which was known to boatmen as 'The Drum'.

After the 6th Lock another canal cut starts along a section

where the river took a very winding course. Along this cut is Ballydrain Lock (5th) which has the reputation for being haunted. Boatmen reported apparitions along this stretch and would never moor their boats nearby. On the left are the grounds of Malone Golf Course whose clubhouse was previously known as Ballydrain House, dating back to the nineteenth century. There is a rather ramshackled accommodation bridge spanning the canal leading to the sizeable island formed between the river and the canal. The canal itself is in pretty poor condition, with sizeable trees and bushes growing in the centre of the canal bed.

This is a tranquil stretch of the towpath, quite rural in character, with numerous fine trees and, in summer, a rich array of wild flowers. It embraces the village and townland of Edenderry which was a key centre of the linen industry when water provided the power. There is a substantial footbridge leading to a nature reserve on the right-hand bank. The 4th Lock is located along this cut and is known as 'Rosie's Lock' after Rosie Ward who flourished as a lock-keeper here around 1834.

The path winds its way through an attractive wooded area with steep banks on the fringes of Barnett Demesne which lies to the left and extends for about 1.2km along the Navigation to Shaw's Bridge. Barnett Demesne and its principal residence, Malone House, were presented to the citizens of Belfast by William Barnett. Malone House was originally a seventeenth-century fort overlooking Shaw's Bridge and was built by Sir Moses Hill. Known then as Castle Carn or Freestone Castle, it was demolished in 1709 and it is believed that some of the stones from the building were used in the construction of Shaw's Bridge. The present house was erected in the nineteenth century but was almost destroyed by terrorists in 1976. It has since been sensitively restored and has tearooms open to the public.

Just before Shaw's Bridge the Minnowburn River, or Purdysburn River as it is sometimes called, flows in from the right hand side having descended from the hills of County Down. The five-arched Shaw's Bridge takes its name from an earlier oak bridge that was erected here in 1655 by a Captain Shaw to transport the guns of Cromwell's army across. This wooden bridge was replaced by a stone bridge in 1698 but this did not last long and was swept away by floods in 1709 to be replaced by the present structure. Shaw's Bridge is now only for pedestrian use and a single spanned concrete bridge to accommodate modern traffic needs was built alongside in 1976. This is another location where the towpath switched sides. However, the cycle route for this tour continues on the same side, entering Clement Wilson Park under the modern concrete bridge.

About 1.5km to the south east of Shaw's Bridge is the Giant's Ring which is worthy of a temporary detour from the towpath tour. It is easy to find by crossing the bridge and following the brown signs. The Ring is a huge mound of earth reaching up to 3.7m (12 feet) in height, 24.4m (80 feet) wide and enclosing a circular area 183m (600 feet) across. Classified as a 'henge' or ceremonial site, it is the largest ritual enclosure anywhere in Ireland. In the centre of the enclosure is a dolmen with a large sloping black basalt cap-stone supported by five uprights. When excavated the chamber formed by the uprights was found to contain cremated bone fragments that have been tentatively dated to late neolithic times (*c.* 3000 BC). Despite its prominence there is no documentary history relating to the site or the area and its past remains shrouded in mystery.

On the left as you pass through Clement Wilson Park are the

remains of a *rath* or 'fort' which was a defended homestead of the early Christian period. It consists of a low, circular platform about 30.5m (100 feet) in diameter and is now planted with trees.

There is another artificial cut for the canal alongside Clement Wilson Park and just past the park's exit you arrive at Newforge Lock, otherwise known as McLeave's Lock (3rd). The towpath crosses the river at the Red Bridge and you enter a delightful stretch of the Navigation where the river broadens out and is bounded on the left by Lagan Meadows Park and on the right by the overhanging trees of Belvoir Park Forest, formerly the home of another local landowner, Lord Deramore. During the Second World War Belvoir Park was used as an Admiralty ammunition dump and the canal boats were used to transport the ammunition to this location from Belfast docks.

On the towpath, at the entrance of Lagan Meadows Park, is an iron post indicating that in 1918 this was the parliamentary and municipal boundary for the Belfast Cromac Division. This is also the start of another canal cut forming a sizeable island of eighteen and a half acres between the river and the canal called Moreland's Meadow. Since 1999 a voluntary group has been actively improving this parkland on which cattle continue to graze. A short cycle around this park amidst impressive cedar trees is a pleasant diversion, particularly during the summer months, and will bring you to a second exit at the site of the 2nd Lock, known as Mickey Taylor's Lock.

There is a noticeable increase in activity along the towpath as you approach Stranmillis and the location of the 1st lock on the Navigation. This was known as Molly Ward's Lock after Molly and William Ward who were lock-keepers as well as inn-keepers here for many years. Sadly both the lock and the tavern are long since gone, with the Belfast Boat Club and car park now occupying the site.

From this point on the river broadens significantly. After a temporary diversion on to the road past the RBAI and Stranmillis Boat Clubs you can resume your journey on a dedicated cycle path along the Stranmillis Embankment towards Belfast Waterfront and Clarendon Dock, the final destination for this tour. Along the route you will encounter a number of impressive bridges with royal associations which come in quick succession as you approach the city centre. These include the modern, four-arched King's Bridge carrying the Ormeau Road, followed by the wide three-arched Albert Bridge built in 1886 to replace the Halfpenny Bridge which was a private toll bridge. Next is the five-arched decorative Queen's Bridge, which stands at the head of Belfast Harbour and at one stage marked the official end of the Lagan Navigation. It was named after the ruling monarch of the time, Queen Victoria. About 50m beyond is the Queen Elizabeth II Bridge, opened by her in July 1966. This is followed by Lagan Weir, built in 1994 to control the tidal impact on the river, and then the M2/M3 Motorway Bridge.

As you cycle along the Belfast Waterfront you cannot ignore its maritime heritage. The massive cranes of Harland and Wolff shipyard, nicknamed Samson and Goliath, dominate the skyline to the east and the Clarendon Dock area to the north has been sensitively refurbished. Despite its tragic end the city of Belfast is very proud of its association with the ill-fated *RMS Titanic*, built in the shipyards of Harland and Wolff in the early years of the twentieth century. The Belfast City Council has designed a *Titanic* Trail that brings visitors to all the important locations associated with the *Titanic* and its chief designer, Thomas

Andrews. Owned by the White Star Line, the *Titanic* was the largest ship of its time, measuring over 274m (900 feet) in length and weighing 46,000 tonnes. On 14 April 1912, four days into its maiden voyage from Southampton to New York City, it collided with an iceberg near Newfoundland and sank with the loss of over 1,500 lives.

Clarendon Dock was the first piece of major infrastructure completed by the Ballast Board, the forerunners of today's Belfast Harbour Commissioners, who occupy the majestic building you see as you approach the docks. Dry Dock No. 1 was built between 1796 and 1800 by William Richie, the pioneer of shipbuilding in Belfast, and is the oldest dry dock in Ireland. It was used commercially until the 1960s. In 1902 the Harbour Commissioners decided to build a new dry dock which they completed in 1911 and it was the largest in the world at that time. The first ship to use it was the *Olympic* which was the sister ship of the *Titanic*.

Near the docks is an interesting church with maritime connections which is worth a visit. Sinclair's Seaman's Presbyterian Church was built in 1857/8 to facilitate visiting seamen. The interior has a number of features with seafaring associations. The pulpit is in the shape of the bow of a ship and the organ has a set of port and starboard lights. There is a clock shaped like a ship's wheel and the collection boxes all take the form of lifeboats.

Belfast is a cycling friendly city and you can if you wish extend your tour northwards along Belfast Lough as far as Whiteabbey using a shared use path which is part of Route 9 of the National Cycle Network, a distance of about 10km. This route initially takes you through the dockland area of Belfast port but then opens out and offers magnificent views of the Belfast hills and across Belfast Lough.

Tour 2
Sprucefield to Ellis' Gut, Lough Neagh
(35 Kilometres)

While the Dungannon motorway now occupies a significant portion of what was formerly the summit of the Lagan Navigation, the tracking of that section by road is not altogether unpleasant. Relatively quiet roads through rolling pastureland take you to Moira where you can return to the tranquillity of the waterway. The serenity of the Broad Water and the more rugged final stages of the approach to Lough Neagh provide variety and interest.

How to get there
Sprucefield is on the outskirts of the city of Lisburn and is approximately 145km from Dublin and 16km from Belfast. It can be reached from Dublin via the M1/N1 road network to Newry and A1 to the Sprucefield roundabout. Then take the turn in the direction of Lisburn. From Belfast use the M1 to the Sprucefield roundabout and once again take the turn in the direction of Lisburn.

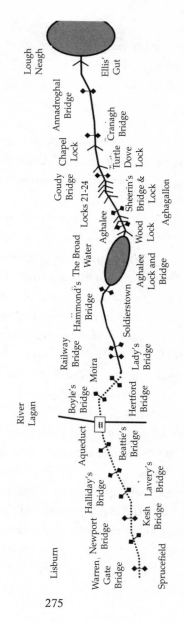

Tour 2 - Lagan Navigation
Sprucefield to Ellis' Gut, Lough Neagh

Key

Bridge

Lock

Lisburn

River
Lagan

Lough
Neagh

Ellis'
Gut

Annadroghal
Bridge

Cranagh
Bridge

Chapel
Lock

Turtle
Dove
Lock

Goudy
Bridge

Locks 21-24

Sheerin's
Bridge &
Lock

Aghalee

Wood
Lock

Aghagallon

The Broad
Water

Hammond's
Bridge

Aghalee
Lock and
Bridge

Railway
Bridge

Moira

Lady's
Bridge

Soldierstown

Boyle's
Bridge

Aqueduct

Hertford
Bridge

Beattie's
Bridge

Halliday's
Bridge

Newport
Bridge

Warren
Gate
Bridge

Kesh
Bridge

Lavery's
Bridge

Sprucefield

275

MAPS

National Cycle Network Route Map Range:

Map *NN9B* Belfast to Ballyshannon – Panel 2 (ISBN 1-901389-21-9) available from the National Cycle Network Information Service of Sustrans.

This tour starts from the same point as Tour 1 but instead of accessing the path to the Union Locks, continue on the Blaris Road passing by the new and old cemeteries and eventually reaching a junction opposite the Maze Prison. The Dungannon motorway peels off in a westerly direction. Turn right and after 200m take the first left turn on to Bog Road which takes you down the left side of the prison. You will get glimpses of the River Lagan which runs broadly parallel to the road and you can note the distance between the river and the independent channel of the canal which now forms the motorway. At the end of Bog Road turn left towards the Down Royal Course. At the race-track are signposts indicating how Route 9 of the National Cycle Network passes across the course. Ignore these signs and instead follow the road which turns sharply in the direction of the motorway. This section of the tour does not follow the Route 9 recommended path in order to keep close to the motorway and to cross it several times so you will get the chance to see as much of the original canal route as possible.

As you cross the motorway for the first time you have a fine view of the original canal route as it cut its way through the lower lying plains of this undulating landscape. At the end of Trench Road turn right passing Hillsborough Elim Pentecostal Church. Having crossed the motorway again go through Meadowbrook

Village and remain on this road which runs broadly parallel to the motorway until you come to a junction that will link you up once again with Route 9. Here you turn left down Hillsborough Road in the direction of Moira past a modern Baptist Church. The church steeple in Moira is prominent in the distance and provides a beacon for your journey towards the town. As you approach Moira you cross the motorway for the penultimate time leading to an extremely busy junction which has to be crossed towards Station Road. After this crossing Route 9 turns left down Drombane Road. Instead, make your way once again towards the motorway to link up again with the canal at Lady's Bridge near Soldierstown, where you can resume your towpath experience.

While there were no locks along the summit level there were several humpbacked bridges along the route that succumbed to the construction of the motorway. The last of these was Hertford Bridge which was located close to the site of the present Moira roundabout. There was also a railway bridge at Newport which fell to the wrecker's ball. Another imposing structure along the summit stretch was an impressive sandstone aqueduct measuring 91.4m (300 feet) in length which carried the canal across the River Lagan not far from Moira. This aqueduct was built between 1782 and 1785 by Richard Owen at a cost of £3,000, funded entirely by Lord Donegall. The loss of these pieces of our heritage is regrettable and the decisionmakers of the 1960s did not appreciate the damage they were doing nor did they have the foresight to see the benefits of retaining a waterway in its complete state for a variety of users.

Lady's Bridge is named after Lady Moira whose family left the area in 1763. She is said to haunt the environs of the canal at midnight dressed in white and carrying a lamp. Just past Lady's

Bridge is the only surviving railway bridge after which you emerge into an exposed area with a good quality towpath. The channel along this stretch is weed filled, even during winter months. After 1km the canal embarks on a gentle but sustained curve to the right leading to the humpbacked Hammond's Bridge, also known as Soldierstown Bridge, which you can pass under. Richard Owen, the engineer who was responsible for the design of the canal from Sprucefield to Lough Neagh, is buried in nearby Soldierstown Village.

Just beyond Hammond's Bridge the canal widens significantly in an area known as the Broad Water, also known locally as Friar's Glen. During the winter months the water is clear and the location is good for fishing. Over the summer, however, broad sections become covered with duckweed, particularly close to where it narrows. This area is serene and is home to a huge variety of wildlife from the ubiquitous swans, herons and moorhens to temporary visitors such as tufted squabs, a large colony of which winter on its shores. Looking across the water you will have a good view of Slieve Croob where the River Lagan rises.

The Broad Water continues for well over 1km before the waterway narrows once again at the site of the bank ranger's house which has been modernised. Take care not to trespass to the front of this house as the cycle path continues to its rear through a section that is bordered on both sides by high bushes forming a pretty tunnel leading to the village of Aghalee. At Aghalee the canal turns gently to the left and you have to leave the canal bank for a while just short of Aghalee Lock (18th) and Bridge. This is the first of ten large falling locks through which the canal descends 21.3m (70 feet) to Lough Neagh. When the canal was abandoned the descending locks were all modified with the insertion of a long concrete slope running from one end of the lock to the other with a narrow channel in the centre. This modification was necessary to maintain water levels as the locks deteriorated.

While it looks as if the towpath is not passable beyond the bridge there is in fact a short canalside walk on the right-hand side a little further on which can be accessed through the housing estate built beside the canal. This walk leads to the second of the two locks at Aghalee known as Wood Lock or Dan Horner's Lock (19th). The extended humpbacked bridge beside this lock has a small archway through which the towpath used to pass. However, it is now overgrown and the path on the opposite side is not passable.

To continue to track the canal it is necessary to once again resort to the roads. Crossing the bridge at Aghalee follow the B12 in the direction of Aghagallon. The canal runs in a parallel line a short distance to your right. Unfortunately, along the next 1km, there are several locks which you will not be able to inspect unless you lock your bike and trek backwards through overgrown terrain from Goudy Bridge. These locks are Sheerin's Lock (20th), Bradley's Lock (21st), Cairn Lock (22nd) and Prospect Lock (23rd). About 1km out of Aghalee is a turn left down Goudy Bridge Road that will bring you down to the bridge itself. On closer inspection you will see that the bridge also has a second arch within its structure to accommodate the towpath. If you look back over the parapets you will see the nearby ruins of the 24th Lock known as Goudy Lock. The towpath from Goudy Bridge has been concreted over and leads after several hundred metres to a lock that once bore the delightful name of Turtle Dove Lock (25th). It was also known as Fegan's Lock after the family of lock-keepers that looked after it. Unfortunately, the lock-house is now in private hands and access to both the lock and onwards is no longer possible. This is unfortunate because great work has been undertaken in clearing the towpath and laying a black-top surface 200m south west of this point and linkage back to Aghalee would be desirable.

Returning to the B12, proceed through the village of Aghagallon and turn right where it is signposted for Lough Neagh. A short way down this road contact with the canal is resumed at Cranagh Bridge where you will see the work undertaken in installing a black-top surface on the towpath back in the direction of Goudy Bridge and also onwards from Cranagh Bridge. Backtracking along this path will bring you to Chapel Lock (26th). The 1km tree-lined section between Cranagh Bridge and Annadroghal Bridge has recently been cleared and a high-quality tarred surface installed. It now forms part of Route 94 of the National Cycle Network. This area is extremely quiet and is a haven for varied wildlife. Before the resurfacing an environmental impact study had to be conducted as it was feared that clearance of the path would disturb the sets of badgers who live in this area. Fortunately it has not done so. The fields to the right are a popular grazing ground in winter months for Whooper Swans but, unlike the shores of Lough Erne, farmers in this area do not receive payment for taking farm animals off the land early to facilitate the swans. A lot of mature trees lie between the towpath and the canal, a strong indication of how long it has been since horses pulled boats along this waterway.

The towpath from Annadroghal Bridge has merged with the adjacent fields. There are proposals to continue the black-top surface all the way to the junction with Lough Neagh but at present there is a dispute in relation to access. It is possible to follow the last 1km of the canal along the bank but there is a barbed wire fence midway to surmount. A short way along this path you will catch the first glimpses of the shores of Lough Neagh. One would imagine the canal would cut straight across to the lake at the earliest point of potential contact yet it does not. Instead it courses along the lakeshore for about 0.5km to Ellis' Gut, apparently because the lake is too shallow at the earlier point. There are ruins of one house on the far side of the canal along this stretch and two other dwellings have been extended and modernised. In two of these houses lived the men who operated the tug boats that brought the lighters across the lake. The third house is the former lock-keeper's house adjacent to the 27th Lock, sometimes known as the Lake Lock. Across from the lock-house is a small island not far from the lake shore. This is Tanpudding Island, said to take its name from the lighters, the flat-bottomed boats or barges used on the Navigation.

Lough Neagh lies 15.2m (50 feet) above sea level and is the largest freshwater body of water in the British Isles and the fifth largest in Western Europe. Broadly rectangular in shape, it occupies an area of over 300 square kilometres and has a shoreline extending to over 140km. Its name is an anglicised version of the Irish, *Loch nEochadh*, the 'Lake of the God Eochaidh'. Eochaidh means horseman and was the name of the legendary king of Munster. There are many stories told in Celtic folklore surrounding the origins of Lough Neagh. Among these is that the lake was formed from the urine of a great horse on which Eochaidh had abducted his father's wife. Another tale with connections to Eochaidh is that in the first century AD he drowned in a well at this location, and that those waters suddenly burst forth and formed the lake. Perhaps the best-known legend is linked to the great Irish mythological warrior Finn McCool. He is said to have created the lake when he ripped up a great swathe of earth to throw at a Scottish warrior who was making his escape via the Giant's Causeway. His shot landed in the Irish Sea to form the Isle of Man. The scientific explanation is that the lake formed about 40 million years ago from a depression created in the Earth's surface by the collapse of basalt rock in an area that was made fragile during the volcanic era, 20 million years earlier.

The lake gets its water supply from eight significant rivers emptying their flow at various points around its shore, with only one river, the Bann to the north, providing an outlet to the sea. It is relatively shallow with the deepest point measuring only 30m while the average depth is no more than 9m. In the days when inland waterways were at their commercial peak Lough Neagh was the hub of great activity, with five canals connected to its shores. Today it retains importance as the primary water source for one-third of Northern Ireland's population. It also supports the largest eel fishery in Europe and a burgeoning leisure and tourism industry.

For those who wish to explore the lake's shore further the Loughshore Trail is a magnificent 182km cycle route around its shores and forms Routes 94 and 96 of the National Cycle Network. As in the case of tours along the towpaths of our inland waterways, the trail enjoys the benefit of a generally level profile, with the highest point at Gortigal only 100m above sea level. A detailed map is available from Sustrans.

SECTION G

THE BOYNE NAVIGATION

HISTORY OF THE BOYNE NAVIGATION

Flowing through some of Ireland's most historical and mystical lands, the River Boyne has been both a witness and participant in events that shaped the country's destiny. The earliest kings of Ireland reigned on its banks and it was the portal through which Christianity entered Ireland. It remains a continuing link with a past that features myth and legend, as well as the hard facts of history which have repercussions to this day. As it meanders its way to the sea at Drogheda the old and new are celebrated by contrasting monuments, such as the burial chambers of Newgrange and the recently built M1 motorway bridge.

My hopes for tracking the River Boyne exceeded expectations. While a towpath was installed along its full length when the navigation was originally built, it fell into disuse a long time ago. I feared the usual encroachments of unhindered growth, poaching of ground by local farmers and erosion by winter swells would have done away with most of its course. Fortunately this is not the case and the navigation is still trackable on its banks for almost all its course although some parts present a formidable challenge during winter months.

One of the main reasons for the towpath's survival in long stretches is that it was built between the river and the artificial cuts and thereby has been isolated from the possibility of merging with the nearby terrain. In addition, there has been a long history of excursions on the riverbank by walkers and fishermen which has helped to keep the growth at bay. An example of this is the delightful 1859 account by Oscar Wilde's father, William, of his journeys along both the Boyne and its tributary, the River Blackwater, which join at Navan.

There are great similarities between the Boyne and the terrain surrounding the River Barrow, although as a cycling experience the Barrow is the jewel in the crown of Ireland's waterways. It is a shame that the Boyne is not open for navigation from Drogheda to Navan. At present boatowners are being denied an enthralling experience. From my journeys along its banks it would appear to be ripe for restoration. It would be easy to make a start by restoring the towpath for the entire course of the navigation which would encourage more people to enjoy the river's enchanting charm!

Construction of the Boyne Navigation was a protracted affair and its subsequent operation was not helped by the fact that it ended up under the control of not one but two separate administrative bodies overseeing different sections. Work on the navigation was started in 1759 by the Commissioners of Inland Navigation under the supervision of Thomas Omer, whose name is associated with several waterways. Over the following 30 years just over 21km of navigation were completed before the project was taken over by local commissioners following the dissolution of the Commissioners of Inland Navigation. These early works were very unsatisfactory and one has to wonder about the competence of Omer as difficulties seem to have arisen with most of the canals he worked on, particularly those that involved canalised rivers such as the Lagan and Barrow Navigations. He did not last long on the Grand Canal either. The upshot in the case of the Boyne Navigation is that by 1789 most of the early works were in a ruinous state despite the considerable sum of £75,000 having been spent on them. As happened with other canalised rivers the engineers had difficulty in maintaining water flows and levels, with flooding in winter months and insufficient depth during the summer.

In 1790 a new enterprise called the River Boyne Company was incorporated mirroring developments with the Grand Canal. The company was charged with completion of the line to Navan and an extension to Trim. There were also subsequent grandiose proposals to run lines from Trim to Athboy and from Navan to Kells. A further proposal was to link in with the Grand Canal at Edenderry and the Royal Canal at Blanchardstown. One of the conditions placed upon the company was the requirement to complete the extension to Trim within five years otherwise it was to forfeit ownership of the Lower Boyne Navigation. The line to Navan was completed by 1800 and records for that year show that up to twelve boats were regularly using the navigation.

The extension to Trim never materialised and as a result administration of the Boyne Navigation became divided, with the lower part in public hands while the upper part was owned by the Boyne Navigation Company. Dual control was a recipe for disaster but persisted through most of the nineteenth century. In 1894, in an effort to resolve the situation, the River Boyne Company transferred its interests to the Board of Works and a new company, the Boyne Navigation Company, was formed to take over the entire system. The impetus created by these new beginnings resulted in further investment directed at improving the waterway by repairing locks and dredging silted channels.

Even allowing for the administrative drawbacks the Boyne Navigation was never a great success and in common with most of Ireland's man-made waterways it changed hands at various intervals. In 1902 the then Chairman of the Grand Canal Company took a seven-year lease on the waterway and operated under the title of Meath Navigation Company. Between 1905 and 1914 a passenger service operated during the summer months using a pleasure steamer called the *Ros na Rhi*. This ventured from Oldbridge to Navan. By 1913 the Boyne Navigation Company's financial position had deteriorated to such an extent it went into liquidation. In 1915 it was bought over by Messrs John Spicer and Company Limited who operated the Boyne and Blackwater Mills and were also prominent bakers. The purchase price was a fairly nominal amount of £500. They continued to operate two horse-drawn boats for about eight months of the year for a number of years after but eventually ceased this in the mid-1920s. After the withdrawal of the Spicer boats the canal was not maintained and quickly became derelict and unusable. Over subsequent years several stretches of the adjoining land were sold off to local landowners which is one of the reasons why the towpath is no longer complete. In 1969 John Spicer handed the remaining parts of the navigation still in his company's ownership to An Taisce.

THE BOYNE NAVIGATION ROUTE OVERVIEW

Like many of Ireland's more significant rivers Celtic legend has a story to tell about the source of the Boyne. Some similarities are apparent with the River Barrow in that both are said to have erupted from the waters of a sacred and mystical well. In the case of the Boyne the well in question is the Blessed Trinity Well, located at the foot of Carbury Hill in County Kildare. In his book, *Beauties and Antiquities of the Boyne*, William Wilde relates the story of how the female curiosity of Queen Boan, wife of the King of Leinster, Nechtain, resulted in her disfigurement by the erupting waters when she defiantly approached the well despite warnings as to what might happen to her. In an effort to hide her mutilation she fled towards the sea and the waters pursued her.

Setting legend aside the River Boyne does indeed rise at Carbury and initially flows westwards towards Edenderry, County Offaly, which it skirts on its northern side. At this stage it is not a very large river and it flows within a short distance of the Grand Canal as that waterway makes its way past Edenderry on its southern side. Not far from Edenderry the river embarks on a sustained curve northwards forming the border between the counties of Kildare and Offaly. Gathering vigour from the Yellow River which flows into the Boyne at a point where the three counties of Meath, Offaly and Kildare meet, it proceeds in a north-easterly direction forming the border between Kildare and Meath until it arrives just short of the Royal Canal near Longwood. Passing under the Royal Canal by a magnificent aqueduct, it meanders deeper into the heart of County Meath to reach Trim, having been fortified by four tributaries: the River Deel; the Kildare Blackwater; the Stonyford River and the Tremblestown River.

From Trim it continues its north-eastern course arriving at Navan where it is joined by the River Blackwater which has made its way down from Lough Ramor in County Cavan. The enlarged river advances through Slane and passes the riverside sites of the megalithic tombs of Knowth, Newgrange and Dowth. It then collects the waters of its final tributary, the Mattock River, and turns sharply eastwards around the site of the Battle of the Boyne to make its final approach to the port of Drogheda, where it enters the Irish Sea. All told, the river measures about 113km from its source in County Kildare to its junction with the sea.

The Boyne Navigation extended only from Drogheda to Navan, a distance of just over 31km. A significant portion of this distance consisted of lateral canals, mostly along the south bank of the river. There were two limited stretches where the canal was constructed along the northern bank. The first of these was at Carrickdexter between Broadboyne Bridge and Slane, and the second was near Newgrange. In all, twenty locks were built along the navigation. At present, nine main bridges span the river over the course of the navigation and there are several small accommodation bridges spanning the lateral canals in various locations. There is also another bridge and a railway viaduct spanning the Boyne estuary. The fact that there are so few bridges along the navigation and none that would present a significant impediment renders this waterway an eminently suitable candidate for restoration to its former navigable glory.

A towpath existed for the entire length of the navigation when it was an operating waterway. This towpath is now patchy but it is still feasible to track the river on its banks using a combination of the surviving towpath supplemented by fishermen's tracks which have served to maintain some definition along the route of the old towpath.

BOYNE NAVIGATION
NAVAN TO DROGHEDA
(31 Kilometres)

This tour brings you through an area saturated in history and will put you in touch with places and events stretching back over several millennia. The fast-flowing waters of the river and the bountiful sylvan settings provide a sensuous backdrop to a journey that takes you past some of Ireland's most impressive sites of cultural or natural heritage. While this tour has been designed as a single route there is so much of interest to be visited and absorbed that you may prefer to undertake it in smaller sections.

How to get there
Navan, County Meath, is 50km from Dublin. From Dublin take the N3 which will bring you directly to the town skirting past the River Boyne for the last 3km. From the North take the M1/N1 to Drogheda or the N2 to Slane and on to Navan via the N51. There is a long-stay car park to the east of the town from which you can easily access the Boyne Navigation. To avail of this facility take the R153, the first turn right after the railway viaduct. The car park is signposted to the left just after Spicer's Mills and Bakery.

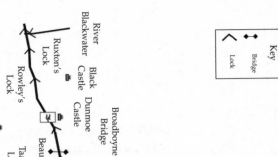

Tour - Boyne Navigation
Navan to Drogheda

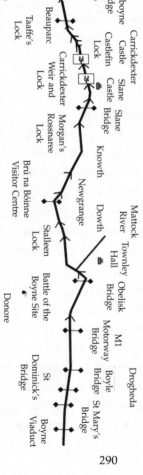

Key

Bridge

Lock

River Blackwater

Navan

Ruxton's Lock

Black Castle

Athlumney Castle

Rowley's Lock

Dunmoe Castle

Broadboyne Bridge

Ardmulchan Castle

Taaffe's Lock

Beauparc

Carrickdexter Castle

Slane Castle

Carrickdexter Weir and Lock

Castlefin Lock

Slane Bridge

Morgan's Lock

Rossnaree Lock

Knowth

Brú na Bóinne Visitor Centre

Newgrange

Dowth

Mattock River

Townley Hall

Obelisk Bridge

Mellifont Abbey

Stalleen Lock

Donore

Battle of the Boyne Site

M1 Motorway Bridge

Boyle Bridge

Drogheda

St Dominick's Bridge

St Mary's Bridge

Boyne Viaduct

MAPS

Ordnance Survey of Ireland Discovery Series:
Map 42 Meath and Westmeath (ISBN 1-901496-06-6)
Map 43 Dublin, Louth and Meath (ISBN 1-901496-82-1)

The long-stay car park near Spicer's Mills is 200m east of the River Boyne's junction with one of its most important tributaries, the River Blackwater. There is access from the car park to an area known as the Ramparts which is the towpath between the Boyne Navigation and the river. A small humpbacked bridge and a derelict lock mark the start of your journey. This is Ruxton's Lock, where boats would lock up to the cut that passed Spicer's Mills, an enterprise that has a long association with the navigation and the last company to operate boats on it. There is a plaque on the bridge noting it was built by Richard Evans, engineer, in 1792. Evans was closely involved with the construction of the Royal Canal and also worked on the Grand Canal. He had a penchant for having his name inscribed on feats of engineering for which he was responsible. A further example of this is the Gratton Aqueduct on the Barrow Line of the Grand Canal and on several bridges along the Royal Canal.

Before leaving Navan it would be remiss not to mention some of the town's history and one of its most famous sons. The Norman, Hugh de Lacy, established the first significant fortifications in the area in the twelfth century. By 1469 it had developed to such an extent that it was granted a charter of incorporation by King Edward IV of England. In more modern times Navan became noted for the manufacture of furniture, and the discovery nearby of the largest lead and zinc mines in Western Europe has ensured that Navan's status as a thriving town endures.

Cycling is often a battle with the elements and one weather feature common in Ireland is wind. In Ireland we have still weather less than five per cent of the time and wind is a regular companion on most cycles. Like sailors, cyclists are always interested in finding how much wind they have to face on their journeys cursing the headwind, welcoming the tailwind and exercising extra care in crosswinds. For devising a meaningful scale on which to measure wind speed, we owe a debt of gratitude to a Navan man, Admiral Sir Francis Beaufort (1774-1857), inventor of the Beaufort Scale, to whom a commemorative plaque is dedicated at St Ultan's School in the town, marking his birthplace. Beaufort enlisted in the Royal Navy at a young age and during his seaborne travels invented a thirteen-point scale to describe wind conditions based on the amount of canvas sail a man of war battleship could hoist with safety. The scale ranged from Force 0, indicating calm conditions, to Hurricane Force 12. These terms are still in use today.

Near the starting point for this tour are the ruins of Athlumney Castle which can be found on high ground almost due south of the car park. It can be reached using the side road off the R153 almost opposite the entrance to the car park. It is obscured from view from the river by the Loreto Convent and is now surrounded by modern housing estates. William Wilde tells of a rather fanciful link between this castle and another building almost opposite on the northern bank of the river, Blackcastle. The two buildings were occupied by sisters who apparently decided upon a plan to prevent their properties from falling into the hands of Cromwell and his men when the latter was travelling through Ireland in the 1650s. Simultaneous fires were to be lit to destroy the properties as soon as the soldiers were spotted. Unfortunately for the sister who occupied Athlumney, her sibling had a wicked plan born out of jealousy which involved her setting fire only to a quantity of dry brush-wood placed on one of the towers of her mansion. While Athlumney was burned to the ground, Blackcastle remained unharmed. A more realistic version of the fate of Athlumney is that it was burned down by its last lord, Sir Launcelot Dowdall, to prevent it being occupied by William of Orange around the time of the Battle of the Boyne in 1690. The graffiti bedecked ruins of Blackcastle, a far more modern structure than Athlumney, can be seen clearly from the towpath. Its demesne is now being redeveloped for housing.

For most of the early part of this tour the towpath lies on a thin finger of land bounded by the river on one side and the canal on the other. It is well preserved and provides an excellent cycling surface. Trees line the route and the south bank of the canal slopes upwards, creating a tranquil corridor for users of this amenity. The sound of water rushing over the first of many weirs encountered along the route disturbs the tranquillity. The smooth waters running up to the weir contrast with the agitated currents that follow. Beyond the weir is an ivy-clad bridge over the canal leading to restored buildings on the south side. While the old towpath runs under the bridge there is also a second arch to accommodate a second path but this is now almost entirely blocked by the growth of many years.

As the river winds away to the left the canal continues in an almost straight line towards Rowley's Lock whose lock-house is still standing but is in a poor state of repair. The small hump-backed bridge at the end of this lock again has a plaque bearing '1792'. The canal and river rejoin shortly after this lock.

Not far along from Rowley's Lock are the remnants of one arch of a bridge which at one time must have crossed the river. In her book, *Ingenious Ireland,* Mary Mulvihill refers to this as Babe's Bridge and describes it as the oldest surviving and unaltered bridge arch in Ireland. She suggests it may date back to 1210 and that its unusual name is derived from the surname of an Anglo-Norman landowner, John le Baube. Perhaps this bridge led to Donoughmore Church and round tower which lie hidden from view on the northern bank of the river not far from here. Given this history it is somewhat surprising that the arch appears to be left in a state of crumbling neglect and there is evidence of further erosion of its stonework.

As the river and canal curl around to the right in parallel courses, the ruins of Ardmulchan Church and graveyard lie straight ahead while on the opposite bank Dunmoe Castle emerges from the cover of a coniferous forest which lines the riverbank. The castle dates back to the fifteenth century and is the former home of the D'Arcy family. Located at the boundary of the Pale it survived attacks by both Cromwell in 1649 and the Williamites in 1690 before succumbing to fire in the late eighteenth century. When William Wilde visited the castle in the 1840s he remarked upon its poor condition and forecast that 'in a few years it will be but a cairn of stone'. Fortunately, it still has the appearance of a castle but it is in a poor state of repair. It can be accessed from the N51 although it is no longer signposted from this road. All that now remains is a high wall between two towers. One of the towers is in reasonable repair but the other is half eaten away. There is a small church and graveyard beside the castle where there is a memorial erected by John D'Arcy in memory of his mother who died in 1881. There is also a curious gravestone immediately beside the church on which is inscribed the following: 'Here lyeth y body of Thomas Casserly who departed this life the 5 day of Aprile in the yeare 1722.' Underneath this inscription is depicted a skull and crossbones – an unusual addition for a tombstone.

Directly opposite Dunmoe Castle is the impressive Ardmulchan Castle, still inhabited by the Galvin family. Unlike the other castles you will encounter along this tour this building is red in colour. It sits proudly on the southern bank separated from the river by the canal. From the towpath you can see a long flight of steps leading up to the castle.

There is little left of Ardmulchan Church which occupies a prominent position on the hillside above the river. A square bell tower and the shell of a church are all that remain. Just below the church are the almost hidden ruins of a lock that was once known as Taaffe's Lock. Along this stretch the canal is overgrown with weeds, although it retains its definition as a viable water course. A sizeable island is created between the canal and the river which has meandered away to the left. This island stretches to the six-arched, stone bridge known either as Broadboyne Bridge or Stackallen Bridge. There is a separate bridge over the canal. The main bridge has the unusual feature of a series of triangular indents along the parapets known as embrasures which were installed to afford pedestrians protection from passing traffic. They now facilitate anglers who may wish to fish from the bridge.

There is a story told of a family who lived beside the river in this vicinity. A stream leading to the river used to pass under a section of their house. Apparently the mother used to bathe the children of the house by dipping them in the stream, which she could access through a trapdoor in the floor of the house. It gives a new meaning to having a house with running water!

Just after Broadboyne Bridge head along the road on the south side for a short distance, passing another lock with no gates remaining, and a restored lock-keeper's cottage. The lock marks the end of the artificial cut and just beyond is a weir and the remains of an old mill known locally as the old cotton mills. Continue down the lane past the mills where you can access the riverbank once again. There is a small stream blocking the path 200m further on but this is easily crossed by means of the well-used stepping stones and supporting wooden rail. After a short journey through mature trees you emerge into a field which can be marshy. Keep to the river's edge and be alert for the thin wires of redundant electrified fencing that may lie invisibly across some sections of the path. You pass the ruins of a small mill building and millrace and then a hill close to the river's edge on which there is a small concrete structure before heading for the fencing that marks the boundary of the Beauparc Estate. There is a small gateway close to the riverbank and it is permissible to pass through the fringes of the estate once you keep to the path that runs immediately beside the river. At times the path is muddy and rugged and you may have to dismount frequently but the effort is worthwhile. Looking across the river the foundations of a former bridge now form small islands. On the north bank you can also see evidence of the considerable work undertaken during the construction of the navigation, with exposed brickwork lining the bank to prevent erosion.

The path takes you across what is effectively the back lawn of Beauparc House. The building is imposing but not pretty from this aspect yet it enjoys an enviable location on an elevated site overlooking a bend in the river. This was the former residence of the Lambart family and is now owned by Lord Henry Mountcharles, the proprietor of Slane Castle, which you will encounter further along. Continuing along the tree-covered path you may find progress slow as the path lies almost at the level of the river and the underground seepage can often render the path quite muddy. There are also a number of fallen trees that are easy enough to pass.

The sound of cascading water welcomes you to Carrickdexter Weir and an area that possesses spectacular scenic beauty. The stretch between this weir and the next in front of Slane Castle must rank as one of the most beautiful stretches of inland water-way in Ireland. The river is enclosed by curtains of mature trees on sloping banks and is best seen on a bright, cold winter's morning when there is not a ripple on the water's surface. The cycling sur-face is perfect, with a carpet of grass providing great comfort. On the north bank are the ivy-clad ruins of Carrickdexter Castle and a short length of canal with the ruins of a lock-house. This is one of the two locations along the navigation where the canal was cut on the northern bank of the river. For the boatmen and their hors-es this meant the tiresome task of switching towpaths, often facil-itated by leading the horse on to the boat and poling across the river. This stretch also marks the junction of the Upper and Lower Boyne Navigations.

There is great temptation to linger at Carrickdexter and its environs and immerse yourself in its captivating beauty. Continuing downstream you will pass an island in the middle of the river channel populated with a number of tall trees where you will often see guillemots perched on the uppermost branches, tak-ing a rest from their seemingly endless fishing forays. As you approach Slane Castle there is a prominent rock escarpment on the right-hand side of the path, known as Maiden Rock or Lover's Leap. There is a fine view of Slane Castle perched on high ground on the northern bank, with its natural amphitheatre which in recent years has played host to some of the world's leading rock stars. The castle is the home of Lord Henry Mountcharles, a descendant of the Conyngham family who acquired the castle in 1703. It was built on the site of an ancient fortress established by the Flemings, at one time lords of Slane. The present structure dates back to 1785 and was designed by James Wyatt and completed by Armagh-born architect, Francis Johnston, one of the most celebrated architects of the late eighteenth and early nineteenth centuries. Johnston is best remembered for designing prominent buildings like the General Post Office on Dublin's O'Connell Street and the Chapel Royal in Dublin Castle. He was also the architect who designed Townley Hall near the site of the Battle of the Boyne, further along here. The castle at Slane was one of the earliest experiments in the revival of Gothic and castellated styles for great country houses that became popular at the end of the eighteenth century. It features a distinctive circular ballroom cum library which was added around 1812, the outside of which can be clearly seen from the towpath. The building was seriously damaged by fire in 1991 and has been painstakingly restored in subsequent years.

Opposite Slane Castle the path deteriorates and can become quite overgrown for a short stretch. A fence with a stile crosses the path just before another disused lock marking the end of a small canal cut. You will just be able to make out the ruins of the lockhouse among bushes nearby. An easy ride right on the water's edge will bring you to the complex river arrangements at Slane. The scene is dominated by the ten-arched Slane Bridge, sometimes referred to as Stone Bridge. Before the bridge is a 183m (600-foot) weir designed to channel water to the mills on the far side of the bridge, with the main channel of the river flowing to the right. There is a also a canal cut starting at the western end of the weir which initially curves back from the river before adopting a parallel course as it passes under the bridge by a separate arch.

Slane is a town saturated with history, that sits proudly on the hills above the Boyne. It is well worth a diversion from the towpath even if it does mean undertaking the steep Mill Hill that leads from Slane Bridge into the centre of the town. A Gothic gate dominates the base of the hill. This was formerly the main entrance to Slane Castle and was built in the late eighteenth century to the design of Francis Johnston. Once you reach the top of the hill you will see one of Slane's most distinctive features, a group of houses placed precisely at the angles of the four corners of the crossroads. These classical style houses date back to the late eighteenth century and at various times have been occupied by notable figures in the local community.

The origins of the town's name are mysterious. One story suggests it is named after Slanius, the youngest of five brothers who ruled the provinces of Ireland at a time when Meath was regarded as a province in itself. C.E.F. Trench, in his booklet entitled *Slane,* refers to Sláine, King of the Fir Bolg, who died and was interred at Slane nearby the Hill of Slane. William Wilde mentions that the early Irish name for the town was *Ferta-Fear-Feig,* 'the graves of the men of Feig'. In Irish Christian history it is best known as the location in which St Patrick lit the first Paschal fire in Ireland in 432 AD.

The Hill of Slane lies on the northern outskirts of the town 1km from the town centre. Apart from its historical importance it offers breathtaking views across the plains of County Meath. On a clear day one can follow the course of the River Boyne across to Drogheda and the Irish Sea, and also view the Dublin and Wicklow Mountains to the south and the Cooley Peninsula to the north.

St Patrick's fire was a brave step at a time when the land was ruled from the nearby Hill of Tara by a High King called Laoghaire who was devoted to a pagan god. The fire could be seen from the king's palace and was regarded as an act of defiance. He despatched a group of men to investigate but St Patrick's powers of persuasion must have been inspiring because the king allowed his subjects to be converted to Christianity while he remained pagan. One of the king's most senior druids, Earc, eventually became the first Bishop of Slane and established a monastery on the hill. The present-day ruins on the hill are of more recent origin and are not connected to Earc. They date back to the early sixteenth century when Sir Christopher Fleming and his wife built a friary for followers of St Francis. The buildings comprise a simple church with a fine bell tower and the remains of a college.

There is a plaque on the northern side of Slane Bridge commemorating the poet, Francis Ledwidge, who was born in Slane in 1887 and was killed at the young age of 30 in the third battle of Ypres in 1917. His family home was a small cottage located just over 1km from the town centre along the N51 to Drogheda. It is now a museum dedicated to the poet and is well worth a visit. Ledwidge was discovered by Lord Dunsany, whose thirteenth-century castle is near the Hill of Tara. He wrote over 200 poems in his short life, mainly about the countryside surrounding his home. His most famous poem is a lament for Thomas McDonagh, one of the heroes of the 1916 Rising. Ledwidge was killed by a bomb that exploded on a road he was working on at

Ypres in Belgium and panels describing his life and featuring extracts from his poetry are on display at the museum. Also in the garden of the cottage is a replica of a memorial that was erected by the city of Ieper, west Flanders at the exact spot where he was killed in Belgium. He is buried in Artillery Woods Cemetery, Boesinghe near Ieper, Belgium.

Returning to the navigation, there is an excellent stretch of towpath leading away from Slane on the south side of the river. Across the river is Slane Mill which at one time was the largest mill in Ireland and was built between 1763 and 1766. Its design resembles more a country house than an industrial building. Initially used as a corn mill, it was later used for the processing of flax and then the manufacture of cotton flour bag cloth. In 1946 it changed to the production of cotton and rayon but ceased business in 1994. It is now occupied by a number of small industries.

The towpath leads to an unusual natural bridge of rock over the canal which locals call Scabby Arch Bridge or as local historian, Mr Trench, describes it, 'Scraggy Arch Bridge'. At this point the canal engineers had to blast their way through solid rock to form the canal channel and the natural arch. It has deteriorated over the years but is still a fascinating spectacle. Locals believe the wreck of a boat, *Lady Boyne,* lies in this general area. The boat caught fire and burned down to the water level before being dragged out of the main channel to the bank where it became buried in mud. It is not visible but locals claim to know the exact location of the wreck.

Further along the towpath is a fine double-chambered lock which is known as Morgan's Lock or Rossnaree Lock. The lock-keeper's cottage stands unusually on the northern bank of the canal and is in reasonable shape, despite having no roof. At the eastern end of the lock is a small humpbacked pedestrian bridge which is barricaded on the far side, but there is a small narrow pedestrian entrance leading to a field. Despite there being no defined towpath after Morgan's Lock it is possible to continue by keeping to the river's edge. Be careful of the wire fence just after Morgan's lock. You have to straddle a couple of barbed wire fences before coming to a delightful area which is extremely peaceful, with the river winding past open fields on the near bank and trees sloping up the bank on the far side.

Quite a challenging section follows, with marshy ground and a couple of small streams to pass. The terrain is quite muddy, particularly in the winter months or after heavy rainfall. There are a couple of weirs straddling the river and divided channels. You emerge in front of the delightfully restored Glen House where you will have to temporarily return to the road. To your left, you see the first glimpse of Newgrange. Remain on the road for about 500m until you come to a car park on the left-hand side with a footbridge leading to the towpath. The path finishes at a petrol station, where you will once again have to return to the road opposite the Boyne Currach Centre. Here a family is trying to revive the art of making currachs that would once have been used for salmon fishing on the river. These small craft, also known as corracles, are an ancient form of horse-skin boat with the hide stretched over a wickerwork frame. There have been reports of them being in use in Ireland as far back as 7,000 years ago for crossing rapid streams and for fishing. The boat contains a single seat and is worked with a paddle.

About 500m further is the entrance to Brú na Bóinne, a designated world heritage site famous for its prehistoric passage tombs. An Interpretive Centre has been opened at the site and there are guided tours operating daily throughout the year. There is also a very pleasant restaurant at the centre. Brú na Bóinne, 'the palace or mansion of the Boyne', is located where the river bends sharply. It is a hugely fascinating place to visit with over 50 monuments and earthworks of which the tombs or passage graves of Newgrange, Knowth and Dowth are the star attractions. It is hard to believe that Newgrange dates back over 5,000 years having been built before the Egyptian pyramids and predating Stonehenge in Wiltshire, England, by almost a millennium. Knowth was built 700 years later around 2,500 BC. Newgrange was excavated between 1962 and 1975 by Professor Michael J. O'Kelly during which he made an astounding discovery revealing the genius of the neolithic people who were responsible for its construction. This was a roof box which rests on the passage roof near the mouth of the tomb and which allows the mid-winter sun to enter the passage. During the winter solstice on 21 December each year the rays of the rising sun penetrate directly into the chamber itself in the form of a narrow beam of light. This phenomenon, which is subject to weather conditions, lasts only up to seventeen minutes. Professor O'Kelly's wife Claire documented the discoveries at Brú na Bóinne in a number of leaflets which are available from the bookshop at the Interpretive Centre.

One of the most fascinating features of Newgrange is that the chamber is constructed in cruciform shape with an elongated shaft. One has to remember that the tomb predates Christianity by several thousand years leading to a lot of speculation as to the significance of the cruciform layout. The guides at the centre advance a number of theories which have been aired over the years, most of which are related to the link between the bones of ancestors and the movements of the sun. In this way the ancestors participated in the celebration of spring, a time of renewal. Perhaps there is a more simple explanation. If one wishes to gaze at the stars or contemplate the heavens the best way to do it is to lie prone on the ground. The extension of your arms outwards provides a relaxed, natural and supportive position and perhaps the neolithic builders, who had a great affinity and respect for the heavens, merely wished to replicate this.

From the bridge that crosses the river beside Brú na Bóinne you will see there is a towpath which runs underneath. However, it is not possible to access the path at this point. Instead you will have to return to the road and proceed eastwards for a short distance where you will find a track off to the left leading to Stalleen Lock and its restored lock-house which you will be able to see from the road. It is very easy to miss this track as it looks like a private entrance but it is documented on the Ordnance Survey map. Before proceeding eastwards it is worthwhile backtracking upstream along the path towards Brú na Bóinne as this is a particularly attractive and scenic part of the navigation. Once again the river is fringed by mature trees of varying species and you will encounter an abundance of wildlife. You can easily appreciate why the ancients chose this location for the resting place of their deceased.

Returning to Stalleen Lock, the next 200km eastwards are awkward and challenging for cyclists as the path is not well defined and is often muddy in places. You will have to frequently dismount to clamber over fallen trees or avoid areas where the bank has subsided. It is not an area that is frequented by too many visitors. However, you will be rewarded for your persistence by visually stunning scenery and tranquil settings. Along the way you will come across another ruined lock and a further 1km on one of the few surviving mileposts along the navigation with the number five engraved on it. The path starts to improve as you approach a small humpbacked bridge that leads to a much-improved track on the north side of the canal frequented by a regular flow of walkers. This track will take you to a road that leads traffic across the river over an iron lattice bridge known as Obelisk Bridge. This is an area which had great significance in the Battle of the Boyne which took place over one single day, 1 July 1690, but which has had enduring impact to the present day.

The battle was fought between William III of England, better known as William of Orange, and the deposed James II. Despite lasting less than a day it was to determine not only the future of Ireland but also the English throne and the balance of power in Europe at the time. By way of an aside there were complex interpersonal relationships between the two men. William was James' nephew and also his son-in-law. His mother was Princess Mary, sister of James and he married his cousin, also called Mary, the eldest daughter of James. Religion played an important part in the conflict also. When James' first wife died he had no male heir and William's wife Mary was next in succession to the throne of England. This would have ensured Protestant succession. However, James remarried and his second wife gave birth to a son in 1687 who now became heir to the throne. Catholic succession seemed assured. This did not go down well with the aristocratic classes in England and William was invited to come to England to lay claim to the throne to ensure Protestant succession. James fled to France and was declared by Parliament to have abdicated by his flight.

Why did the pivotal battle take place in Ireland? James came to Ireland the previous year to lead an army assembled by one of his supporters, Richard Talbot, in the hope of reclaiming his throne. He also received help from French forces who landed at Kinsale in 1690. William responded by bringing a multinational force comprising Dutch, Danish, English and Irish troops. Exchanges had taken place at various locations before the definitive battle on the banks of the Boyne close to Obelisk Bridge. The Jacobite army of 26,000 men camped at Donore located on rising ground a short distance to the south of the river. William's army, which outnumbered their opponents by at least 10,000, camped on the opposite bank and set up headquarters near Mellifont Abbey about 4km from Obelisk Bridge. There is an information panel at a viewing area on the north side of the bridge that details the location of both forces and the course of troop movements during the battle. The area leading away to the north skirting Townley Hall Forest Park is now known as King William's Glen.

The Williamites outmanoeuvred the Jacobites by despatching a force of 10,000 troops to cross upstream at the fords of Rossnaree. The intention was to cut off any Jacobite retreat. James mistakenly believed this was to be the location of the main crossing and moved significant forces to his left wing. However, the main crossing took place at Oldbridge, downstream from Obelisk Bridge when the tidal river was at its lowest point. William himself crossed the river further downstream at Drybridge, which you will reach shortly. Before the day was out the victory was with the Williamites and James had fled to Dublin before returning to France where he died in exile in 1701. Despite his death the Jacobite campaign persisted for several decades until it was finally crushed at the Battle of Culloden Moor in 1746. Its legacy in Ireland is long lived and the Battle of the Boyne still raises passions on both sides of the religious divide, particularly around its anniversary each year.

Before moving downstream you may wish to visit Mellifont Abbey, the first Continental-style monastery built in Ireland before the Norman invasion. Approximately 4km from Obelisk Bridge, it can be reached by taking the road up King William's Glen in the direction of Tullyallen and following the signposted directions. The abbey was founded in 1142 by Maelmhadhog O'Morgair, better known as St Malachy, who persuaded St Bernard of Clairvaux to send a group of his Cistercian monks to help establish a monastery. The importance of the abbey is evidenced by the fact that when the abbey church was consecrated in 1157 the ceremony was attended by no fewer than seventeen bishops in addition to the Archbishop of Armagh, as well as the High King of Ireland and many local chieftains. Its foundation introduced the European monastic life to Ireland and at its height was the mother-house to 22 monasteries which traced their filiations to it. At the time of the suppression of Irish monasteries by Henry VIII in 1539, Mellifont was handed over to a succession of families, eventually becoming the property of the Moore family who held the title Earls of Drogheda. The Moores later disposed of the abbey in the early eighteenth century after which it was left vacant. Today the ruins are in far better condition than when William Wilde reported on them during his visit in 1859. The main parts of the abbey survive as low walls which were unearthed during excavations. From the ruins that remain it appears to have been a fairly extensive and impressive group of buildings. The most prominent surviving structures are an unusual octagonal lavabo where the monks used to wash their hands before eating and a roofed building to the left of the site which was the Chapter House. There is a visitor's centre at the site that is open during the summer months.

Returning to the navigation, continue on the road which runs on the north bank of the canal from Obelisk Bridge before crossing to the south side by a narrow bridge. A little back from the new motorway bridge is another lock, the first on the navigation. There is a plaque on the lock wall commemorating David Jebb, the engineer who supervised construction of this part of the navigation in 1778. A short cycle beyond the impressive motorway bridge is the start of an excellent path leading to the centre of Drogheda and the official end of the navigation. The area is known as Drybridge and it is noted on an information panel beside the path that this was the location where King William crossed with about 3,500 of his mounted troops. This point also marks the boundary between County Meath and County Louth.

St Oliver Plunkett, one of Drogheda's most famous inhabitants, described the town in the seventeenth century as being 'the most noble city of my diocese'. Writing almost 200 years later, William Wilde did not share his view and in turn described it as 'one of the dirtiest, worst sewered and most ill-ventilated towns in Ireland'. A lot has changed since Wilde's time. Drogheda derives its name from an anglicised version of the early Irish *Drochat Átha*, 'the bridge of the ford'. It is an interesting town from an historical perspective and its story has been influenced by the various peoples who settled within its confines over the years, all of whom have left structural remnants of their occupation. The Normans were the first to create an urban development but during their time there were in fact two towns separated by the river. The two towns came together in 1412 forming a strategic Royalist outpost of the Pale. A strongly fortified town with thick protecting walls, portions of which still survive to this day, it has over the years been subjected to various attacks with sometimes tragic results. During the 1641 rising it survived a siege lasting over three months. It was not so fortunate in 1649 when Oliver Cromwell's parliamentary forces breached the walls despite stubborn resistance and savagely slaughtered many soldiers, as well as some of its citizens, including women and children. It was last attacked during the Irish Civil War in 1922 when Free State forces attacked a Republican garrison stationed in the town.

Many interesting buildings stand out among the town's skyline as you approach from the western side and a tour of these is a worthwhile diversion. Probably the best place to start is at Millmount Fort, the martello tower that dominates the southern bank. Built on the site of a Norman motte and bailey, the present tower dates back to 1808 and is part of a complex of buildings that include the town's museum. Near Millmount is Drogheda's Heritage Centre which is housed in a former Church of Ireland church where you can view Cromwell's Mound, from where the parliamentarian forces bombarded the town's walls. Part of the old town walls can be seen in the old church grounds.

Crossing the river, one of the most prominent buildings is the Gothic style Catholic Church of St Peter's. The church houses the national shrine of St Oliver Plunkett. Born at Loughcrew near Oldcastle, County Meath in 1629, he was ordained in 1654 and subsequently became Archbishop of Armagh taking up residence in Drogheda in 1670. At a time when persecution of Catholics was increasing he became one of the victims of the outfall of what is known as the Titus Oates plot. According to this, Charles II, brother of King James, then Duke of York, was going to be overthrown by the Jesuits. Protestants were to be massacred and the French were to invade Ireland. While he knew there was no truth in the story, the king nevertheless gave an order in Ireland that bishops, Jesuits and regular priests should leave the country by 20 November 1678. Oliver Plunkett was arrested in December 1679 and for the next eighteen months was subjected to false charges and sham trials in Ireland and subsequently in London. Despite perjured witnesses and no evidence, he was convicted of high treason and was hanged, drawn and quartered at Tyburn on 1 July 1681. He was canonised on 12 October 1975 and his head and some of his bones are preserved in reliquaries in the church.

There are several other attractions. The imposing St Laurence's Gate is a well-preserved barbican of the thirteenth century. A barbican gate is one which is built forward of the main entrance as an extra fortification. Normally barbicans had holes in the floor for dropping rocks or hot liquids on attackers below. The Magdalen Tower occupies the highest point on the north bank and is the belfry tower of a once extensive Dominican Friary dating back to 1224. There is also St Mary's Abbey, one of the oldest structures in the town which, disappointingly, is poorly cared for. Despite its prominent belfry tower surrounding a Gothic archway it lies down an unattractive laneway surrounded by garages and has been subjected to graffiti.

One structure that cannot be ignored is the Boyne Viaduct Railway Bridge with its fifteen arches and a curved central steel span sitting 30.5m (100 feet) above the water. The present steel girder structure dates back to 1932 replacing an earlier latticed cast-iron bridge designed by Sir John McNeill (1793-1880) and erected in 1855. The original bridge was a milestone in bridge building. It was designed as a lattice of cast-iron girders in order to minimise its weight, given that it had to span a deep gorge and broad estuary and had its foundations in a soft river bed. When finished it was the longest lattice construction of its type in the world.

Below the bridge is the estuary where the River Boyne completes its journey before entering the Irish Sea between Baltray and Mornington. The R150 will take you parallel to the estuary mouth where you will be rewarded by a close-up view of an unusual square tower known as Maiden Tower, which dates back over 500 years, and a small pillar of solid masonry called 'Lady's Finger'. William Wilde tells of one legend associated with this tower, said to have been built by a lady to watch for the return of her fiancé from an overseas adventure. By earlier agreement his return would be marked by a white flag if his trip had been successful and a red one if it had not. On approaching the coast he saw the tower and mistakenly believed that the town had been taken by an invader so he raised the red flag. In despair the lady immediately threw herself from the tower.

Appendix I

USEFUL CONTACTS

WATERWAYS IRELAND
Eliot House, 5-7 Belmore Street, Enniskillen, County Fermanagh, BT 74 6AA, Northern Ireland
Tel.: 0044 28 66323004
E-mail: information@waterwaysireland.org

WATERWAYS IRELAND EASTERN REGIONAL OFFICE
Floor 2, Block C Ashtowngate, Navan Road, Dublin 15
Tel. : 01 8680148
Fax.: 01 8383647

WATERWAYS IRELAND VISITOR CENTRE
Grand Canal Quay, Dublin 2
Tel.: 01 6777510
Please note that while this facility is open all year round during winter months it is closed on Mondays and Tuesdays.
Opening hours are 9.30am to 5.30pm.

INLAND WATERWAYS ASSOCIATION OF IRELAND
Tel.: 1890 924991
E-Mail: waterways@iwai.ie

SUSTRANS (NORTHERN IRELAND)
Mc Avoy House, 17a Ormeau Avenue, Belfast BT2 8HD, Northern Ireland
Tel.: 0044 28 9043 4569

Appendix II

WEBSITE ADDRESSES

www.waterwaysireland.org
The website of Waterways Ireland, a 32-county body established in 1999 with a brief to manage, maintain, develop and restore the inland navigable waterways principally for recreational purposes.

www.iwai.ie
The website of the Inland Waterways Association of Ireland. It is an extensive website with information on all the inland waterways of Ireland. There is also a mailing list to which you can subscribe but this is mainly oriented towards boatowners.

www.royalcanal.org
The website of the Royal Canal Amenity Group, founded originally by Dr Ian Bath and which now has many satellite sections along the route of the canal. The Group's members devote their spare time to restoring the Royal Canal to its former glory.

www.leisureways.ie
A commercial website used to advertise a canal boat hiring facility based at Thomastown, County Westmeath.

www.canalways.ie
A commercial website used to advertise a canal boat hiring facility based at Rathangan, County Kildare.

www.cyclingireland.ie
The official website of Cycling Ireland, the governing body for cycling in Ireland and to which most of the established cycling clubs of Ireland are affiliated. There is information on these clubs, plus details of events being held throughout the country. Cycling Ireland caters for all aspects of the sport including road racing, leisure cycling, track racing, mountain biking and cross-country. The contact address for Cycling Ireland is Kelly Roche House, 619 North Circular Road, Dublin 1

www.irishcycling.com
An extensive website providing information on cycling clubs, events, news and links to other cycling websites. It also has a message board facility.

www.mycyclingclub.com:
This website is for mountain bike enthusiasts and is the site of the Mountain Biking Association of Dublin which meets every Sunday at 11am at the Yellow House, Rathfarnham, Dublin 16 for outings.

www.enigmatixuk.com:
The website of M & M Baldwin, Booksellers and Publishers who specialise in books on inland waterways. They are based at 24 High Street, Cleobury, Kidderminster, England.

www.americancanalsociety.org
This is the website of the American Canal Society which was established in 1972 to promote historic canal research and the preservation and restoration of canals. The site concentrates on American canals but there is interesting and useful information on canals in general. The annual

membership subscription is $20.

www.sustrans.org.uk & www.nationalcyclenetwork.org.uk
These websites are associated with Sustrans (Sustainable Transport) a practical charity whose work involves designing and building routes for cyclists and walkers.

Appendix III

DISTANCE TABLE – GRAND CANAL

From Sea Lock to Main Line	*Kilometres*
Westmoreland Sea Lock, Ringsend	0.0
Mc Mahon Bridge, Ringsend	0.6
Maquay Bridge and 1st Lock, Grand Canal Street	1.2
Mc Kenny Bridge and 2nd Lock, Lr. Mount Street	1.4
Huband Bridge and 3rd Lock, Upr. Mount Street	1.6
Macartney Bridge and 4th Lock, Baggot Street	2.0
Eustace Bridge and 5th Lock, Leeson Street	2.6
Luas Bridge	3.1
Charlemont Bridge and 6th Lock	3.2
La Touche Bridge and 7th Lock, Portobello	3.6
Emmet Bridge, Harold's Cross	4.2
Parnell Bridge	4.6
Camac Bridge, Dolphin's Barn	5.0
Herberton Bridge	5.4
Griffith Bridge, Junction with Main Line,	
Luas Bridge and 1st Lock, Suir Road Bridge	6.0
2nd Lock, Goldenbridge footbridge	6.6
3rd Lock, Blackhorse Bridge, Inchicore	7.6

4th Lock	8.0
5th Lock	8.4
Kylemore Road Bridge	8.6
6th Lock	8.8
7th Lock, Ballyfermot Bridge	9.6
8th Lock	10.4
M50 Bridge	11.2
9th Lock, Clondalkin Bridge	12.2
10th Lock	12.6
11th Lock	13.0
12th Lock, Lucan Road Bridge	16.0
Gollierstown Bridge	17.4
Hazelhatch Bridge	20.6
Aylmer's Bridge	22.4
13th Lock	23.4
Henry Bridge	24.6
Ponsonby Bridge	27.0
14th Lock, Devonshire Bridge	29.4
15th Lock	30.0
Railway Bridge	32.0
Sallins Bridge	33.2
Junction with Naas Line	34.0
Leinster Aqueduct	35.0
16th Lock, Digby Bridge	37.2
17th Lock, Landenstown Bridge	38.2
18th Lock	39.6
Burgh or Cock Bridge	40.8
Bonynge or Healy's Bridge	42.6
Binn's Bridge, Robertstown	44.8
19th Lock, Lowtown and Lowtown Marina	46.2
Junction with New Barrow Line	46.4
Bond Bridge, Allenwood	48.0

Shee or Scow Bridge	49.4
Light Railway Bridge (lifting)	51.0
Hamilton Bridge	53.2
Bord na Móna Bridge, Kilpatrick	54.4
Hartley Bridge, Ticknevin	56.6
20th Lock, Ticknevin	57.4
Blundell Aqueduct, The Tunnel	62.0
Downshire Bridge, Edenderry Line	63.8
Colgan's Bridge	64.2
George's Bridge	64.4
Rathmore Bridge	65.2
Cartland Bridge	66.8
Trimblestown Bridge	68.8
Rhode Bridge	73.2
Toberdaly Bridge	74.2
Light Railway Bridge (lifting)	75.8
Killeen Bridge	78.8
Molesworth Bridge, Daingean	81.4
Bord na Móna Bridge (fixed span)	84.4
Chevinix Bridge, Ballycommon	86.8
Campbell's Bridge, over Kilbeggan Line	87.0
21st Lock, Ballycommon	87.2
22nd Lock, Cappyroe Bridge	88.6
23rd Lock	89.2
24th Lock, Celtic Canal Cruisers	92.2
25th Lock, Cappincur Bridge	92.8
26th Lock	93.6
Bury Bridge, Tullamore Harbour Junction	95.0
Kilbeggan Road Bridge, Tullamore	95.4
27th Lock, Cox's Bridge	95.8
28th Lock	96.2
New Bridge	96.4

Railway Bridge	96.6
Shra Bridge	97.8
29th Lock, Ballycowan Bridge	99.6
Huband Aqueduct	100.0
Charleville Aqueduct	101.0
Corcoran's Bridge, Rahan	103.6
Becan's Bridge, Rahan	104.8
Henesy's Bridge	105.8
30th Lock, Ballincloughin Bridge	106.6
31st Lock, Cornalour Bridge	107.4
Plunkett Bridge	111.0
Light Railway Bridge (swivel)	115.4
Derry Bridge	116.4
Macartney Aqueduct, Silver River	118.6
Armstrong Bridge, Gallen	121.6
Noggus Bridge	122.2
32nd Lock, Glyn Bridge	123.0
Judge's Bridge	124.2
33rd Lock, Belmont Bridge	125.0
L'Estrange Bridge	127.6
34th Lock, Clononey Bridge	128.6
Griffith Bridge, Shannon Harbour	130.0
35th Lock	130.6
36th Lock, junction with Shannon	131.0

DISTANCE TABLE – KILBEGGAN BRANCH

Distance from junction with Main Line
at Ballycommon to: *Kilometres*

Campbell's Bridge	0.0
Brook's Bridge	1.0
Odlum's Bridge	2.2
Tong's Bridge	3.5
Wood of O Bridge	4.0
Whelan's Bridge	6.1
Murphy's Bridge	6.9
Lowertown Bridge	8.2
Grange Bridge	10.1
Skeahanagh Bridge	12.5
Kilbeggan Harbour	13.1

DISTANCE TABLE – BARROW LINE

Distance from junction with Main Line
at Lowtown to: *Kilometres*

Littletown Bridge	1.4
Ballyteigue Bridge	2.8
20th Lock, Ballyteigue	2.4
21st Lock, Ballyteigue	3.6
22nd Lock, Glenaree Bridge	8.4
Rathangan Bridge	12.4
23rd Lock, Spencer Bridge	13.2
Wilson's Bridge	15.4
Umeras Bridge	17.8

24th Lock, Macartney's Bridge	20.8
Shepherd's Brook or High Bridge	22.2
Monasterevin lifting bridge and Barrow Aqueduct	23.0
Junction with Mountmellick Branch	23.2
25th Lock, Moore's Bridge	23.4
Clogheen Bridge, Dublin Road	24.0
Old Bridge	26.4
Fisherstown Bridge	29.2
Courtwood Bridge	31.0
Gratton Aqueduct	32.6
Vicarstown Bridge	34.8
Camac Aqueduct	36.2
Ballymanus Bridge	36.8
Milltown Bridge	41.0
26th Lock, Cardington Bridge	44.4
Lennon's Bridge	44.6
27th Lock, Athy and Augustus Bridge	45.2
28th Lock, junction with River Barrow	45.6

Appendix IV

GRAND CANAL TIMELINE

1751 Commissioners of Inland Navigation established.

1756 Construction of Grand Canal started.

1763 Thomas Omer, engineer, completes three locks and 16km (ten miles) of canal westward from Clondalkin.

1765 Canal completed to River Morrell by Dublin Corporation in order to obtain a water supply.

1772 The Company of Undertakers of the Grand Canal incorporated.

1773 Work started on city sections and foundation stone of 1st Lock laid by Earl Harcourt.

1777 Commencement of water flow from the River Morrell to the City Basin near James' Street.

1779 Canal navigation opened to Sallins.

1780 First passenger boat began service to Sallins.

1784 Passenger boat service extended to Robertstown.

1785 Barrow Line reached Monasterevin.

1789 Branch canal to Naas completed by Kildare Canal Company.

1790 Construction work started on the Circular Line link to River Liffey.

1791 Barrow Line completed to Athy.

1796	Ringsend Docks completed.
1797	Main Line completed as far as Daingean.
1798	Main Line reached Tullamore.
1803	Main Line to the Shannon finished but problems with subsidence.
1804	First trade boat passed through the canal to the Shannon.
1808	Grand Canal Company acquired the Naas Branch.
1810	Naas Branch extended to Corbally.
1824	Ballinasloe Branch started.
1827	Mountmellick Branch started.
1828	Ballinasloe Branch opened to navigation.
1830	Kilbeggan Branch started.
1831	Mountmellick Branch opened to navigation.
1834	Fast passenger ('fly') boat service inaugurated.
1835	Kilbeggan Branch opened to navigation.
1852	Passenger boats taken out of service.
1950	Grand Canal Company merged with Coras Iompair Éireann (CIE).
1960	Trade boats taken out of service by CIE.
1961	Ballinasloe, Mountmellick, Kilbeggan and Naas Branches officially closed to navigation.
1974	James' Street Harbour closed to navigation.
1986	Office of Public Works took over responsibility for Grand Canal system.
1987	Naas Branch re-opened to Naas Harbour.
1996	Responsibility for Grand Canal system transferred to the Department of Arts, Culture and the Gaeltacht, now the Department of Arts, Heritage, Gaeltacht and the Islands.
1999	Waterways Ireland assumes responsibility for all Ireland's inland waterways including the Grand Canal system.

Appendix V

DISTANCE TABLE – BARROW NAVIGATION

Distance from Athy to:	*Kilometres*
Ardreigh Lifting Bridge	1.2
Ardreigh Lock	1.5
Ardreigh Bridge	3.9
Kilmorony Bridge	4.5
Tankardstown Bridge	6.5
Levitstown Lifting Bridge	6.9
Levitstown Lock	7.0
Maganey Bridge	10.2
Maganey Lock	11.6
Bestfield Lock	15.8
Graiguecullen Bridge, Carlow	18.5
Carlow Lock	18.7
Clogrenan Lock	20.2
Milford Bridge	23.4
Milford Lifting Bridge	24.2
Milford Lock	24.3
Rathvinden Lock	28.4
Leighlinbridge	29.4

Rathellin Lock	31.8
Bagenalstown or Lodge Lock	33.9
Royal Oak Bridge	35.0
Fenniscourt Lock	37.4
Slyguff Lock	39.8
Upper Ballyellin Lock	42.3
Goresbridge	43.7
Lower Ballyellin Lock	44.7
Ballytiglea Lock	47.3
Ballytiglea Bridge	48.7
Borris Lock	49.8
Ballingrane Lock	52.3
Clashganna Lock	54.5
Ballykennan Lock (double)	55.6
Graiguenamanagh Bridge	58.1
Upper Tinnahinch or Graiguenamanagh Lock	58.5
Lower Tinnahinch Lock	60.2
Carriglead Lock	61.6
St Mullins Lock	64.7

Appendix VI

Barrow Navigation Timeline

1537   An act of parliament outlaws construction of weirs across the River Barrow to raise water levels for fishing or milling without providing a flash-lock in the weir to allow boats to pass.

1703   Committee of Irish House of Commons appointed to bring in a bill to make the River Barrow navigable.

1709   Report issued in which it was estimated that the River Barrow could be made navigable from Athy to the sea for £3,000.

1715   Local commissioners established to carry out work to make many rivers in Ireland navigable, including the River Barrow.

1751   Commissioners of Inland Navigation established.

1759   Commissioners asked for £2,000 to fund removal of obstructions in the River Barrow from Monasterevin to the sea.

1761   Work commenced at Carriglead and later extended to the stretch between St Mullins and Graiguenamanagh.

1783   Work completed upstream to Clashganna.

1790   Barrow Navigation Company incorporated and took over the completed works.

1800   'Drag line' or towpath completed from St Mullins to Athy. Ten lateral canals and locks finished. Four of the original locks enlarged to accommodate boats of up to 80 tons.

1803   Directors General of Inland Navigation provide grant aid to complete the navigation to a depth of 0.5m (1.5 feet).

1812   Navigation completed to Athy at an estimated cost of over £220,000. Depths in the river were reported as very unsatisfactory over succeeding years.

1834   New lateral canal and lock constructed at Clogrenan.

1871   Dividend of six per cent paid to shareholders.

1894   Grand Canal Company purchased Barrow Navigation Company for £32,500.

1922   Report by Canals and Inland Waterways Commission cited frequent delays caused by defects in the navigation and low water levels in summer.

1935   Compensation of £18,000 paid to Grand Canal Company due to increased silting in the lateral canals and faster currents in winter caused by Upper Barrow Drainage Scheme.

1950   Coras Iompair Éireann (CIE) assumed control of Navigation.

1959   Commercial trade withdrawn by CIE.

1986   The Office of Public Works (OPW) took over responsibility for Navigation.

1996   In common with other waterways the Barrow Navigation was taken over by the Waterways Service of the Department of Arts, Culture and the Gaeltacht, and then became part of Dúchas, The Heritage Service of the Department of Arts, Heritage, Gaeltacht and the Islands.

1999   Waterways Ireland assumed responsibility for all Ireland's inland waterways including the Barrow Navigation.

Appendix VII

Main Line	*Kilometres*
Dublin North Wall, lifting bridges and sea lock. (Start of Spencer Dock)	0.0
Sheriff Street drawbridge	0.3
High level railway bridges	0.9
Railway loop line, lifting bridge, (end of Spencer Dock)	1.1
Newcomen Bridge, North Strand Road and 1st Lock	1.2
Clarke Bridge, Summerhill Parade	1.4
Clonliffe Bridge, Russell Street	1.9
Binns Bridge, Drumcondra Road and 2nd Lock (double)	2.3
3rd Lock (double)	2.6
4th Lock (double)	2.8
Junction with Broadstone Branch (filled in)	3.0
Westmoreland Bridge, Cross Guns and 5th Lock (double)	3.2
6th Lock (double)	3.5
Railway Bridge and 7th Lock, Liffey Junction	4.7
Broome Bridge	5.3
Reilly's Bridge, Ratoath Road and 8th Lock	5.9

9th Lock	6.5
Longford Bridge, Dublin City-County boundary and 10th Lock (double)	7.5
11th Lock (double)	9.0
New Bridge, Dunsink Road	9.4
Ranelagh Bridge	9.6
Blanchardstown bypass bridge	9.7
M50 Motorway Aqueduct	9.8
Blanchardstown bypass bridge	9.9
Talbot Bridge and 12th Lock (double), Blanchardstown	10.0
Granard Bridge, Castleknock Road	10.2
Kirkpatrick Bridge, Carpenterstown	11.8
Kennan or Neville Bridge, Porterstown	12.7
Callaghan or Carhampton Bridge, Clonsilla	13.9
Dublin & Meath Railway Bridge (piers only)	14.7
Pakenham Bridge Barberstown	15.1
Collins Bridge, Coldblow	16.9
Dublin-Kildare county boundary, boat-slip and amenity area	18.0
Cope Bridge	18.9
Ryewater Aqueduct	20.3
Leixlip Spa and Louisa Bridge	20.7
Deey Bridge and 13th Lock	22.3
Carton Demesne Wharf and Pike Bridge	24.2
Mullen Bridges	26.3
Maynooth Harbour, boat-slip and footbridge	26.5
Bond Bridge	27.0
Jackson's Bridge and 14th Lock	28.7
Bailey's Bridge	30.0
Chambers Bridge and 15th Lock, The Maws	30.8
Kilcock Harbour, Shaw's Bridge and 16th Lock (double)	32.4
Allen or Spin Bridge	33.5

Kildare-Meath county boundary	35.3
Ryewater feeder, Mc Loghlin's Bridge and 17th Lock	
(Ferns or Ferrans Lock) (double)	36.2
Meath-Kildare county boundary	39.7
Cloncurry Bridge and Kildare-Meath county boundary	42.1
Enfield Bridge and amenity area	45.2
Enfield Harbour and boat slip	45.3
River Blackwater Aqueduct and Meath-Kildare	
county boundary	48.9
Kilmore Bridge	49.7
Moyvalley Bridges	51.4
Ribbontail Bridge (footbridge)	53.4
Kildare-Meath county boundary	53.8
Harbour and Longwood Road Aqueduct	55.2
River Boyne Aqueduct	55.5
Blackshade Bridge	57.6
Hill of Down or Killyon Bridge	60.1
Ballasport Bridge	61.4
Meath-Westmeath county boundary	63.8
D'Arcy's Bridge	67.3
Riverstown feeder, Thomastown Harbour and Bridge and	
18th Lock	68.6
19th Lock	69.1
20th Lock	69.5
21st Lock	70.0
Riverstown Bridge and 22nd Lock, Killucan	70.4
23rd Lock	70.8
24th Lock	71.3
25th Lock and start of summit level	71.5
Footy's Bridge	71.7
Nead's or Heathstown Bridge	73.7
Lifting accommodation bridge	74.7

Down's Bridge	77.0
Footbridge	77.9
Baltrasna Bridge	80.5
Saunder's Bridge	83.8
Harbour (Piper's Boreen)	84.1
Culverted crossing, site of Dublin Road or Moran's Bridge, Mullingar	84.6
Lough Owel Feeder	85.3
Mullingar Harbour, dry dock, low level footbridge, Scanlan's Bridge and boat slip	85.5
Footbridge (Loreto Convent)	85.7
Railway Bridge	85.9
Footbridge	86.1
The Green Bridge	86.3
New Bridge	88.0
Footbridge, Mullingar Race Course	88.1
Kilpatrick Bridge	89.6
Bellmount Bridge	90.9
Ballinea Harbour and Ballinea Bridges	91.6
Shandonagh Bridge	94.0
Coolnahay Harbour, 26th Lock, end of summit level and Dolan Bridge	96.1
27th Lock	96.5
28th Lock	97.0
Walsh's Bridge	97.5
Kildallan Bridge	99.0
29th Lock	99.1
30th Lock	99.5
31st Lock	99.7
32nd Lock and Kill Bridge	100.4
33rd Lock	101.0
34th Lock and Balroe Bridge	102.2

Balroe Feeder	102.7
35th Lock, Ballynacarrigy Harbour	104.0
Ballynacarrigy Bridge	104.2
36th Lock and accommodation bridge	105.7
Kiddy's Bridge	106.2
37th Lock and accommodation bridge	106.9
38th Lock and Kelly's Bridge	107.2
Ledwith's Bridge	107.7
Blackwater River (passes under canal via 3.7m wide tunnel)	108.6
Bog Bridge	110.0
Westmeath-Longford county boundary	110.4
Quinn's Bridge	111.3
Whitworth Aqueduct over River Inny	111.9
Scally's Bridge	112.0
Culverted road crossing, Abbeyshrule	112.7
Webb's Bridge, Abbeyshrule Harbour and boat-slip	112.8
39th Lock and Draper's Bridge, Tinnelick	114.3
Allard's Bridge	116.0
Guy's Bridge	117.1
Molly Ward's Bridge	117.6
Fowlard's Bridge	118.7
Toome Bridge	120.3
Chaigneau Bridge and Ballybrannigan Harbour (near Ballymahon)	121.9
Culverted road crossing and site of Longford Bridge	123.4
Archie's Bridge and Quay	124.2
40th Lock and accommodation bridge, Mullawornia	125.6
Pake or Tirlicken Bridge and culverted road crossing	126.5
Foygh Harbour and Bridge	127.9
Cloonbreany Bridge	129.5
Culverted road crossing, Island Bridge and Mosstown Harbour, Keenagh	131.4

41st Lock and Coolnahinch Bridge	132.8
Ards Bridge	134.6
42nd Lock, Ards	135.0
Lyneen or Ballinamore Bridge and culverted road crossing	135.9
Lower Lyneen or Crossover Bridge	137.0
Junction with Longford Branch, Cloonsheerin	137.8
43rd Lock and Aghnaskea Bridge, Killashee	139.1
Killashee Harbour, 44th Lock and Savage Bridge	139.8
Ballydrum Bridge	140.7
Culverted road crossing and Begnagh Bridge	142.9
Bord na Móna culverted crossings	144.4
45th Lock, Rinmount	144.8
Richmond Bridge, Richmond Harbour and dry dock, Cloondara	145.5
46th Lock, leading into Camlin River	145.6

Distance Table – Longford Branch

Distance from Cloonsheerin Junction with main line	*Kilometres*
Cloonsheerin Bridge	0.3
Aghantrah Bridge	1.6
Newtown Bridge	3.1
Cloonturk Bridge	4.2
Knockanboy Bridge and culverted road crossing	4.9
Churchlands Bridge and culverted road crossing	5.8
Farranyoogan Bridge	7.1
New terminus south of railway	8.4

Appendix VIII

ROYAL CANAL TIMELINE

1751   Commissioners of Inland Navigation established.

1755   Survey made by Thomas Williams and John Cooley for a canal from Dublin connecting to the north Shannon at Termonbarry.

1756   Commissioners of Inland Navigation opted in favour of the more southerly Grand Canal route.

1789   Reviving the old plans for a canal from Dublin to Termonbarry, the Royal Canal Company is established with funding from Government and private subscription.

1796   Canal, including Ryewater Aqueduct, completed to Kilcock.

1805   Canal reached Thomastown.

1806   Canal completed to Mullingar.

1807   Royal Canal Hotel at Moyvalley opened.

1808   Canal completed to Coolnahay at the western end of the summit level.

1811–   Parliament initiated investigations into the company's affairs as
1813   indebtedness increased to £862,000 and disputes arose as to the best course to the Shannon.

1813   Directors General of Inland Navigation assumed control of the canal following dissolution of the Royal Canal Company and undertook to complete the canal at public expense.

1817   Canal completed at a total cost of £1,421,954.

1818   The New Royal Canal Company incorporated to take over the canal.

1830   The Longford Branch is opened.

1845   Canal is purchased by the Midland Great Western Railway Company with the intention of laying a railway line to the west alongside.

1873   Spencer Dock link to the River Liffey is completed.

1877   Broadstone Harbour filled in as forecourt for the railway terminus.

1927   Further section of Broadstone Branch filled in.

1938   Amalgamation of railway companies resulted in ownership of the canal being transferred to the Great Southern Railway Company.

1944   Great Southern Railway Company became part of Coras Iompair Éireann (CIE) thus giving the canal a new owner.

1939-   Brief revival of trade during the Emergency Years of the
1945   Second World War.

1946   LTC Rolt navigated the canal and recorded his trip in *Green and Silver*.

1951   Last bye-trader, James Leech, of Killucan, ceased to operate.

1955   Douglas Heard's *Hark* was the last officially recorded boat to pass through the canal.

1956   Broadstone Branch filled in completely.

1961   Canal officially closed to navigation.

1974   The 'Save the Royal Canal' campaign began and the Royal Canal Amenity Group was formed.

1986   Office of Public Works took over responsibility for the canal.

1990   74km restored between 12th Lock and Mullingar.

1996   In common with other waterways, the Royal Canal was taken over by the Waterways Service of the Department of

Arts, Culture and the Gaeltacht, and then became part of Dúchas, The Heritage Service of the Department of Arts, Heritage, Gaeltacht and the Islands.

1999   Waterways Ireland assumed responsibility for all Ireland's inland waterways including the Royal Canal.

Appendix IX

DISTANCE TABLE – THE SHANNON-ERNE WATERWAY

From unction with the River Shannon	*Kilometres*
Leitrim Moorings and Bridge (no. 1)	0.3
Killarcan Lock (16)	1.0
Killarcan Bridge (no. 2)	1.7
Tirmactiernan Lock (15)	1.8
Crossycarwill Bridge (no.3)	2.3
Drumduff Bridge (no. 4) and Lock (14)	3.4
Newbrook Road Bridge (no. 5)	3.6
Newbrook Lock (13)	3.8
Lisconor Bridge (no. 6) and Lock (12)	4.4
Kilclare Lower Lock (11)	5.2
Kilclare Bridge (no. 7) and Middle Lock (10)	5.4
Kilclare Upper Lock (9)	5.6
Kilclare Road Bridge (no. 8)	6.0
Scrabbagh Bridge (no. 9)	6.3
Drumaleague Lough	7.1
Letterfine Cutting (entry)	7.3
Letterfine Road Bridge (no. 10)	7.5

Roscarban Bridge (no. 11)	7.9
Letterfine Cutting (exit), Lough Scur	8.5
Lough Scur (end)	10.3
Keshcarrigan moorings and village	10.5
Rossy Footbridge (no. 12)	11.1
Lough Marrave	11.4
Kilmacsherwill Bridge (no. 13)	12.5
Castlefore Lock (8) and Bridge (no. 14)	13.2
Drumany Bridge (no. 15)	13.6
Derrinkip Bridge (no. 16)	14.9
Muckros Lough	15.5
St John's Lough	16.6
Derrymacoffin Bridge (no. 17)	17.5
Ballyduff Road Bridge (no. 18)	18.6
Ballyduff Lock (7)	19.0
Creevy Bridge (no. 19), Ballinamore Golf Club	20.7
Ballinamore Quay	22.7
Ballinamore Lock (6)	22.8
Ballinamore Navigation Road Bridge (no. 20)	23.0
Ardrum Lock (5)	23.9
Aghoo Road Bridge (no. 21)	26.4
Aghoo Lock (4)	26.8
Lisnatullagh Bridge (no. 22)	28.9
Carrickmakeegan Bridge (no. 23)	30.7
Garadice Lough (entry)	31.3
Garadice Lough (exit), Haughton's Shore	35.0
Ballinacur Road Bridge (no. 24)	35.2
Woodford Lough (entry)	35.3
Ballmagauran Lough (entry)	36.4
Derrycassan Lough (entry)	38.0

Coologe Lough (entry)	39.4
Coologe Bridge (no. 25)	40.0
Skelan Lock (3)	40.6
Ballyheady Bridge (no. 26)	44.4
Ballyconnell Moorings	49.0
Ballyconnell Road Bridge (no. 27)	49.2
Ballyconnell Weir	49.5
Ballyconnell Lock (2) and Accommodation Bridge (no. 28)	49.9
Scotchtown Island (west end)	51.0
Scotchtown Island (east end)	51.4
Cloncoohy Cut (entry)	51.7
Cloncoohy Bridge (no. 29)	52.0
Cloncoohy Cut (exit)	52.7
Dernagore Cut (entry)	53.0
Dernagore Cut (exit)	53.4
Corraquill Lock (1) and Bridge (no. 30)	55.1
Senator George Mitchell Bridge (no. 31)	58.1
Aghalane Quay	59.0
Drumard Lough	62.8
Upper Lough Erne	63.4

Appendix X

1780	Work starts on a navigation of the River Erne proposed by Richard Evans.
1792	Work on Evans' canal ceases due to financial problems.
1793	William Chapman starts work on making the Woodford River navigable but runs out of funds the following year.
1842	Passing of Act to promote drainage of lands and improvement of navigation in Ireland supplemented by further Acts between 1845 and 1847 paving the way for the Ballinamore-Ballyconnell Canal.
1846	Drainage works for Ballinamore and Ballyconnell district started on 30 June.
1847	Navigation works commenced as part of famine relief employment.
1858	First official trial on the canal.
1860	Navigation formally passed over to the Navigation Trustees. A separate group established to oversee the drainage works.
1867	Navigation closed.
1873	*Audax* is the last boat to pass through the navigation for 120 years.
1878	Last meeting of Navigation Trustees took place on 26 April in Dublin.

1906	Royal Commission on Canals and Waterways recommend that waterway should be maintained as a drain but also that navigation should be kept in good order.
1936	Leitrim County Council terminated the appointments of the Drainage Trustees.
1969	IWAI call for survey to be conducted on the canal and for its restoration as a navigable waterway.
1971	*Irish Press* hints at restoration as part of North-South co-operation.
1989	ESBI tasked with execution of restoration project.
1990	Restoration work gets underway.
1993	Traffic commenced on newly-restored waterway.
1994	Shannon-Erne Waterway officially opened on 23 May.

Appendix XI

DISTANCE TABLE – NEWRY CANAL

Distance from Dublin Road Bridge to:	Kilometres
Needham Bridge	0.8
New Street Bridge	1.1
2nd Lock	1.7
3rd Lock	2.4
Motorway Bridge	3.3
4th Lock	3.6
5th Lock	4.3
Bridge to Carnbane Industrial Estate	4.5
Accommodation Bridge	5.2
Forsythe's Lock (6th Lock)	5.9
Steenson's Bridge	6.2
7th Lock	7.5
Jerretspass	8.6
8th Lock	9.8
First Railway Crossing	12.1
9th Lock	12.2
Gamble's Bridge	12.3
Second Railway Crossing	13.1

10th Lock	14.6
11th Lock	15.8
Poyntzpass Bridge	15.9
Acton's Visitor Centre	18.1
Scarva Bridge	20.5
Scarva Community Centre and Footbridge	20.7
Cusher River Aqueduct	21.4
Campbell's Lock (12th Lock)	22.0
Terryhoogan Bridge	22.1
Terryhoogan Lock (13th Lock)	22.3
A51 Bridge	24.7
Knock Bridge	28.5
Moneypenny's Lock (14th Lock) and Museum	29.5
Whitecoat Bridge	31.2
Bann Bridge, Portadown	33.1

Appendix XII

NEWRY CANAL TIMELINE

c. 1640   Colonel George Monck proposes digging a navigable trench between Portadown and Newry.

1703   First survey carried out by Francis Neill.

1729   Act of Parliament provides for funding.

1730   Construction of canal commences.

1736   Thomas Stears replaces Richard Castle as canal engineer.

1741   Construction completed.

1742   Canal opened to navigation.

1769   Extended ship canal opened.

1800   Control passed to Directors General of Inland Navigation.

1811   Completion of ten year programme of refurbishment and improvement.

1812   Passenger service commenced.

1829   Newry Navigation Company takes over the reins.

1850   Completion of extension of ship canal and Albert Basin.

c. 1900   Newry Port and Harbour Trust take control.

1937   Last vessel negotiated passage through canal.

1947   Inland canal officially closed to navigation.

1954   Canal becomes a designated watercourse.

1974   Operations of ship canal cease.

1980s- Canal purchased by the local Councils of the districts through
1990s   which it passes.

2000   With the help of Sustrans the towpath is cleared and a
        black-top surface installed for the majority of the route
        from Newry to Portadown.

Appendix XIII

Distance Table – Lagan Navigation

Belfast Boat Club, Stranmillis
(previously Molly Ward's Lock) to: *Kilometres*

Shaw's Bridges	3.6
Lagan Meadows	6.0
Rosie's Lock (4th) Edenderry	6.4
Drum Bridge	8.4
McQuiston's Lock (7th) Mossvale	9.4
Ballyskeagh High Bridge	10.9
Lambeg Bridge	12.1
Hilden	12.8
Island Civic Centre Lisburn and 12th Lock	15.2
Moore's Bridge	16.1
Union Locks, Sprucefield	17.3
Warren Gate Bridge	17.5
Newport Bridge	20.2
Boyle's Bridge	29.2
Lady's Bridge	30.1
Railway Bridge	30.2
Hammond's Bridge	32.0

Appendix XIV

LAGAN NAVIGATION TIMELINE

1637	Early proposals to make Lagan navigable.
1753	Passing of Act for the Lagan Navigation by Irish Parliament.
1756	Construction starts on Belfast to Lisburn section under supervision of Thomas Omer.
1763	Canal completed to Lisburn and the *Lord Hertford* owned by James Gregg was the first boat to pass through the canal.
1765	Having arrived at Sprucefield work ceases due to financial problems and flooding in the river sections.
1779	Establishment of Company of Undertakers of the Lagan Navigation.
1782	Appointment of Richard Owen as engineer to supervise construction of section from Sprucefield to Lough Neagh.
1794	Completion of canal to Lough Neagh at a total cost of £108,231 and formal opening by the Marquess of Donegall.
Early 1800s	Local businessmen buy controlling interest in Lagan Navigation Company and set about improving the navigation.
1843	New Lagan Navigation Company incorporated to take over the canal. Passing of new Lagan Navigation Act.
1888	Lagan Navigation Company takes over administration of Ulster Canal and the Tyrone Navigation (Coalisland Canal).

1954   Lagan Navigation Company dissolved and canal transferred to Ministry of Commerce. Western end, from Lisburn to Lough Neagh, officially abandoned.

1958   Remainder of canal officially abandoned.

1960s   Motorway built over the section from Moira to Lisburn making restoration of the canal impossible.

Appendix XV

DISTANCE TABLE – BOYNE NAVIGATION*

Ruxton's Lock, Navan to:	*Kilometres*
Rowley's Lock	2.6
Taaffe's Lock	5.1
Broadboyne Bridge	6.6
Castlefin Lock	8.6
Carrickdexter Lock and Weir	10.4
Slane Bridge	13.2
Scabby Arch Bridge	15.1
Morgan's Lock	15.5
Brú na Bóinne Interpretive Centre	21.5
Stalleen Lock	23.0
Obelisk Bridge	27.0
M1 Motorway Bridge	28.7
Boyle Bridge	31.2
St Dominick's Bridge	31.4
St Mary's Bridge	31.8
Boyne Viaduct	32.6

*Approximate distances

Appendix XVI

BOYNE NAVIGATION TIMELINE

1759	Commissioners of Inland Navigation commenced work on Boyne Navigation under the supervision of Thomas Omer.
1789	Commissioners of Inland Navigation dissolved and local commissioners appointed to supervise Lower Boyne. Only 21km of navigation completed to date.
1790	River Boyne Company incorporated.
1800	Completion of line to Navan. Proposals to run lines from Trim to Athboy and from Navan to Kells.
1835	Office of Public Works assumes control of Lower Boyne Navigation while Upper Boyne Navigation remains under the control of River Boyne Company.
1894	Newly-incorporated Boyne Navigation Company takes over the entire system thereby stopping dual control of Navigation.
1902	James McCann granted seven year lease of navigation and operated under the title of Meath Navigation Company.
1913	Boyne Navigation Company went into liquidation.
1915	Messrs John Spicer and Company Limited purchased the Navigation.
1920s	Last horse-drawn boats withdrawn from service and canal

allowed to go derelict.

1969   John Spicer hands over remaining parts of Navigation to An Taisce.

BIBLIOGRAPHY

Barrow, Lennox, *Irish Round Towers* – Irish Heritage Series No. 8, Dublin, 1976

Blair, May, *Once Upon the Lagan – the Story of the Lagan Canal*, Belfast, 2000

Byrne, Patrick, *Irish Ghost Stories*, Dublin, 1965

Casey, Christine, and Rowan, Alistair, The Buildings of Ireland – North Leinster, London, 1993

Clarke, Peter, *The Royal Canal – The Complete Story*, Dublin, 1992

Conaghan, Michael, Gleeson, Oliver, and Maddock, Alison, eds., *The Grand Canal – Inchicore and Kilmainham*, Dublin 1994

County Kildare VEC, *Towpaths Trails*, Kildare

Cumberlidge, Jane, *The Inland Waterways of Ireland*, Cambridgeshire, 2002

Delany, Ruth, *Ireland's Royal Canal 1789-1992*, Dublin 1992

Delany, Ruth, *The Grand Canal of Ireland*, Devon, 1973

Delany, Ruth, *A Celebration of 250 Years of Ireland's Inland Waterways*, Belfast, 1986

Delany, Ruth, Addis, Jeremy, and the Inland Waterways Association, *Guide to the Grand Canal of Ireland*, Dublin, 1975

Delany, D.R., and V.T.H., *The Canals of the South of Ireland*, Devon, 1966

Delany, Ruth, Kidney, Paul, and Borner, Walter, eds., *The Shell Guide to* the River Shannon (includes the Shannon-Erne Waterway & the Erne Navigation), Dublin, 1996

Dwyer, Kevin, *Ireland – The Inner Island - A journey through Ireland's Inland Waterways*, Cork, 2000

Flanagan, Patrick, *The Ballinamore & Ballyconnell Canal*, Devon, 1972

Flanagan, Patrick, *The Shannon-Erne Waterway*, Dublin 1994

Hadfield, Charles, and Skempton, A.W., *William Jessop, Engineer*, Devon, 1979

Harbison, Peter, *Beranger's Antique Buildings of Ireland*, Dublin 1998

Harbison, Peter, *Guide to National and Historic Monuments of Ireland*, Dublin, 1992

Heron, Marianne, *The Hidden Houses of Ireland*, Dublin, 1999

Hopkins, Frank, *Rare Old Dublin – Heroes Hawkers and Hoors*, Cork, 2003

McCormack, John, A., *Story of Dublin – The people and events that shaped the city*, Dublin, 2000

McCutcheon, W.A., *The Canals of the North of Ireland*, Devon, 1965

Malet, Hugh, *In the Wake of the Gods*, London, 1972

Malet, Hugh, *Voyage in a Bowler Hat*, London, 1960

Meehan, Cary, *The Traveller's Guide to Sacred Ireland*, Glastonbury, 2002

Mulvihill, Mary, *Ingenious Ireland*, Dublin 2002

O'Reily, Joe and Killally, Caitriona, *Through the Locks*, Westmeath

Ó Riain, Flann, *Townlands of Leinster*, Dublin, 2000

O'Sullivan, T.F., *Goodly Barrow – A voyage on an Irish River*, Dublin 2001

Ransom, P.J.G., *Holiday Cruising in Ireland, a Guide to Irish Inland Waterways*, Devon, 1971

Rolt, L.T.C., Green and Silver, London, 1949

Rothery, Seán, *A Field Guide to the Buildings of Ireland*, Dublin, 1997

Simms, Angret, and Andrews, J.H., eds., *Irish Country Towns – The Thomas Davis Lecture Series*, Dublin, 1994

Somerville-Large, Peter, *The Irish Country House – A Social History*,

London, 1995

St John Joyce, Weston, *The Neighbourhood of Dublin*, Dublin, 1988

Warner, Dick, and Fallon, Niall, *Waterways – By Steam Launch Through Ireland,* London, 1995

Waterways Service, Guide to the Royal Canal of Ireland, Dublin 1997

Wilde, William R. The Beauties of the Boyne and its Tributary, the Blackwater, Galway, 2003

INDEX